Freud, Marx and Morals

FREUD, MARX AND MORALS

HUGO MEYNELL

BARNES & NOBLE BOOKS
TOTOWA, NEW JERSEY

First published in Great Britain 1981 by
THE MACMILLAN PRESS LTD

First published in the USA 1981 by
BARNES & NOBLE BOOKS
81 Adams Drive
Totowa, New Jersey, 07512

ISBN 0–389–20045–X

Printed in Hong Kong

British Library Cataloguing in Publication Data

Meynell, Hugo Anthony
  Freud, Marx and morals. – (New studies in
  practical philosophy).
  1. Ethics
  I. Title   II. Series
  170   BJ1012

  ISBN 0-333-29521-8

Barnes & Noble ISBN 0–389–20045–X

Contents

Author's Note

A version of chapter 2 has appeared in the *Journal for the British Society of Phenomenology* (May, 1971); one of chapter 3 in *Philosophy* (October, 1970); one of chapter 6 in *The Philosophical Quarterly* (April, 1971). Parts of chapter 1 have appeared in *Religious Studies* (January, 1970) and part of chapter 4 in *New Blackfriars* (January, 1974). They are reproduced here by kind permission of the editors of these journals.

My thanks are due to Linda Chalton, Peggy Craven, Eileen Harris and Rose Purdy, for typing the manuscript.

TO IVOR AND JOAN LECLERC
in gratitude for much kindness

Editor's Foreword

A great deal of recent philosophical discussion about morality has turned on the following question. Are moral judgements, in the last logical analysis, grounded in principles of right or wrong, to which men simply decide that they will adhere; or, in certain facts about human nature, which necessarily determine what can, or cannot, count as its well-being? The schools of ethical theory called emotivism or prescriptivism incline to the former view and those called descriptivism or neo-naturalism to the latter.

In this book, Dr Meynell makes a distinctive contribution to the debate. He enters the lists armed with ideas which he has gleaned from various modern authors, most notably Freud and Marx. In all these writers he discovers a notion which he calls 'effective freedom'; and he contends that this conception takes us to the heart of the matter where morality is concerned. In seeking to elucidate it, he contends that there is a 'loose entailment' between what *is* the case concerning human nature and what *ought* to be the case in human conduct.

The attempt to show how the conception of human nature which we find in such popular authors as Freud and Marx can shed light on the fundamental issue about morality in analytical philosophy will, I think, interest all Dr Meynell's readers, whether they agree with his conclusions or not.

W. D. HUDSON

Introduction

Many people are only too eager to provide us with answers to the important question of how we ought to live our lives. But the answers which they give are, to say the least of it, various and conflicting. It is tempting simply to avoid undue attention to this awkward fact, and to plump for the answer which appeals to one's emotions, and, assuming its rightness, condemn without a hearing all rival claimants. Such a solution once adopted may last a person for a lifetime. Alternatively, he may move abruptly from one rival solution to another, repressing all doubts and difficulties during his periods of commitment.

But suppose someone fails to share the confidence of any one moral sect that all its rivals are absolutely and obviously wrong. He may then sincerely ask to which of the available general solutions it is most reasonable and responsible to give his allegiance. Or, having decided to adopt one position, he may notice that there are conflicting applications and interpretations of it, between which he wants to make a reasonable and responsible choice. Or again he may believe that one general interpretation and application of one overall viewpoint is clearly right, and yet wonder whether others may not have something useful to contribute on certain issues. How is such a person to proceed? It is this kind of problem that the present book is intended to clarify.

In many human societies and cultures of the past, it may have been not unreasonable to assume without question that one particular general account of what one ought to do and why was the correct one, and to be sure as a consequence of the wrongness of rival accounts. But in contemporary Western society a person has to be blind and deaf not to have constantly thrust on his attention general views on the matter which are radically discrepant with his own. He may allay his doubts by assiduously cultivating the company of like-minded people, by refusing to attend to the arguments advanced against his own position, and by treating the alternatives with unreflective contempt, But however common such an attitude is in practice, it is difficult to see how it can survive sustained reflection. It would be a considerable mental and moral feat for a person to put it clearly and distinctly to himself, 'I assume my basic moral and political position without any serious consideration of the alternatives, and dismiss its rivals as unworthy of consideration just because they differ from the basic position I have thus arbitrarily and unreflectively adopted.' When this problem of ultimate justification is faced, it is apt to lead to moral scepticism and cynicism. The subject stands confronted by a number of accounts of what he ought in general to do, each convincing if he can bring himself to accept it uncritically, each extremely vulnerable if he starts bringing up awkward questions, and asking by virtue of what it is preferable to its rivals. He may well conclude that all overall moral and political views are equally arbitrary, 'right' for those to whom they happen to appeal, 'wrong' for those to whom they do not.

This book has been written in support of the conviction that moral dogmatism and moral scepticism are not the only available options; that the data are available on the basis of which a rational morality may be constructed and vindicated against opposing views. It summarises a number of influential accounts of the nature of man, and the moral conclusions which have been and may be drawn from them. It tries to bring out how these might be combined into a single consistent view. I hope it will give some pleasure and bring some comfort to readers who like to bring reasonable reflection to bear on their moral commitments. But if its effect were merely to give a little pause to those who are hostile to this sort of mental activity, it would to some extent have succeeded in its purpose.

What I attempt to establish may conveniently be summed up in the following four theses:

(i) What is good depends to a great extent on what tends to promote the flourishing of individuals and communities;
(ii) A number of influential modern writers have shed light on what constitutes or contributes to human flourishing;

(iii) There is a single thread running through their various accounts; namely, that what I shall call 'effective freedom' both is itself an aspect of human flourishing, and is a virtually necessary means of securing other aspects of it;

(iv) All that has been said can be reconciled with some trends in contemporary moral philosophy, and supply a justifiable corrective to others.

1 Morality, Happiness and Epistemology

In this chapter, I wish to expound and defend a thesis which may seem a truism: that good action is largely a matter of promoting satisfaction and fulfilment among human beings, and diminishing their unhappiness and frustration. But its defence is by no means a trivial matter, since 'subjectivist' and 'relativist' views of morality which are inconsistent with it are widely prevalent; not only are these defended by philosophers, but they are taken for granted by many educated people.

Now what one might call the strong utilitarian position, that goodness is to be *defined* in terms of contribution to happiness, may involve the 'naturalistic fallacy', may be vulnerable to arguments adduced by G. E. Moore, R. M. Hare and others. These matters will be considered at length in chapter 6, where I will try to defend the thesis against some of the more sophisticated objections which may be raised against it. Suffice it for the moment to say that I am not committing myself to the strong utilitarian position; that I am not saying that goodness is to be *defined* in terms of happiness, fulfilment, and so on, but only that the question of how far anything contributes to human happiness and fulfilment *has a vital bearing on* the question of whether it is good. I think that this proposition is usually doubted only because it is wrongly confused with the strong utilitarian thesis.

We seem to have a kind of preliminary grasp of what it is to be a fulfilled human being, and what it is to fail to be such, which does not appear to have changed much since the dawn of civilisation. This is admittedly corrected and amplified as our knowledge advances, to a degree that is gravely underestimated by those systems of morals which depend on a very detailed account, available to intuition, of the nature of man.

Thus philosophers have taken one another to task for assuming that there is such a thing as the 'nature' of man as such, from which moral rules for human beings might be deemed to derive.[1] But though it may be true that there is no single set of necessary conditions which must be fulfilled by a flourishing and fully realised human individual or community, it is surely the case that such individuals and communities must at least approximate to some kind of norm. A fulfilled and happy human life cannot be lived in conditions like those of Auschwitz or the Warsaw Ghetto; that human beings cannot on the whole fulfil themselves under such conditions of physical deprivation and social disruption is an objective fact about human nature as such, and not something which we simply make to be true by judging it to be so, nor yet something which applies only to some individuals from some backgrounds. To the degree that human nature is basically homogeneous, the very general principles according to which human beings may be happy or fulfilled, or fail to be so, whether individually or as groups, will also be homogeneous. And these principles seem centrally constitutive of morality.

There is a difficulty here which has been much canvassed by moral philosophers in the course of the present century: that while what we *can* do may certainly be inferred from the kind of creatures that we are, it is by no means clear how what we *ought* to do can be so inferred.[2] The missing link here, or at least the most important one, is reference to happiness or fulfilment: that we ought *on the whole* to do what conduces to the happiness or fulfilment of people including ourselves. What is apt to contribute to man's happiness depends on the kind of creature that he is, what he has come to be in the course of evolution; and so ultimately what is morally good depends on this as well.

Such an account of goodness seems at first sight to fall foul of the usual arguments against what is called ethical 'naturalism', the thesis that 'good' is definable or at least somehow reducible in non-moral terms. But these arguments are valid, at least against that kind of 'naturalism' which would define goodness in terms of contribution to happinesss, only so far as the qualification 'as a whole' or 'in general' is left out of the statement of the naturalist's principles; this is what makes the difference between the position which I am trying to commend and the 'strong' utilitarianism which I would admit to be capable of such refutation. In special cases, like that well-known one of the 'punishment' of an innocent man in order to appease a destructive mob, we are liable to argue that the principle of happiness should yield to that of justice;[3] but this does not by any means imply that it is not of the essence of moral argument that the happiness of oneself and of others is not *on the whole*, apart from such special cases as that in which the principle of happiness conflicts with that of justice, a valid court of appeal.[4] If a man denied that *on the whole* one ought to do what promotes happiness, he would not just be advancing an odd moral point of view, but would be showing that he did not really understand what is meant by 'ought'. There are certain moral judgements which, while they are not tautologies strictly speaking, are such that one would be inclined to say, of one who did not assent to them, 'he does not know the *meaning* of "morally good"!' And a man who really did not know that one ought on the whole to act in such a way as to promote people's happiness, and acted and felt as though he did not know it, would be not so much ignorant as inhuman or insane.[5]

It might be objected that it is one thing to be concerned with questions of fact, of however general a nature, and another to be concerned with the logic of moral discourse. But I would agree with the point made by Mary Warnock, that it is impossible to get any very useful picture of moral discourse until one has some idea of the situation, of human misery, desire, happiness, frustration, and so on, within which moral discourse has application.[6] One might as well try to understand 'the logic of modern physics' without reference to the experiments carried out by modern physicists, or the practical effects of their discoveries. And indeed, as concepts like 'energy', 'mass', and 'particle' change somewhat as we learn more and more about the nature of material bodies, so it might be expected that concepts like 'love', 'hate' and 'goodness' will change, peripherally if not centrally, as we find out more about human beings, their actions and their motives.

I have been in effect commending the suggestion, made by some recent philosophers, which indeed on the face of it seems obvious enough, that what is morally good or bad depends to a large degree at least on what it is for human beings to flourish:[7]

that good actions tend in general to promote their flourishing, bad actions to militate against it. The notion of 'flourishing' straddles the still rather fashionable distinction between 'fact' and 'value', and is intended to do so. The main difficulty in considering it is that many of the ways of analysing and describing the development of individual human beings and their relationships within society, so far as they aspire to be 'objective', do not do so. For the behaviourist, the wretchedness of the child who is regularly beaten by its drunken father or victimised by its selfish mother, is just one pattern of behaviour, the happiness of the child brought up in an atmosphere of love and mutual helpfulness, another – provided he sticks to his behaviourist last. In his 'objective' scrutiny, however thorough in its own terms, the colossal difference between happiness as such and misery as such has somehow evaporated. On the other hand, those students of human affairs who have applied existentialist or psychoanalytic terms to understanding them, and are quite capable of articulating adequately in their own terms the difference between the two situations which I have just described, have not impressed their scientific colleagues as providing the kind of empirical backing necessary to validate their theories – which in any case conflict as much with one another as with the canons of orthodox science. It would seem that the widespread philosophical dogma that facts are facts, and values are values, and never the twain shall meet, is vindicated by the theoretical chaos in the study of human beings, as individuals and in society, from which we might be expected to derive some account of human flourishing.

I do not think the main difficulty is the paucity or irrelevance of the ascertained facts; there is enough of such material and to spare. The problem is rather to provide some co-ordination of the facts which have been ascertained; and it is this problem on which I wish to concentrate attention.

When an individual is at odds with his society or a part of it, and feels that it more or less frustrates his chances of leading a happy and fulfilled life, it is very difficult at first sight to see by what criteria one can recognise to what extent he is in the right in his complaints against society, and to what extent society is justified in restraining him according to the standards of conduct which it explicitly (for example by law or the long-established customs expressed in moral saws) or implicitly (by the pressures which it *de facto* if not *de jure* applies) enforces upon its members. It may be asked in despair, if conformity with the expectations of one's society is not the criterion of good conduct, whatever other such criterion could there be? And yet there are few who maintain this view so consistently as to hold, for example, that the torture of criminals is right in those societies where it happens to be generally approved. Indeed, on such a view, the notion of the betterment of a society's laws and moral principles makes no sense, since these laws and principles are themselves the standards by which what is good, for those who live in that society, is decided. If appeal is made to the happiness of individuals within that society (an appeal that was made by Bentham and the other English Utilitarians, with immense effect upon society of a kind which most people, whether consistently with their own principles or not, would regard as 'good'), it may be objected that 'happiness' is a concept so vague as to provide no effective criterion at all.

Bentham tried to provide a basis for morality by establishing a systematic science of 'pleasure', and so in effect of happiness or flourishing.[8] Some, including a large number of contemporary philosophers, would say that his effort was bound to fail by its very nature; while others might say that in fact not enough was known about human beings as individuals and in society for such a science to be possible at that time. The former hypothesis has actually been thought in many circles to be capable of proof. I have already given some reasons, which I will develop later on,[9] for holding that the alleged proof is fallacious, and that the truth or falsity of value-judgements depends – contrary to a belief still widespread among philosophers – on the truth or falsity of statements of fact. Important, if not paramount, among these facts is the extent to which the thing, action or person concerned contributes to or frustrates the general happiness, flourishing or fulfilment of human beings. If this is so, the second hypothesis, that Bentham's attempt to construct an objective science of value failed because the relevant facts were not available to him, may be seriously entertained. Rather than rehearsing mere theoretical possibilities, it will be useful to examine actual findings which seem to have a bearing on this subject.

Eugene Heimler has made up a questionnaire which is designed to test a person's social viability. It may be felt that such a test presupposes that the judgement of society on the deviant individual is necessarily correct; but in fact the test, as I shall suggest, provides criteria for assessing the health of a society in relation to the individuals who comprise it, as well as the health of the individual in relation to his society. Heimler's questionnaire was answered by a number of patients residing in mental hospitals, a number of other persons who were of concern to their local health departments for reasons of mental health, and a control group consisting of patients admitted for physical ailments and a random selection of personal friends and acquaintances of the psychiatrists who were conducting the inquiry. The questions were related to five main areas of living in which one can achieve more or less satisfaction: (i) financial; (ii) sexual; (iii) through family relationships; (iv) through friendship; and (v) through work and interests. These seemed to correspond to and develop out of the following kinds of satisfaction available to the small child: (i) security in relation to basic needs; (ii) sensual pleasure though being fed, caressed, and cared for; (iii) affection given and received; (iv) the feeling of being with someone and not alone; and (v) play activities directed towards the mother and later towards toys. The test consisted of five questions asked about the subject's achievement of each of these kinds of satisfaction, and the total theoretically possible score was one hundred. Four marks were given for the answer 'Yes' to each question, two for 'Perhaps', and none for 'No'.[10] The group of those who were of concern to their local health departments for reasons connected with mental health scored less than sixty on average; the control group more. The group of patients resident in mental hospitals scored less than thirty. Those who score a third or less on this test, it is concluded, are not a part of ordinary society, having failed to find, it may be assumed, enough satisfaction within that society to make life at all tolerable to them; those who score a half or less are the concern of social workers; those who score over half tend to function more or less adequately in society.[11]

Whatever 'human flourishing' is, I think one would wish to say that, *ceteris paribus*, those who sought out psychiatric treatment flourished less than those who did not. People who are happy, fulfilled, and satisfied in relation to their environment do not seek such treatment. Hardly anyone goes to see a psychiatrist, ready to dispense a considerable fee, in order to tell him of his overall happiness, confidence and success in life, any more than one takes time off work, or spoils a comfortable evening, in order to complain to a general practitioner about one's exceptionally good health. Indeed, it is characteristic of those who leave mental hospitals for good, or permanently discontinue psychiatric treatment, that they describe their change of state in some such way as that they 'get more out of life' than before, or are more 'satisfied', often specifying the particular aspects of their lives of which this is especially true. (This has been confirmed by a large survey of the opinions of ex-patients and their relatives; it is not founded merely on chance experience and guesswork.)[12]

Let us say that a group of any size, from a family to a nation-state, is 'healthy' to the extent that its members would approach a score of one hundred on Heimler's test, except so far as falls below this score were determined by organic lesions and other characteristics of individuals such that social pressures had neither precipitated their *malaise*, nor were capable of curing or alleviating it. In other words, a social group is 'healthy', on the definition of this term just proposed, to the extent that it promotes 'flourishing' in individuals, approximately as measured on Heimler's scale, both within it and outside it. A criminal gang in which morale was high would be an example of a group which is comparatively 'healthy' in respect of its effect on its own members, but is by no means so in its effect on other people.

This last point is of some importance, as it indicates that Heimler's scale or something like it could at least theoretically serve as a criterion for the 'health' of a social group in relation to individuals, and that it does not beg the question whether the attempt of the individual to put his society in the wrong may be justified. R. D. Laing very properly took T. Lidz to task for assuming, in his talk of schizophrenia as 'a failure of human adaptation', that the absence of those qualities in an individual which are such as to make him accepted as 'sane' by his group is necessarily a defect in the individual himself, and not rather symptomatic of a defect in the group. Laing quotes with approval a complaint that the language commonly used in the clinical description of schizophrenics is a veritable 'vocabulary of denigration', with its predisposition to terms like 'failure', 'lack' and 'loss'. One must not exclude *a limine* the possibility that the cracked mind of the schizophrenic may *let in* light.[13] Why, Laing asks, should one not assess schizophrenia as a *successful* attempt *not* to adapt to society?[14] Unfortunately Laing provides no very clear picture of the kind of society to which such adaptation might be of positive worth, though his sardonic comment that millions of 'sane' people have deliberately killed and maimed millions of their 'sane' fellows in the course of the present century is surely to the point.[15] He has many criticisms to make of 'modern' society; but one may well question the apparently implicit assumption that other societies were any better. It is all very well taking Athens of the fifth century B.C. as one's paradigm of a good society,[16] so long as one forgets that it was run on the basis of slavery, the subjection of women, and colonial exploitation, and that it was at least as belligerent as most other societies recorded in history. Heimler's test and the scale that results from it, however, offer some prospect of finding a clear set of criteria by which not only an individual's adaptation to his society, but also a society's adaptation to the requirements of individuals inside and outside it, can be reliably assessed. For it is an account of human flourishing or happiness which, while it reflects the *subjective* feelings and assessments which one might reasonably suppose to be of the very essence of happiness, is yet capable of *objective* testing and measurement.

I have laid what may seem an undue amount of emphasis on Heimler's work; but it seems to me to exemplify principles which have a long and respectable ancestry in ethics – and in general in those forms of inquiry which take man as such for their subject, as opposed to man in his role as physical object – but which have declined in prestige owing to the spectacular success of the physical sciences. Unfortunately Aristotle, who was a master of these principles, at one time had a demonstrably bad influence on the physical sciences. But, to take one notorious example, if Aristotle's teleological principles of explanation broke down in the physical sciences, or were found to be replaceable, it does not immediately follow, though it is often assumed, that the same must in the last resort apply to the human sciences.[17] Before inquiry into the nature of morals can be taken very far, some attention has to be given to the relation of explanation in the human sciences to explanation in the natural sciences.

When we try to understand any event whatever, we are trying to arrive at one of two kinds of explanation of it. The first is the kind that we would look for in the case of a hailstorm, or of an attack of measles, or the vicissitudes of a piece of sodium dropped into a saucepan of water. The second kind, in terms of motive, purpose and so on, is what we characteristically look for when we are trying to explain human actions. 'Why did he spray those roses?' 'Because he was trying to kill the greenfly on them.' 'Why has he just started talking about the significance of the existence of erratic blocks for the science of geology?' 'Because he is trying to impress one learned colleague who is in a position to advance his career, and annoy another against whom he has a long-standing grudge.'

I do not suppose that anyone would deny that we all do look for explanations of these two kinds, and that we find them at least relatively satisfactory when we get them; opinions differ, however, on the significance of this. Aristotle seems to have regarded natural phenomena in general as somehow purposive; one might put it that he extended the type of explanation which we characteristically demand for human action to nature at large.[18] The disposition to do this is said to be typical of the primitive mind which is inclined to ask, when the rain spoils the crops, why the gods are angry, rather than to what atmospheric conditions the high or unseasonable rainfall is due.

As is well known, the deliberate refusal to look for this kind of explanation of phenomena was at the root of the scientific revolution of the seventeenth and succeeding centuries. Biology remained for some time a stronghold of teleology, since it is obvious that, if you wish to understand the phenomenon of nest-building among birds, you must take into account that nests are in some sense *for* the laying of eggs and the rearing of young. However, in time Darwin's theory provided an overall account of how even biological teleology could ultimately be subsumed under a scheme of explanation involving nothing in the way of final causes. In the case cited, the Darwinian explanation would be roughly that, at an early stage in the evolution of nest-building birds, only those specimens which were genetically programmed to build nests and lay their eggs in them were in fact successful in rearing offspring – or at least that they were more successful in doing so than others, and thus the trait became predominant and ultimately universal in the various species concerned.

Let us call the type of explanation that we use typically for natural events 'type A explanation', that kind which we use for human actions 'type B explanation'. Given that the yielding of type B to type A explanation has been so successful in physics and chemistry, and ultimately in biology, it is no wonder that the same principle should be expected to hold for psychology as well. And it is in fact very commonly held in effect, by persons strongly influenced by scientific culture, that once we know enough, type B explanation will be seen to be as dispensable in human affairs as it has been found to be in the realm of nature at large. After all, man is a part of nature; and so it might be reasonable to suppose, at least on first considering the matter, that it is only a matter of time before human thought and behaviour can be explained by the very same principles which have already proved so fruitful in physics, chemistry and biology. The psychological theories developed by B. F. Skinner are a thorough and impressive application of this assumption.

It is sometimes maintained that type B explanation is not really scientific at all. But this thesis is ambiguous: on one understanding of it, it is a mere matter of definition; on another, it begs some very important questions. Understood in the former way, it amounts to nothing more than the stipulation, 'do not call an explanation "scientific" unless it is of type A'. This leaves open the possibility that there may be explanations which are of predictive value, and yet only of type B and so not 'scientific'; and also that some events may not be capable of 'scientific' explanation at all or, at best, not until some time in the indefinite future, while they are readily amenable here and now to explanation of other kinds. If the thesis is understood in the second way, the implicit stipulation may rather be, 'do not look for type B explanations, since they are of no predictive value.' The last clause, however, is certainly false. To say that one man is setting out to please another man, or to annoy him, may be a perfectly good explanation of certain elements in his behaviour, and furthermore give rise to expectations about his subsequent behaviour which may or may not be fulfilled.

It seems evident enough that how we act in order to influence an event depends on how we understand it. A primitive might sacrifice an ox in order to prevent excessive rainfall. Such an action would make sense if the agent assumed that his god had been punishing him for the inadequate quantity or quality of his ritual performance by the sending of the rain. Evidently we ourselves do not understand meteorological phenomena in this sort of way; the fundamental difference between our point of view on the matter and that of the primitive is that he thinks of the weather in terms of the activities of a conscious agent, whereas the modern on the whole does not. But when the modern wishes to influence a person, given at least that he regards that person as sane and responsible, he behaves in the same kind of way as the primitive in our example did in relation to his weather-god. He tries to find out such things as how the person to be influenced envisages his situation at present, what state of affairs he intends to bring about, and what good he seeks to achieve by this. One can of course influence an agent without taking account of the fact that he is an agent, by physical or chemical manipulation. To influence him *as* an agent, however, is to do such things as convincing him that his situation is not such as he conceives it to be, or showing him that he will not bring about the state of affairs which he intends by acting as he does, or that neither the good which he thinks will accrue from that state of affairs, nor any other good, will in fact do so.

We may distinguish, then, between two fundamental kinds of influence on an agent's behaviour: (a) that which treats him *as an agent* in the kind of way that I have just described, and (b) that which affects him by means such as one might apply to an inanimate object, plant or lower animal. One of the central points at issue, for example, in contemporary disputes about the treatment of mental illness, is whether or in what circumstances the sufferers ought to be treated in the first kind of way – as agents, by the methods of persuasion customarily used upon agents – or in the second kind of way, which does not take into account their status as agents.

'But in the end', it may be objected, 'type B explanation will altogether be replaced by type A explanation – when our knowledge of brain chemistry and physiology has sufficiently increased.' Does scientific explanation bid fair to rule out or render out of date or superfluous explanation in terms of agents, their motives and purposes? It appears to me that it does not and could not, for the following reason. On what grounds, it may be asked, should the scientific world-view itself be accepted? The answer is, presumably, because human investigators, over the course of several centuries, have come to assert its constituent propositions as a result of having tested them by means of observation and experiment, against their rivals. To have done this, they must *deliberately* have carried out the experiments and made the observations, *in order to* determine whether the propositions in question were probably or certainly true. But such a process is certainly a matter of agents acting in accordance with motives and purposes, in fact, of what is subject to B explanation. Thus to rule out B explanation, allegedly because it was incompatible with the scientific world-view, would in fact be to rule out the possibility of oneself, or anyone else, accepting the scientific world-view because there was good reason for him to do so. In fine, if the scientific world-view has the consequence of ruling out B explanation, it is self-destructive. I conclude that one cannot in the last resort consistently *both* maintain the scientific world-view, *and* hold that it rules out B explanation. And one cannot reasonably accept any version of the scientific world-view which does rule out such explanation.[19]

It is obvious that I have raised many controversial points in the philosophy of mind and the philosophy of action. While I cannot deal with these at length short of a treatise on most of the main topics of philosophy, some comment does seem necessary and in order. As I see it, there are at least four positions which might be taken up about those entities which are at once physical events, and so presumably subject to A explanation, and human actions, and thus characteristically to be submitted to B explanation:

(i) That B explanation is mistaken in principle, being at worst incoherent, at best applicable to no real state of affairs;

(ii) That B explanations are logically reducible to A explanations;

(iii) That events subject to B explanation are entirely causally determined by events subject to A explanation;

(iv) That B explanation is to some degree really independent of A explanation – for example, that an event which might or might not have occurred by the operation of laws whose articulation would be a matter of A explanation actually did occur owing to some B explanation.

Only the first of these is inconsistent with the thesis that I wish to argue for here, that human actions really are at least in many cases subject to B explanation. Suppose that the second or the third were true, as is apparently believed by many contemporary philosophers;[20] that the sets of physical events either identical with or expressive of human judgements, decisions and so on, were subject to physical and chemical determination; the thesis which I am trying to argue would not be affected, since it is to the effect only that B explanations are not wrong in principle, not on their having this or that causal or logical relation with A explanations and the events subject to them.

Human actions as such, then, cannot but be characteristically subject to B explanation, explanation in terms of ends *for* which they are performed. By applying this result to that arrived at earlier in the chapter, on the nature of human satisfaction and its relevance for morality, one may determine in addition what is characteristic of good human action. Human action as such is *for* ends; good action in general is *for* human satisfaction, not of course, in typical cases at least, merely that of the agent himself, but that of all those whom he is liable to affect by his action.

Good action, then, is at least largely a matter of finding out what tends to promote the satisfaction of persons, and acting accordingly. It would thus seem that to be morally good is at least largely a matter of acquiring, or perhaps rather of not losing, a kind of knowledge; but the fact that it is not merely so, and the fact that the knowledge concerned is of a special kind, has made people fail to see this. Now some have stressed the role of experience, some rather that of the construction of hypotheses, in the acquisition of knowledge; but I think few would deny that it is characteristic of knowledge in general that, in order to acquire it, one has to cultivate three mental dispositions: one has to be attentive to the data of experience; one has to be intelligent in thinking of ways in which the data might be accounted for; and one has to be reasonable in preferring that account evolved by intelligence which best fits the data in hand.[21] That this is so may be brought out by a couple of examples of knowledge: that water consists of hydrogen and oxygen, and that Queen Victoria outlived her husband. Men have not always known that water consists of hydrogen and oxygen. Before anyone had discovered hydrogen or oxygen, or had hit on a method by which water might be divided into its constituent elements, there was no reason for supposing that water was not the pure element which it had always been taken to be. The truth that water consists of hydrogen and oxygen is not to be come by, again, by sheer attentiveness, by observing and recording what is evident to the innocent eye or to any of the senses; it has been propounded as the result of a long history of persons thinking up theories, working out their consequences for observation, and then testing them. It is, in other words, the fruit of the sustained exercise not only of *attentiveness* to data available to the senses, but of *intelligence* in thinking out theories, and *reasonableness* in determining which of the theories thought out accords best with the evidence. The historical case is not dissimilar in principle; anyone who doubts the proposition mentioned about Queen Victoria may be invited to exercise his intelligence in thinking up a possible alternative explanation of the evidence available to our senses (in books and so on), and his reasonableness in showing that it fits the evidence better than the conventional one.

I have suggested that three kinds of mental activity are necessarily involved in coming to know, and have illustrated this by a couple of simple examples. The suggestion may also be commended by the fact that it amounts to a synthesis of empiricism, which stresses the role of experience in coming to know, and rationalism, which emphasises rather the significance of intelligence and reason; and that it does so without apparent inconsistency. If it is true, the empiricist is quite right to maintain the indispensable place of appeal to experience in most knowledge-claims. But he seems to underestimate the role of intelligence, in envisaging possibilities and formulating hypotheses, and of reason, in judging that one of the possibilities is probably so in that it seems best to square with the evidence. It is one thing for an astronomer to make a series of observations of successive positions of the planets as observed from the earth; it is another thing for it to occur to him that the earth and the planets might go round the sun rather than the sun and the planets going round the earth; and another thing again for him to judge that the sensory evidence which he has collected fits the former hypothesis rather than the latter. The rationalist has just the opposite defect to that of the empiricist. He sufficiently stresses the importance of constructive intelligence in the business of coming to know; but he does not sufficiently attend to the fact that, of all the possibilities which the constructive intelligence may set up of what *might be* so, only that *is* so which is confirmed by the data of experience.

It may be objected that an account of knowledge might reconcile the conflicting claims of rationalism and empiricism, and still be wrong. But the position which I have outlined is susceptible of a more powerful defence; that its denial is actually self-destructive. Suppose someone were to say that he knows that it is not the case that one comes to know by attending to evidence, by thinking out possible explanations for it, and judging as certainly or probably true the explanation which best fits the evidence. Is his claim to knowledge justified? If it is, it can only be because he (or perhaps his authority) has attended to the evidence which bears on the subject; has envisaged the possible explanations for this evidence; and judged to be so the explanation that best fits the evidence. In what else could such justification consist? But if that were the case, he would have come to know by employment of those very mental capacities which he denied were involved in coming to know. However, if he were not justified, there would be no point in taking his claim to knowledge seriously.

The examples cited from science and history illustrate another important characteristic of knowledge; that human beings, by employment of the appropriate mental capacities, may come to know what would have been the case if they had never come to know it, or even if they had never existed. Let us say that a man exhibits the capacity of 'cognitive self-transcendence'[22] so far as he comes to know what is the case independently of his knowing it. It is clear that the sciences, purporting as they do to consist of knowledge of states of affairs which would have obtained even if scientists had never existed to investigate them, presuppose that human beings are capable of self-transcendence. It follows from this that an alleged conclusion of science, from which the impossibility of cognitive self-transcendence can be validly inferred, must be false. Thus the view that human thinking is nothing more than an indirect route to human pleasure, or simply a reflex of economic and social forces, and cannot transcend these to the extent necessary for gaining knowledge of what is independent of human beings and their social situation, may be refuted on the ground that it presupposes cognitional self-transcendence in the act of propounding doctrines from which its impossibility may be inferred.

A scientist may assert what he thinks to be the truth, because the evidence as he sees it supports him, even when this goes against his inclinations, desires or fears. Now such assertion of what is believed to be true, on the grounds that it is believed to be true, is only one kind of responsible action. A man may also go against the pressure of desire or fear in trying to defend someone else who is attacked in the street, or in giving the lie to some powerful and influential person, because this seems to him a good thing to do. Let us call this capacity to act according to a reasonable judgement of what is best, as opposed to under the influence of emotion or desire, 'moral self-transcendence'.[23] The existence of moral self-transcendence, like that of cognitive self-transcendence, may be shown by the fact that any denial of its existence is self-destructive. Suppose someone tells us that it does not exist. Does he say so as a result of a responsible decision to inform others of the truth as he sees it? Or does he do so for some other reason, for example, to gratify other members of his family or political party, or to curry favour with his boss and thus enhance his career prospects? In the former case, he has performed an act of moral self-transcendence in the act of denying the existence of any such thing; in the latter case, there is no reason to take him seriously.

It may be objected that, by way of exception at least, a man who spoke out of such corrupt motives might be saying the right thing for the wrong reasons. At least the authority to which he was submitting, say out of fawning obsequiousness or craven fear, could be saying the right thing for the right reasons. But in this case, so far as moral self-transcendence were denied to the speaker himself, it would at least have to be attributed to the authority to which he submitted, if one were to have good reason for taking what he said seriously. A further objection might still be made, that the truth could be stated, by sheer coincidence, by a man who was following only for corrupt motives the doctrine of an authority who was asserting and promulgating it only for corrupt motives. But in that case, anyone who accepted it reasonably and responsibly as the truth, rather than submitting to it from some other kind of motive, would be exemplifying moral self-transcendence in doing so.

It seems that the same basic epistemological principles which apply to scientific and historical investigation apply also to states of affairs much more closely relevant to morality; though to be sure the means of our knowledge of these states of affairs has not been and presumably cannot be refined to the degree of technical precision which characterises the procedures of the physical scientist or the historian. Is my daughter happy or is she not, as a result of what I do or say? I have no more direct access to her possible feelings of well-being or distress than I have to Queen Victoria during the later years of her reign. But my finding out whether she is unhappy or not is a matter of my observing her behaviour, of my considering all the ways in which that behaviour might be accounted for, and of my assenting to that belief about her feelings which seems best to account for it. Is she really unhappy, or is she shamming? To decide between these two possibilities, I might ask myself whether she has been in the habit of shamming in the past, or whether she has in the present adequate motives for doing so, and observe whether her expression generally changes abruptly when she believes she is no longer being taken notice of, and so on.

It might be objected that the elaborate paraphernalia of hypothesis and deduction is grossly misapplied to our everyday knowledge of one another. One needs years of specialist

training to become a scientist or historian; whereas our disposition to apprehend one another's feelings is learned at our
mothers' knees or probably not learned at all. Now I admit that
the detailed application of the dispositions involved in coming
to know is very different in the two kinds of case; but I insist that
one basic set of dispositions is involved just the same. In the
everyday case of the kind relevant to morality, as in the
scientific and historical cases, I am liable to err so far as I fail to
attend to the evidence available to my senses, or so far as I fail
to think up a sufficiently wide range of ways in which it might
be accounted for, or so far as I fail to select from within that
range the hypothesis which best does justice to the evidence.
Rather than following what Bernard Lonergan has called the
'transcendental precepts' of attentiveness, intelligence, and
reasonableness,[24] I may err respectively through inattention,
stupidity, or silliness; through inattention which does not
advert to all the relevant data on the matter in hand, through
stupidity which cannot think out the full range of ways in which
it might be accounted for, through silliness which fails to
adjudicate upon the various accounts in accordance with their
confirmation by the evidence. We tend towards the truth on all
matters whatever so far as we follow these precepts; we tend to
fall into error so far as we fail to do so.

    The attaining of truth and avoidance of error about the real
needs and feelings of those with whom we come into contact is
not, of course, as in the case of history or of science, at all a
matter of mastery of technical rules and procedures. It is a
matter of setting ourselves against the tendencies within us,
deriving from our personal or social situation and history, to
overlook part of the available evidence relevant to a decision, or
one of the possible explanations for it, or the fact that one of the
explanations that we have envisaged best fits the evidence.
Sloth, fear, desire for comfort, love of power, or even a half-
conscious relish for the sufferings of other people, may impose
blocks on our attentiveness, intelligence and reasonableness.
Suppose that I am a university teacher who has taught the
same topic in exactly the same way for many years, and to
change my performance in any way would require unwonted
effort on my part. A student tactfully suggests to me that I
might be interested in a certain new book which deals with the

subject; but what I hear about the contents of the book makes
me fear that it might oblige me to reconsider my whole attitude
to the subject, and so necessitate the reorganisation of my
course from scratch. Is it not rather tempting for me somehow
to fail to hear, or later fail to remember hearing, what the
student has said; or for me to attribute what I have heard to a
conceited desire on the part of the student to take his teacher
down a peg? It is to be feared that such vices are not confined to
individual teachers, but have not been unknown to characterise
whole academic communities. In matters concerned with morality, we have motives for the avoidance of truth which are less
immediately relevant to science or history (though motives of
this kind, which may properly be called 'ideological', may
affect our conclusions even there),[25] where ignorance is due
more commonly to other causes than self-deception. Suppose
again that I have evidence which strongly suggests that a
student is being victimised by a member of the staff of a
teaching institution – school, university, or polytechnic – who is
senior to myself, and whose opinion of me is liable to affect my
career, pay and all, for better or for worse. Is it not tempting for
me in such a case either to fail to scrutinise the evidence for the
victimisation with much care, or to accept or concoct some
story which justifies my superior's attitude towards the
student? In a case like this, I am motivated by sloth or fear or
ambition in such a way that I either fail to advert to the
evidence available to my senses, or abuse intelligence and
reason in order to give an account of it which suits my own
convenience rather than the evidence itself.

Someone will say, 'But such knowledge of the needs and
feelings of others cannot be the essence of moral goodness. In
each of these cases one might come to a correct judgement on
how matters stood, and yet act irresponsibly.' That one can
know all the relevant facts in a case, and still act irresponsibly, I
grant. However, that one can still act irresponsibly when one
knows the state of the case, does not entail that one can act
responsibly when one does not know the state of the case. To
express the matter somewhat more technically, the fact that
knowledge of the relevant facts is not a sufficient condition of
good action does not mean that it is not a virtually necessary
condition of it.[26] Thus the objection raised above may be met by

the suggestion that cultivation of the kind of knowledge, and avoidance of the kind of self-deception, which I have described, are a large part but not the whole of moral goodness. (If this is true, one can see that Plato's equation of virtue with knowledge, even if incorrect in the last analysis, is at least profound and plausible).[27] If one is to do what is good as well as know what is true, one must, in addition to being attentive, intelligent and reasonable, be responsible as well.[28] The application of the first three dispositions to discovery of the truth in matters of science, history and ordinary life, I have already briefly described. Moral goodness seems to consist of cultivation of the fourth disposition, and those applications of the first three, in family, professional or political life, which are most closely connected with morals. To be responsible is not only to have the disposition to come to a fully attentive, intelligent and reasonable judgement as to what is good, but to have the disposition to decide and act accordingly.

Observance of the first three precepts is a necessary condition of observance of the fourth, simply because one cannot take a responsible decision about a situation of which one is ignorant. And while observance of the first three precepts does not of itself entail observance of the fourth, it does at least promote it, as a matter of psychological fact. To act at once clear-sightedly and irresponsibly is at least rather rare. For example, it would require a perverse kind of moral courage, of which I think few are capable, for the teacher in our first example to put it clearly to himself: 'The student is quite right; I ought to change my course, and perhaps my whole method of teaching. But I'm just too damned lazy, and so will set out to discredit or ridicule the student instead.' Or, in the second case: 'Professor So-and-so is grossly victimising that student. But I daren't risk my career and my standard of living by pointing this out, and so will keep silent on the matter, or tell lies if I have to speak about it at all.' Just the same considerations apply to moral issues of a more public nature. Classes and groups are as subject to self-deception as are individuals. It is of the essence of moral and political responsibility that one should be concerned to draw attention to the distinction between the sectional aims of groups, and especially one's own group, on the one hand, and the public interest on the other. For examples of what it is to draw attention to such distinctions, one might take the work of Sakharov in Russia, or Ralph Nader in the United States, or, on a humbler but still impressive level, the activities of our own Television Consumer Unit. Attention to such matters will not, of course, stop people behaving badly, but at least it will hinder their doing so, through counteracting the processes of self-deception, the constrictions of attentiveness, intelligence and reason, by means of which they provide themselves with excuses.

To stress, as I have done, the importance of the individual's exercise of his own mental faculties in determining what is the case, and what he ought to do about it, is not to deny that there is any place for submission to authority, or for taking things on trust. If anyone is to learn anything at all, he must at least provisionally accept on trust a great many beliefs and moral attitudes from his community and especially from his parents and teachers. Since no one can find out for himself everything which is relevant to the conduct of his life, it would hardly be very intelligent, reasonable or responsible of him not to accept many such beliefs and attitudes. But there is plenty of opportunity for exercise of these mental faculties, or for failure to exercise them, in deciding whether to submit to any particular claimant to authority, in choosing between rival claimants and in determining the conditions and limits of submission to an authority accepted in principle. Submission to or rejection of an authority, altogether or on any particular issue, may be due rather to strength of desire, envy or timidity, than reasonable and responsible decision.

It will be noted that, on the view I have put forward, intellectual and moral qualities in agents are far more closely related than they would appear to be on the basis of much recent philosophy. It might be objected that, if the view were right, to be good would be more or less the same as to be clever. Since to be good and to be clever are evidently very different things, the view from which such a conclusion may be validly deduced must be wrong. The answer is, surely, that the clever are indeed better than the stupid at coming to know the needs and feelings of other persons, so long as their motives are good. But unfortunately, when their motives are bad, they are much better at rationalisation and what one might call the more active forms of self-deception. Where suffering or injustice are really gross and palpable, it may cynically be suggested, it takes a really clever person either to fail to advert to them or to concoct plausible justification for them.

If the general achievement of happiness and satisfaction, and the general avoidance of suffering and frustration, are criteria for what is of positive value, then exercise of the dispositions of attentiveness, intelligence, reasonableness and responsibility, and the free action in which this culminates, may be justified as both intrinsically and instrumentally valuable. They are intrinsically valuable in that intense satisfaction may be got out of their exercise as such; and instrumentally valuable in that one cannot, except incidentally by way of a fluke, act for the best, either in technical matters or in politics or in the affairs of ordinary life, without attentiveness, intelligence and reasonableness in establishing the relevant facts, and responsibility in acting accordingly.

Let us say that a man has 'effective freedom' to the extent that he is attentive, intelligent and reasonable in judging what is to be done, and capable of acting accordingly.[29] One tends to be happy so far as one acts with such effective freedom in relation to one's own long-term satisfaction, and good so far as one does so in relation to that of people in general. Thus a degree of effective freedom seems necessary if one is to be either good or happy; but Plato's conclusion, that virtue and happiness are the same in the last analysis, should not immediately be inferred from this.[30] There seems no reason why a man should not exercise his effective freedom in achieving happiness for himself at the expense of moral goodness, or moral goodness at the expense of happiness; even if short of effective freedom he can scarcely be either happy or good.

In this chapter I have been concerned to labour the obvious, but for all that often disputed point, that what is a good human action depends very largely at least on the sort of being that man is and the ways in which, as a consequence of the sort of being that he is, it is open to him to achieve happiness and fulfilment. I have also tried to summarise the nature of the mental qualities and dispositions necessary for the performance of good actions. More technical objections to this highly 'objective' account of the nature of morality will be considered in chapter 6 below. It will be the object of the examination and comparison of authorities in the intervening chapters to determine further the nature and preconditions of human happiness and fulfilment, in the light of man's inheritance of animal instinct, the contingencies of his individual development, and his economic circumstances and social position.

2   On Driving People Mad: Laing

Much of the contemporary dispute as to the causation of 'mental illness', or indeed as to whether 'mental illness' can properly speaking be said to exist at all, seems to depend on the question of whether the states so described are subject to B or to A explanation.[1] It is of some interest that while physiological explanation of neurotic or psychotic behaviour would be explanation of type A, psychoanalytic explanation of it would certainly be of type B. That is to say, neurotic symptoms as described in psychoanalytic terms are essentially purposive, though the purpose is not one that the patient acknowledges; though he can, sure enough, be brought to acknowledge it in certain circumstances and it is central to the whole theory that he can do so. Now it is not uncommon for psychiatrists to look for 'psychogenic' or type B explanations of neurosis, while saying that in the case of psychosis the causes will be found to be mainly or exclusively physiological. This is apt to be asserted not only in the case of the so-called organic psychoses – where disorders of thought and behaviour are correlated with known organic lesions and chemical abnormalities – but also in the so-called functional psychoses of schizophrenia and manic-depression, where no such lesions or abnormalities have been established.

Much of the work of R. D. Laing consists in effect of the adducing of evidence that, at least in the case of schizophrenia, type B explanation is the most useful and fruitful one available.[2] When a man is suffering from an organic ailment, we do not, at least nowadays, generally think it useful to ask him, 'What do you *mean* by it?' That neurotic illnesses, even in those extreme hysterical cases where a limb is paralysed, do have a 'meaning' in this sense, was arguably the greatest discovery of Freud.

Now Laing's clinical experience and research is such as to suggest that, if we want explanations of the bizarre patterns of thought and behaviour which are labelled 'schizophrenic', we should ask 'Why is this person doing this?', expecting an answer in terms of the aims of his life and the relationships he is trying to establish with other persons and things, rather than 'Why is this happening to him?' – in fact, that we should look for type B rather than type A explanation of his behaviour. Schizophrenia, according to Laing, like neurosis on the Freudian view,[3] is the result of a strategy evolved by an individual to cope with a situation in which he thinks he finds himself or has found himself. It is sometimes lamented that non-physiological accounts of schizophrenia put its understanding right outside the limits set by classical medicine. But Laing might retort that the successes of classical medicine have been precisely in the realm of proven organic deficiency or malfunction, where it may readily be admitted that type A explanations arc appropriate: in those aspects of cure which concern what is *happening* to a patient (like mumps or nettlerash) rather than what he is *doing*. And his plea, in its simplest terms, is that our understanding of schizophrenia, which is one kind or a number of related kinds of human thought and behaviour, should be of a piece with our understanding of the rest of human behaviour. In general, when we see someone going through a complicated series of actions, we seek an explanation in terms of *what he is trying to achieve* by what he does; we are not interested in electrical or chemical events within his brain or nervous system. That the explanation of schizophrenia will turn out to be of a piece with explanation of human thought and activity of non-schizophrenic kinds is surely not less reasonable a claim, on the face of it, than that it will turn out to be in terms of the organic lesions and physiological abnormalities which are the subject matter of classical medicine.

Even if the difficulties already mentioned in the way of reducing type B explanation to type A explanation could be overcome, this reduction would hardly amount to an impugning of Laing's claims, which are just as important from a practical point of view if taken to imply only that *in terms of the relevant sciences as they are at present* the aetiology of schizophrenia is a matter either wholly or partly of type B explanation rather

than of type A. Freud did not regard his own type B explanations of neurotic symptoms as precluding in the long run the
discovery of type A explanations for them; he merely claimed
that in the meantime, *faute de mieux*, his own type B explanations
could constitute both a theory of the aetiology of the neuroses
and a source of suggestions as to how their symptoms might be
alleviated or cured. It would be no serious aspersion on Laing's
kind of explanation if it were regarded in the same provisional
way.

It is difficult to see any good *a priori* reason for denying that
the behaviour of some or all of those who are regarded as
schizophrenic might be subject to type B rather than type A
explanation; that is to say, that such behaviour might become
comprehensible once it was shown how the agent understood
his situation, and consequently what his motives and purposes
were in regard to it. Whether this is or is not the case – whether
schizophrenia is to be understood in terms of type A or type B
explanation now or in the future – can be determined only by
actual research.[4]

It is essential to Laing's position that the behaviour of those
classified as schizophrenics is to be understood, and so can best
be influenced, in the same general kind of way as the behaviour
of other agents. This is as much as to say that, if one wishes to
understand the behaviour of a schizophrenic, one must get to
know such things as how he envisages his situation, what he
hopes to achieve out of it and in what respect he thinks that
achievement will be worthwhile. Someone might argue somewhat as follows: 'Granted that the schizophrenic's action is
intelligible in some cases in the light of what he deems his
situation to be, we cannot assume in his case, as we can in the
case of a person who is mistaken in the usual kinds of ways and
for the usual kinds of reasons, that his ideas about his present
situation are to be understood as due merely to mistaken, but at
least intelligible, reflection on the course of his past and present
experience. Thus a normal but ignorant person might well
refuse to believe that the sun is larger than the earth; though we
disagree with him, at least the course of reasoning by which he
reached his erroneous conclusions is in principle clear to us.
The sun certainly does not look larger than the earth; it takes a
great deal of sophisticated reflection before it becomes at all

natural to believe that it is in fact so. But in the case of the schizophrenic our disagreement is much more fundamental than this: we do not have the feeling that, if we were a little more stupid or less educated than we are, or if we had had certain experiences without access to certain information, we would say what he says or act as he acts. This is what makes it so plausible to look for explanations in terms of abnormal chemistry of the brain, or something similar.'

But it is precisely Laing's contention, which he supports by a weight of evidence, that the schizophrenic's words and actions *can* be understood as the result of a series of attempts to construe, and to act in relation to, the situation in which he actually is or has been. Here again is a matter which cannot be settled either way *a priori*, but only by consideration of the available evidence.

It seems characteristic of those schizophrenics investigated by Laing that: (a) they have come to experience themselves and their environment in an unusual way, owing to their attempts to cope with certain kinds of difficulty within that environment; (b) they express, in some of their more bizarre utterances, a kind of poetic analogy with what the sympathetic enquirer may eventually find their real situation to be.

It will be convenient to summarise Laing's account of schizophrenia under the following headings:

1 The Family and Interpersonal Background of Schizophrenia.
2 The Schizoid Condition.
3 The Change from the Schizoid Condition to Schizophrenia.
4 Truth expressed in Delusion.
5 The Recovery of Sanity.

1   *The Family and Interpersonal Background of Schizophrenia*

That the future schizophrenic patient may be genetically predisposed is admitted by Laing. It appears that the patients studied, when babies, had difficulty with the expression and implementation of their instinctual needs. But what is remarkable is that all or most of those in the early environment of the patient took this very feature as a token of goodness and stamped with approval the absence of self-action. The combination of almost total failure by the baby to achieve self-instinctual gratification, along with the mother's total failure to realise this, can be noted as one of the recurrent themes in the early beginnings of the relation of mother to schizophrenic child.

When it was first guessed that some features in the relationship of mother to child might predispose to schizophrenia in the child, there was a tendency towards a witch hunt for 'schizo-phrenogenic mothers'. But to admit the importance of the relationship between mother and child in the aetiology of schizophrenia is not to be committed to regarding it as of exclusive importance. All that is at issue is whether there are 'some ways of being a mother that impede rather than facilitate or "reinforce" any genetically determined inborn tendency there may be in the child' to fail to achieve the relatively confident and useful interaction with his fellows which is characteristic of the majority of people. In any case, the evidence goes to suggest that what contributed to schizo-phrenia in the child is the whole family situation rather than merely the behaviour of the mother. Over and over again, it seems in retrospect that parents have regarded with alarm what the investigators felt to have been normal signs of growing up in the child and adolescent – like engaging in normal domestic activities on its own initiative.[5]

Recurrent in the description of the lives of schizophrenics by their families is a division into three main stages; during the first of which they were exceedingly 'good', until they abruptly became so 'bad' that it was quite a relief to realise that they were really 'mad'. Reports of an early model childhood come, after prolonged experience of these cases, to have a rather sinister ring – especially as so often the ideas of 'goodness' and 'normality' held by the families concerned seem applied to what is rather indicative of inner deadness. It is just this deadness, this lack of independent liveliness and initiative, which appears to receive the highest commendation in these families. The effect of the family attitude may be augmented by a remarkable isolation from the human environment at large, which again is characteristic of these families. It tends to be extremely difficult for the future patient to make direct relationships with others outside the family, at an age when most young people would be doing so. For example, in the case of Lucie's contacts with other people, 'the way she saw them, how she thought they saw her, and how she saw herself, were all equally mediated by her father backed up by her mother.' When people do at length break away from their families, often they have been so affected by them that they are unable to make use of their apparent freedom.[6]

The family tends to see the prospective schizophrenic in terms of a stereotype, departures from which are either not acknowledged at all, or stigmatised as bad or mad. They tend to be unable to see things from his point of view, or even to acknowledge that it is 'really' his point of view, whatever he himself may have to say about it. The patient Claire admitted that she had been well provided with material things when she was a child, but complained that she as a person, who had feelings and desires which she tried to express, was completely ignored. Claire's mother insisted that Claire's feelings were just like her own; when occasionally the recognition appeared to be at the point of breaking in upon her that this might not be so, her only response was alarm and puzzlement. One is struck in this case, as in very many similar ones, by 'the imperviousness of the mother to the daughter as a person separate to and different from herself'.[7]

Of June in her earliest years, her mother's account never varied; June used to be happy, boisterous, and affectionate. This account seemed quite impervious to June's own statements to the contrary. Whenever the account did not exactly fit June, so far as her mother was concerned there was only one explanation – that she was ill. This 'essentialism' in their view of the prospective patient, this 'Procrustean identity' that they impose upon him, again seems characteristic of these families. In the case of Ruth, her parents *both* denied that Ruth led the kind of life that she, and they on other occasions, said she did lead, *and* attributed that kind of life to 'mad' or 'bad' behaviour on Ruth's part. 'Thus, she is said to drink excessively, while, simultaneously, she is said not to drink at all'.[8] Her mother tells the interviewer, 'She's brought people home – when she's been ill she's brought people home she normally wouldn't tolerate, you know, these beatniks'; Father adds, 'There have been writers and God knows what'. When Ruth asserts herself in any way against the parental view of her real essence, by going where she wants with whom she chooses, or wearing clothes she likes, her parents infer that an attack of her illness is coming on. Hazel, though already an adult, has never once had a boy or girl friend in the house; according to her mother, though not according to Hazel, this is what Hazel wants. The wife of David, again, *really* agrees with him. Whenever she does not do so, it is a sign that she is ill. In this case, neither the husband nor the parents of the patient – all of whom, it ought to be added, were devoutly religious – seemed to have any understanding of the patient's point of view, or of the fact that they had no understanding of it.[9]

Not only is the prospective patient very often seen in terms of a sterotype, but the attitudes of his family towards him tend to be confusingly contradictory. Maya said that her parents constantly put difficulties in the way of her reading what she wanted to; they denied this with laughter. When Maya mentioned her Bible reading as an example, her father, still laughing, asked why she wanted to read the Bible anyway when she could find out better about that kind of thing from other books. Again, the father and mother constantly winked at one another when the whole family was interviewed together. The interviewer commented on this after twenty minutes of the interview; at which the parents denied they were doing it, went on doing it, and went on denying that they were doing it.

All of us have a tendency to doubt the validity of our perceptions when other persons do not confirm them; and it is worth reflecting on what might be expected to happen when the reality of states of affairs which we seem to perceive is habitually denied by those who are most intimately involved with us.[10]

2   *The Schizoid Condition*

Jean, in order to get any real satisfaction out of her life in a very 'Christian' family, had been compelled at an early age to 'split' (as she herself put it) her personality. First, at the age of nine, she had gone to the cinema with a friend and the friend's parents without letting her own parents know. Having got away with this, she went on leading a double life. She wore make-up, went to the cinema and went out with boys – all without telling her family. As a corollary to this she systematically cultivated a split between a true inner self, whose thoughts and desires were in accordance with her secret life, and a false outer self which acted and spoke according to what was felt to be proper within the family circle. Jean felt acutely guilt-ridden as a result of this duplicity.[11] Now of course everyone has sometimes to conceal his feelings from others or at least to fail to reveal them; it is only when the habit of thinking and feeling in one way, and speaking and acting in a way which is wholly other, becomes more or less unremitting owing to inner predisposition or outer circumstances or both, that one may reasonably surmise that the consequences might ultimately be pathological.

The schizoid disconnects his speech and actions from his thoughts and feelings out of motives of fear and hatred; the unpleasant consequences of speaking and acting as he feels are too great for him to bear. But his inner world, since it has no real interaction with the outer, becomes progressively more and more impoverished, futile and empty. Unfortunately such withdrawal from others, in order not to be hurt by others, does not work in the long run, since no one feels more at the mercy of others than the schizoid. He may try to forestall being got at by others by getting at them. As one patient said, 'I emphasise people's faults to regain my self-possession'. A more unequivocal withdrawal seems to be at the basis of the behaviour of a patient who had been severely 'depersonalised' for some years; she described her attitude as due to a desire to play possum – in effect, to feign deadness in order not to be killed. The chronic insecurity of some schizoids will make them compulsive sticklers for neatness. One patient said, 'I don't know how to deal with the unexpected. That's why I like things neat and tidy. Nothing unexpected can happen then.' Genuine and spontaneous interaction with others is what is at once most longed for and most dreaded in such cases. Now everyone sometimes has moods in which life seems to him futile and meaningless; in the case of the schizoid these seem to be particularly frequent and severe. Within the inner world of his fantasy, the schizoid is omnipotent and free; in real projects, he is subject to agonies of humiliation. There are two main obstacles to the individual getting out of his state of isolation: anxiety and guilt.[12]

Schizoid false selves, when they are 'good' rather than absurdly 'bad', as sometimes happens,[13] are very compliant with others; but this compliance tends to caricature. The schizoid is liable to be a model child or husband, or an admirably industrious clerk. But his posture becomes more and more stereotyped, and bizarre features develop. The false self tends to assume more and more of the characteristics of those on whom its compliance is based; as this tendency increases, the underlying hatred becomes more and more evident. (It is to be remarked that this compliance and impersonation may be with and of a fantasy figure rather than a real person.) For instance, the father of James had a habit of asking guests at his table whether they were sure that they had had enough to eat; but James's own solicitations became compulsive and beyond all reasonable bounds, and a general embarrassment and nuisance. James sensed the aggressive implications in his father's habit and, by exaggerating them, exposed them to general ridicule and anger. Thus by his satirical comment he evoked from others feelings which he had about his father, but which he dared not express directly. A compliant daughter, again, may be using her very compliance, with its singular exaggeration, as a means of attack.[14]

The schizoid needs to be seen and recognised by others as he is; but others are at the same time a threat to him. Rose had a way of embarrassing people in order to convince herself that she was real, that she could have a real effect on other people. She herself came to realise that the more she withdrew from other people, the more vulnerable she became. The more she cut herself off from other people, the more she felt threatened by inner disintegration. The result of such desire and fear is that the schizoid is apt to compromise by seeking out company, but never being himself in it. He is inclined to laugh at what he does. not think is funny, to make friends with people he does not like, to dress ostentatiously, to speak loudly – and in general to draw attention at once to and away from himself. James's behaviour was due to a compound of resentment of others and contempt for himself, which resulted in a bizarre product of shown and concealed feelings. He had eccentric ideas; he was a theosophist and astrologer, in spite of his genuine understanding of more orthodox scientific theories. That he could share with others these odd notions of his may be guessed to be one means by which he preserved his sanity. A girl schizoid was fantastically and irrationally unpunctual for interviews with her doctor, and was in general very secretive about herself and what she was doing. Her speech was listless, and she sedulously avoided talking about herself, but would discuss politics and economics instead.[15]

3   The Change from the Schizoid Condition to Schizophrenia

It is not always possible to specify the exact borderline between the sane schizoid individual and the schizophrenic. The psychosis has sometimes an abrupt, sometimes a gradual, apparent onset. It seems that the potential schizophrenic's outer appearance of normality is preserved by more and more desperate means. What was in the first instance a guard or barrier for the self to hide behind becomes a gaol; the person has engaged in 'a deliberate cultivation of a state of death-in-life as a defence against the pain of life'. Once a certain point has been passed, efforts either at further withdrawal or at re-establishment of authentic interaction with the world will lead straight to psychosis – whether the sufferer decides to murder his true self once and for all, or to be honest in spite of everything. In either case, the adaptation to reality of the false self will have seemed to the subject (to judge from what is claimed by many patients) to be a more and more shameful, futile or ridiculous pretence. It seems that when the false self has been externally a pretty normal person, who is not notice-ably bizarre in speech or behaviour, that there occurs one of those sudden onsets of insanity which seems totally unprepared in the subject's previous history. A man who was twenty-two years old and previously quite normal by his family's account, put out to sea in a small boat, and when he was picked up said that he had lost God and was trying to find him. A father of a family who was in his fifties, on a picnic and in sight of other picnickers, plunged naked into a river to wash away his sins, saying that he had never loved his wife and children.[16]

The kind of behaviour shown by these two people, for all its prima-facie absurd quality, is only too tragically intelligible, in

terms of reaction to a trivial and meaningless life in the first
example and, in the second, to guilt at having pretended to
have feelings that one should have had but did not have. In
other cases, the impossibility of the patient's position in life and
the intelligibility of his 'mad' acts and sayings as a response to
it, come out quite clearly, at any rate when the circumstances
are taken into account. Maya was regularly told by her parents
that she felt what she did not feel she felt, and that she was not
in the habit of performing actions which she remembered quite
vividly that she was in the habit of performing. She accused
them of trying to 'obliterate' her mind – a way of speaking
which seems to convey very well how deeply and radically
confusing their attributions must have been to her. But she had
been taught that this view by her of her parents was merely a
symptom of illness. So inevitably she sought refuge in her
private shell. But *this* was to exhibit the schizophrenic characteristic of being 'withdrawn'. Her denial that she was the
subject of her thoughts – 'I don't think, the voices think' –
appeared to be an effort to evade the barrage of criticism and
invalidation by her family of what she said and thought.

Lucie, a chronic schizophrenic, was inclined to wonder
seriously about the significance of life, and was rather awkward
in the company of those who seemed to her merely to chatter
superficially, rather than trying to say what was important and
worthwhile.[17] 'She was never sure whether they talked superficially on purpose, or whether they really did not know what
they seemed to be denying. With anyone with whom she could
genuinely talk, she was not . . . in any way "withdrawn", or
"asocial" or "autistic".' Jean had delusions to the effect that
her parents and husband were dead, and that her husband was
not really her husband. 'Unable to express, and inwardly
forbidden to feel, dissatisfaction with, or disappointment in,
her husband, she said he was not her husband. Not daring to
reject or defy her parents openly, she did so quite clearly but in
a way that is "schizophrenic".'[18]

4   *Truth expressed in Delusion*

A sympathetic attention to what the schizophrenic is saying,
and an attempt to grasp what he is trying to express, may

provide a real insight into his state in life. One's understanding of his statements is often analogous to one's grasp of the meaning of an obscure poem. Laing's theories are reminiscent of those of Freud and Jung in that what is at issue is a matter of *interpretation*, of what the patient *means*, rather than of the physical *causes* of his words and actions. A schizophrenic may be subject to the delusion that he is an 'unreal man', or that he is 'made of glass' or 'transparent'.[19] But is it not remarkable that these expressions convey, albeit in a disconcertingly concrete way, feelings that, in a milder form no doubt, no one is altogether a stranger to – feelings of unreality and vanity, and the uncanny conviction that others can read one's thoughts?

Lucie – faced by behaviour on her father's part that the whole of the rest of the family admitted was unreasonable, but that she was not allowed to react to as such, confronted with constant bewildering contradiction between what her mother said and what her mother said she said, and largely bereft of those contacts with the outside world which might to some extent have confirmed her perception of her situation – tried to make some sense of it all as follows:

> I can't trust what I see. It doesn't get backed up. It doesn't get confirmed in any way – just left to drift, you know . . . I know some truth about things, and yet I can't defend it – I don't think I've got a real grasp of my situation. What can I do? How can I get on my feet again? I'm not certain about anything. I'm not certain about what people are saying, or if they're saying anything at all. I don't know what really is wrong, if there is anything wrong.

This was the occasion for her psychiatrist to diagnose 'thought-disorder'; perhaps one may grant to her that there is some difficulty in conceptualising that relation between the acting subject and his world which *no one* has yet succeeded in conceptualising adequately.[20]

The schizophrenic who tells you that he has committed suicide may know perfectly well that he has not cut his own throat or thrown himself into a canal. After all, given the apprehension of the relation between the self and the body which is characteristic of the schizoid, the self and the throat may have a rather tenuous relationship. It is not too difficult to get at the sense that a 'depersonalised' patient is trying to convey when he says that he has murdered himself, or lost himself. He may for instance have deliberately set out to obliterate all feeling from himself as a way of evading the slights and humiliations which he fears at the hands of others. The individual is led to 'kill' his 'self' in this way not only out of anxiety, but out of a crushing sense of guilt. As one patient put it, 'I had to die to keep from dying . . . I guess you had to die emotionally or your feelings would have killed you'.[21]

In many cases, once some kind of rapport has been established between doctor and patient, interpretation of the patient's speech and actions is relatively easy. But in other cases, one has to translate out of 'schizophrenese'. This may be illustrated by the example of a patient who, in the official terminology, was subject to depersonalisation and derealisation, and suffered from autism and nihilistic delusions. Much of what she said is readily intelligible if one starts by trying to understand it rather than regarding it simply as a symptom caused by illness; she felt she was not a person, that she was unreal, that she wanted to become a person, that she was at once empty and powerfully destructive. But beyond this point her communications do seem to be utterly unintelligible. Her accusations against her mother in particular seem wild and far-fetched. When she says, for instance, that her mother is responsible for the murder of a child, she is alone in a world that no one can share.[22] It is at such a point as this that a detailed study of the family background may prove helpful.

It must be admitted, of course, that research into the family history of a schizophrenic is an arduous and chancy business, since it is so difficult to establish who, if anyone, in the family situation is speaking the truth. But one important aspect of the matter appeared in this case from interviews with the patient's family and involved the very minimum of extrapolation or interpretation. All of the really 'significant others' in her life, interviewed at the time of her illness, saw her life in the three stages already mentioned: there was an early one when she was 'good', normal and healthy; but later, 'her behaviour changed so that she acted in terms of what *all* the significant others in her world unanimously agreed was "bad" until, in a short while,

she was "mad"'. The nature of the reports of the transition
between the two last stages gives a clue to the meaning of her
delusions. It was a relief to her family when, instead of saying
such wounding and terrible things as that her mother wouldn't
let her live, she said instead that her mother had murdered a
child. As her mother said, 'I'm glad that it was an illness after
all'. The hint thus provided, of a cryptic connection between a
sane appraisal of the patient's situation and the content of her
delusions, gives a clue to other features of her madness as well,
like her insistence that she was a 'tolled bell'.[23] She was or had
been a 'belle' who did precisely what she was told, without her
heart being in what she did. Another psychotic feature was that
she said her name was 'Mrs Taylor'. She was conveying that
she was 'tailor-made', a 'tailored maid' cut out to suit other
people in all her overt words and actions. This kind of psychotic
statement, in its elliptical, punning and parabolic nature, may
be quite impossible to decipher without the help of the patient
himself. The patient's experience in this case was that her
mother, in the areas of conflict between them, had to be right,
totally right; but she herself felt that in order for her to be able to
exist, to breathe, her mother must admit herself wrong about
some things. At last she began to convert the way she felt about
her relationship to her mother, which she could not and dared
not avow, into physical fact; to talk as though her mother had
literally murdered a child. It was a relief to her family when
they could pity her for being 'mad', and hence no longer felt
compelled to vindicate themselves by condemning her as 'bad'
or 'wicked'.[24]

5 *Recovery of Sanity*

It is important to distinguish sharply between mere restoration
of the *status quo ante* and genuine therapy. In cases of the first
kind, the patient merely gives up the struggle, and plays at
being sane by retreating once more into schizoid shut-upness.
The recovery of Jean, the member of the deeply religious
family, seems to have been just such a return to 'normality'.
During her 'breakdown', she had fleetingly, and to be sure
somewhat frenetically, expressed her real feelings, while her
family prayed, successfully it is to be feared, that she would get

'better' – on their own terms. The means of genuine therapy seems to be to make contact with the original self, which seems to remain a possibility even in the most apparently far-gone cases.[25]

It goes without saying that incomprehensibility is the great barrier in getting to know a schizophrenic. Even when he is *trying* to tell someone about himself, his speech is difficult enough to follow. And he has many motives for not trying: it seems, from what schizophrenics themselves say, that obscurity and complexity are deliberately used as a smokescreen behind which to hide. As one patient explained, the schizophrenic is apt to feel crushed and mangled even by ordinary conversational exchanges. Understanding by another, however much of a relief it may be to him in some respects, constitutes a threat to the defensive system which he has erected. Much of his outward behaviour is analogous to underground passages which appear to lead to the citadel which one is trying to enter, but which in fact lead nowhere. The schizophrenic is apt not to be inclined – why *should* he be? – to reveal himself to any philandering passer-by. Binswanger thus has good reason to advise the therapist not to try to get too near the patient too soon.[26]

The schizophrenic is often deliberately distracting in what he says, but will occasionally throw in something really significant to see whether the doctor has the intelligence and concern to follow it up. When he finds someone who he has any reason to believe can and will help him, there is no more need to resort to distractions. (This throws an interesting light on the remark I once heard from a psychiatrist, that Laing seems never to have met any real schizophrenics.) The first step to cure may actually be when the patient comes to express hatred for the doctor. One might indeed have expected this, since the doctor will be reopening the patient's wounds in establishing personal contact and so getting inside his defences.[27] Not the least significant of the barriers to real cure, as opposed to mere re-establishment of the *status quo ante*, may be the patient's family. Every step in Mary's achievement of autonomy and maturity – at least as these were seen by Laing and his colleagues – were stigmatised by her parents as so much evidence of selfishness and conceit. Maya thought that her main task in life was to become a person in her own rights, to act on her own initiative and independently of her parents. But any steps she took towards achieving this were and had been consistently regarded with alarm by her family.[28]

Having summarised what I take to be Laing's account of schizophrenia more or less without comment, I shall raise and answer a few objections and add some final comments. It is perhaps worth emphasising that this chapter is in no sense an apologetic for all or most of the views which Laing expresses in his books. Thus objections to any general moral or political doctrines which may be attributed to him, whether such objections are well-founded or not, simply are irrelevant to the point at issue.[29] I am concerned only with Laing's account of schizophrenia as it is found in the two books summarised. I mention this only because of the common practice in controversy of discrediting an author's views on one subject by criticising his treatment of another.

With this preliminary caution, I will consider objections one by one:[30]

(a) 'Why should not the schizophrenic have affected the behaviour of his family, rather than the family that of the schizophrenic, as Laing assumes?' That the effect should be mutual does indeed seem likely on the face of it, and is not in the least inconsistent with Laing's account, which merely emphasises the way in which the family affects the schizophrenic rather than the way in which the schizophrenic affects the family.[31] Certainly, if Laing himself, or someone else who claimed to support his views, were to state or to imply that the schizophrenic's behaviour had no reciprocal effect on his family's treatment of him, he would almost certainly be wrong. As to Laing's emphasis on the one side, one may perhaps plead with Kierkegaard that it is difficult at once to provide a corrective and the corrective of that corrective.

(b) 'It may be that the same genetic factor has influenced the behaviour both of the schizophrenic and of his family. This is certainly the case with Huntingdon's chorea, which is known *both* to be hereditary *and* to occur in families which are highly eccentric in other respects.' Now it appears to me, from what I know of the evidence – for example Kallmann's research and the discussion which it has provoked[32] – that the existence of a hereditary predisposition to schizophrenia is virtually certain. But Laing himself *admits* the possibility of genetically predisposing factors,[33] which admission is indeeed in no way incompatible with his general account.

(c) 'The wide acceptance of Laing's account would put an intolerable strain on the families, and especially the mothers, of schizophrenics. The unhappiness which would arise from their feelings of guilt would be intensified by the witch hunts to which they would be subjected by psychiatrists.' This is certainly a point which ought to be borne in mind when one considers how Laing's theories ought to be implemented, if they are true; but it really has no bearing on the question of whether they are true or not. Those doctors who prescribed thalidomide for the prospective mothers of 'thalidomide babies' must have many feelings of guilt and regret, for which they deserve a great deal of sympathy from those who have the good luck not to be involved; but this has no bearing on the truth of the proposition that the drug which they prescribed had the appalling results usually attributed to it. In any case, Laing's researches provide flimsy grounds at best for those who would argue that the families of schizophrenics are in some absolute sense worse than other families. They merely tend to support the view that dispositions which are surely almost universal, when carried beyond a certain point, and brought to bear on someone who is to a certain degree vulnerable in the relevant respect, tends to result in schizophrenia.

(d) 'Laing's schizophrenics are very untypical cases.' If this is true, there might be several reasons for it; one perhaps being, as Jung suggested long ago, that many schizophrenics stop being at least typically 'schizophrenic' when approached with understanding and respect. And even if it is granted that his cases remain untypical when the attitude of the psychiatrist is taken into account, Laing's theory may still provide a useful avenue of approach to the treatment of *some* schizophrenics. How untypical the cases discussed by Laing are, if they are untypical at all, can be decided only by extensive research into the responses of schizophrenics to different kinds of treatment, and into the normality or abnormality of their family backgrounds.

(e) 'The validity of Laing's account depends on acquisition of information about the schizophrenic's early life, and the history of his relations with his family. But reliable information about these is impossible to get, owing to the subjective bias of all concerned.' Such bias is admittedly difficult to reveal and allow for all at once; but it can all the same progressively be shown up for what it is when a sufficient number of circumstances and other relevant viewpoints are taken into account. The procedure which has to be followed in order that a relatively fair picture may be obtained is rather like that of detective work, as Laing remarks; rather like that of historical research. One should view an account with increasing suspicion the less self-consistent it is, the less it is corroborated by other circumstances and witnesses, and the more the giver of the account has to gain by his story being accepted. The facts that such information is often difficult to get and to evaluate, and that it cannot be quantified by the procedures usual in the physical sciences, provide no grounds whatever for supposing that it is not relevant to the psychiatrist's purposes.

(f) 'Laing seems intent on blaming the family, and perhaps especially the mother, for the condition of the schizophrenic. But the important question is not who is to blame for the situation, but how it may best be coped with.' But the point of Laing's account is not the assigning of blame as such, but rather an analysis of the nature and causes of schizophrenia, in order not only that patients should in future be more effectively cured, but that they should be prevented so far as possible from falling ill in the first place. Whether blame is appropriate, and to what extent it is so, is another matter.

(g) 'If therapy is to be reliable, it ought to be based so far as possible on scientific psychological theory. Laing's account, whatever its virtues may be in other respects, certainly is not scientific'. This objection has already in principle been dealt with;[34] but something more remains to be said. Let us take as a paradigm case of a scientific psychological theory Skinner's theory of operant conditioning. Now therapy on Laing's account consists, in essentials, in (a) getting to understand the patient's point of view, and (b) finding or creating an environment for him in which, given that point of view, he can interact with his fellows in a way which is fairly satisfying to all parties.

It can scarcely be denied that there is a difference of some kind between, on the one hand, getting to understand the patient's point of view and taking it into account in preparing him to re-enter society and society to receive him, and on the other hand, readjusting him to society without taking his point of view into account. Now it is true, as a matter of logic, either that Skinner's theory of operant conditioning is subtle enough to preserve this difference, or that it is not. If it is, well and good: Laing's account is not in essential conflict with Skinner's theories; Laing's stipulations amount merely to the insistence that one kind of operant conditioning rather than another is the most effective in achieving the desired result. If Skinner's theory is not sufficiently subtle to preserve the difference, then Laing's clinical experience is only one among many indications that there is something inadequate in the whole theory of operant conditioning as providing a basis for the explanation of human behaviour.

(h) 'There is reason to think that Laing's methods are the very opposite of therapeutic, since patients, by being encouraged to talk about the delusions which are constitutive of their illness, will have them reinforced.' This objection neglects the very great difference between merely being encouraged to repeat some bizarre statement and being asked to explain or account for it. To be asked to explain or account for what one says or does is by no means necessarily to be encouraged to persist in saying or doing it.

(i) 'It is surely an argument in favour of the biochemical theory of the causation of schizophrenia that states very similar to it can be brought about by means of drugs.' It is perhaps worth bearing in mind the parallel with depression. I understand that it is agreed on all hands that one may be depressed either *about* some situation or other, or *owing to* some organic condition. These forms of explanation are of course not mutually exclusive. One who is organically so predisposed may get depressed for some trivial reason; in such a case, both the reason for the depression, and the physical causes of it, would have to be taken into account if one were to arrive at a complete explanation. It has been pointed out as well that a cutting of the *corpus callosum* between the hemispheres of a person's brain induces signs and symptoms closely analogous to neurotic dissociation and to self-deception; I do not know whether anyone would want to argue from this that cases of self-deception should not be explained as a rule as at least primarily due to a subject's motives for avoiding adverting to some unpleasant fact.[35] I cannot see why this should not also be the case with schizophrenia; that causes of the kind described by Laing and physiological causes should not both contribute in different proportions to different cases. Also it seems not unlikely on the face of it that repeated experience of a certain kind of situation, and of the emotions associated with it, may have long-term effects on the biochemistry of the brain.[36]

Mention of self-deception invites a speculation with which it seems fitting to conclude this chapter; on the relation between schizophrenia and self-deception by members of the patient's family. It is remarkable how often the 'bad' behaviour of the schizophrenics described by Laing, before it is finally decided that they are 'mad', consists in their drawing attention to oppressive or inconsistent features in the behaviour or discourse of their families, which the families themselves are unable to face. Self-deception certainly seems to be at the root of the so-called 'double-bind', when one person A, typically a parent, puts another B in a situation in which whatever B does will be wrong. The fact that A can always get away with blaming B will save him from making the humiliating discovery of pathologically vindictive elements, for example, in his own character. It has been argued that repetitions of such situations as this are liable to lead ultimately to schizophrenia in B.[37] That we would rather drive our nearest and dearest mad, than acknowledge defects in our own characters, is a reflection on human nature perhaps more melancholy than implausible.

It is worth summarising what is to be learned from Laing, on the general problem with which this book is concerned. Above all he brings out the extraordinary capacity of a certain kind of self-deception in some people to give rise to suffering in others. A restriction of my own effective freedom, through sloth, fear, self-indulgence or self-esteem, may result in a total denial of effective freedom to one or more persons in my environment. A full appreciation of this fact is bound to have a profound effect on one's judgement of what kinds of action are good and bad, and in what degree. Is it not to be plausibly inferred, for example, that one kind of parental behaviour, which is almost universally tolerated and very widely commended, is objectively worse than many kinds of indictable crime? Laing's case-histories bring out with wonderful lucidity and force a typical pattern of oppression existing between members of families; Marx's work, as we shall see, shows just the same kind of relation between the classes of society.

3 Man as Animal: Lorenz

Man is related to non-human animals, and shares many of their characteristics as a result. What can be inferred from this about the actions and dispositions which promote his flourishing and consequently, given the overall validity of the arguments of the first chapter,[1] about what human actions and dispositions are good or bad?

The argument of Konrad Lorenz's *On Aggression*, so far as it is relevant to the purposes of this book, is reducible to the following nine theses, the last five of them directly relevant to morality and based on the first four:

1. Personal bonds of love and friendship occur only among animals which are aggressive towards other members of their own species.
2. Love and friendship have evolved phylogenetically from, and in certain circumstances may turn back into, intra-specific aggression.
3. Intra-specific aggression does not often lead conspecifics to kill one another, at least in the natural state; powerfully armed animals have evolved by natural selection to have strong inhibitions against the killing of members of their own species.
4. The condition of men in palaeolithic times developed markedly in them aggression between tribal groups; in inter-tribal warfare, the 'warrior virtues' were at a premium from the point of view of survival.
5. Aggression between man and man is to a large extent an innate rather than a socially imposed characteristic, and is hence hardly to be removed, though it may indeed be ameliorated, by appropriate education and social organisation.
6. Specifically moral and other-regarding dispositions also depend on inherited instinct, and not merely on the inhibition of such instinct or its restraint by reason.

7. The redirection of aggression outside one's community is a possible solution to the problem of discharging aggression.

8. With the invention of long-range weapons, the expression of man's aggressive impulses towards other members of his species has tended to become less compensated by corresponding inhibitions than formerly.

9. The conditions of modern life leave people with no adequate scope for the discharge of their aggressive impulses, and this is a prime cause of violence and neurosis.

I shall summarise the material with which Lorenz supports each of these theses, and conclude with some comments.

1   *Personal bonds of love and friendship occur only among animals which are aggressive towards other members of their own species.*

In explaining any trait characteristic of animals, especially when it is widespread among many different and unrelated species, the zoologist is bound to ask what survival value it has. It is at first difficult to see what survival value there could be in aggression between members of the same species. Darwin noted that it was better for the prospects of a race if the strongest male among those available took possession of the female; and to this end, a fight resulting in the loser making himself scarce is evidently one available means. More recently it has been remarked that intra-specific aggression tends to spread a species over its available habitat, so that overcrowding, with bad consequences for the food supply, does not occur. It seems that this last effect constitutes the most important survival value of intra-specific aggression. It also seems that the personal bond, that is the state in which two or more members of the same species treat each other with special discrimination, came into existence at that point in evolution where the co-operation of two or more aggressive animals was necessary; and usually this was for the tending of the brood. It is remarkable that only aggressive animals form personal bonds of this kind. Now aggression is millions of years older than personal friendship and love. Most present day reptiles are aggressive towards other members of their own species, and there is every reason to suppose that their ancestors were at least equally so. But the personal bond appears only in one group of fishes, in birds and in mammals – all of which groups have developed fairly recently by evolutionary standards.[2]

2   *Love and friendship have evolved phylogenetically from intra-specific aggression, and in certain circumstances may turn back into it.*

This is the central thesis of *On Aggression*, from which the others are all more or less derivative; I shall therefore give a fair amount of space to Lorenz's defence and illustration of it. Among some aggressive and brightly coloured fish, it is to be observed that there is peaceful coexistence only between individuals in a conjugal pair; on the other hand, such a pair will be more aggressive than will single fish towards outsiders. The male of a pair of cichlids is in the habit, moreover, of delivering a furious attack on his mate which in the event bypasses her narrowly and finds its goal in another cichlid – which in natural conditions is apt to be the territorial neighbour. In the very early stages of cohabitation between a pair of cichlids, the partner must always appear from the same direction, in the same manner, with the same lighting; otherwise each fish regards the other as a stranger to be fought. If a captive couple is put into another aquarium at this stage, the whole process of pair-formation may be wrecked. But 'the closer the acquaintanceship becomes, the more the picture [of the mate] becomes independent of the background'. In aquarium cichlids, where aggression which would normally be vented on the territorial neighbours is denied outlet, the result is sometimes the killing of one of the partners. Experienced keepers have occasionally been made aware that glass partitions, with cichlid pairs on each side, were being blurred by a growth of weed, by the fact that a cichlid male was getting very rude to his wife.[3]

In some geese and ducks, the female will incite her mate to attack another member of the species; in others, the action of 'inciting' seems to have become entirely stylised, and there are many intermediate states:

> While the message of inciting in ruddy shelduck and Egyptian geese could be expressed in the words 'Drive him off, thrash him!', in diving ducks (and dabbling ducks) it simply means 'I love you'. In several groups, midway between these

two extremes, as for example in the gadwall and widgeon, an intermediate meaning may be found, 'You are my hero. I rely on you.'

(These 'meanings' are to be inferred from the situations which the actions fit, into which, as Wittgenstein might have said, they are woven in the elementary language-games of the various species of ducks and geese concerned.)[4] This series of examples is an especially striking illustration of what may be said to be the central thesis of *On Aggression* – that activities arising from redirected aggression form and maintain bonds of love and friendship between conspecifics. The behaviour of aggression redirected to love, for example between a pair of ducks, becomes itself a relief of the instinctual drive; thus the behaviour *is* the bond. A bird or other animal in losing its mate loses the only object on which it can discharge the drive; hence the restless searching that ensues for the lost partner. Between living mates, there results 'that magic elastic band which, in geese, ravens or jackdaws, evidently pulls harder as the mates get further away from one another'.[5]

It appears that evolution has in general solved the problem of preventing inter-marital fighting not by inhibition of aggression, but by its redirection against the hostile neighbour. In the so-called 'dance' of cranes, 'the whole procedure says as clearly as human words, "I am big and threatening, but not towards you – towards the other, the other, the other".' A mallard pair will engage in their own greeting ceremony most intensely when they find one another again after a long period of separation. Disintegration of fighting inhibitions seems to threaten the partners every time they separate; this explains the appeasement ceremony which there is at each reunion. In human beings as well we find greeting between lovers and friends excited and intense in proportion to the length of time of the separation. Some types of human greeting give special plausibility to the idea that the greeting smile has evolved through the ritualising of redirected threatening. 'The friendly tooth-baring of very polite Japanese lends support to this theory.' Many orientals smile in this way; and it is remarkable that when smiling most intensely they do not look straight at the person greeted, but past him.[6]

The general conclusion seems to be that, in the course of phylogenesis, 'greeting has evolved from threatening by way of redirection and ritualisation.' In individual development, however, it is greeting from the first. In the case of the greylag goose, it is the so-called 'triumph ceremony', the stylised procedure of greeting, which holds the pair together; sexual intercourse does not seem to play such an important role. In the female of this species, copulation and the triumph ceremony cannot readily be performed with different individuals. Also, the goose finds it more difficult than does the gander to enter into a new triumph-ceremony relationship after she has lost her partner. However, an often widowed or divorced (female) goose is comparatively very ready to enter a new triumph-ceremony relationship or to copulate, not being inhibited by the maidenly restraint which is typical of virgin geese. A goose deprived of its partner by mischance will at first search round actively for it; when this search is unsuccessful, the bereaved goose loses all courage and runs away even from the youngest and weakest members of the flock. Everything observable in the bearing of a goose which loses its mate corresponds to what is to be seen in human grief. In goose as in man, it is in the neighbourhood of the eyes, due to a certain characteristic set of the muscles, that the characteristic signs of deep grief are to be seen.

If, in the greylag goose and in man, highly complex norms of behaviour, such as falling in love, strife for ranking order, jealousy, grieving etc., are not only similar but down to the most absurd details the same, we can be sure that every one of these instincts has survival value, in each case almost if not quite the same in the greylag as in man.[7]

The triumph ceremony, when it reaches a very high level of intensity, becomes more and more ominously similar to the aggression which is its prototype. Usually this sinister de-ritualisation subsides, but in a very few observed cases the partners have started beating one another with a severity out of all proportion to that of the usual squabbles between geese. The usual sort of fight lasts only a few seconds or at most a minute or two, whereas this particular kind may last five minutes. Once this has happened between triumph-ceremony partners, they seem sedulously to avoid one another. When they do chance to come face to face, their reaction can be described only as one of embarrassment. The peculiar bitterness of matrimonial quarrels in man is evidently closely comparable. It is difficult to avoid the conclusion that in all true cases of love the measure of latent aggression is so high that, on the rupturing of the bond, hate regularly makes its appearance. Hate, as opposed to ordinary aggressiveness, is directed towards a particular individual, just as love is.[8]

It is remarkable that geese reared in isolation from their peers are very disturbed in relation to their environment, particularly its social aspect; in this they show a vivid analogy to hospitalised human children. Especially strongly affected is the capacity for dealing with novel situations: rather than actively exploring its environment and searching for new stimuli, the goose who has been deprived of normal contacts will avoid any new stimulation and react to it as though it were painful. The geese seem slowly to recover; it is not yet known how complete such recovery can be. 'As yet none of our experimental geese [i.e. those reared in isolation] has paired'.[9]

The argument with which Lorenz supports the second thesis which I distinguished should now be summarised, since one may lose sight of it in the welter of corroborative detail. To explain how any structural or behavioural characteristic of a species has evolved is to show both how it has survival value for that species and how it could have arisen by plausible mutations from those of earlier forms. Given sexual reproduction, it is evidently necessary for conspecifics not to avoid one another in all circumstances; but given the necessity for the spread of a species over the available habitat to avoid overcrowding, aggressive behaviour towards conspecifics seems also to have survival value. So far all that has to be reconciled are the need to associate long enough for copulation, and general aggression against other members of the species. But if young are to be reared and protected, association of two or more animals for this purpose will evidently have survival value within the general context of intra-specific aggression. But how could such a profound modification of behaviour come about? Lorenz argues that it does so by the redirection of aggression from the mate to other members of the species. In the absence of alternative explanations, this one surely has some plausibility; it is confirmed to some extent by the fact that all animals which form personal bonds are aggressive towards other members of their own species, and more impressively by the apparent presence of all degrees of such redirection and sublimation in nature.

3   *Intra-specific aggression does not often lead conspecifics to kill one another, at least in the natural state; powerfully built animals have evolved by natural selection to have strong inhibitions against the killing of members of their own species.*

In all the very heavily armed carnivorous mammals, intra-specific aggression is limited by strong inhibitions. The present dangers to human civilisation are due precisely to the fact that man has *not* got a carnivorous mentality; he is basically harmless, devoid of natural weapons for killing prey, and therefore without such strong inhibitions against killing his own kind as such creatures must have in order to survive as species. This is not to deny, of course, that man has *some* inhibitions of this kind; a little introspection will suggest that at moments of great aggressive feeling one does not so much want to kill one's enemy as to beat him sufficiently to make him feel one's superiority.[10]

The gentleman's horror at the idea of striking any woman, which one might expect to be determined rather narrowly by culture, is shared by a wide range of species of animals. Not only do dogs refuse to bite bitches, even under severe provocation, but there are inhibitions against fighting females in hamsters, goldfinches and even a few reptiles. The male bullfinch, who accepts any number of attacks from his wife without becoming aggressive, evidently impresses her in so doing. It is worthy of notice that this and other examples of chivalrous behaviour, such as feeding the mate in birds, are privileges falling to the higher ranking of two animals.[11]

4   *The condition of men in palaeolithic times developed markedly in them aggression between tribal groups; in inter-tribal warfare, the 'warrior virtues' were at a premium from the point of view of survival.*

Sometimes natural selection comes to operate as a form of competition within a species which does not help the species as such to survive. The Egyptian goose will incite her male partner to fight, and if he loses will tend to go over to the victor. This fighting urge is probably of no survival value whatever to the species, but is a result of intra-specific selection. The hen of the argus pheasant reacts sexually to huge eye-spots on the wings of the male. A cock with really big eye-spots can scarcely fly; and the result is that it is precisely the leaver of most descendants who is most liable to be eaten by predators. Here, as in Western man's hectic competitive life, 'competition between members of a species causes selective breeding without any relation to the extra-specific environment.' Forty thousand years or so ago, in the early Stone Age, man had mastered the dangers which threatened him from nature to such an extent that the pressure exerted by one tribe upon another became the chief factor determining human evolution. So it is that man has developed those 'warrior virtues' which are still unfortunately so widely regarded as unequivocally desirable. The greatest dangers to man's survival at present stem from the fact that those instinctive dispositions which enabled our ancestors to survive in inter-tribal fighting now realise themselves most effectively in war; these are 'readiness to sacrifice oneself in the service of a common cause, disciplined submission to the rank-order of a group, mutual aid in the face of deadly danger, and above all, a superlatively strong bond of friendship between men'. That such admirable qualities flourish in war makes many decent people fail to see war for the abominable evil that it is. Intra-specific selection in man works also in the direction of self-assertion and the amassing of property, and in general against simple goodness.[12]

5   *Aggression between man and man is to a large extent an innate rather than a socially imposed characteristic, and is hence hardly to be removed, though it may indeed be ameliorated, by appropriate education and social organisation.*

That the aggressive tendency is innate in man as well as in other animals seems an inescapable conclusion from the evidence. I suppose most people would accept that this is the case for the non-human animals; but in man, matters are widely supposed to be different. The erroneous underlying assumption

is that 'animal and human behaviour is predominantly reactive
and that, even if it contains any innate elements at all, it can be
altered to an unlimited extent by learning'. This superstition,
dear as it is to ideologues both eastern and western, flies in the
face of the evidence. The central nervous system does not have
to wait for stimuli, whatever the ideological pressure in favour
of its doing so. A captive male ring-dove deprived of female
company first courted a previously ignored white dove, then a
rolled-up newspaper when deprived of that, and finally a
corner of his cage. It appears that the threshold-value of
eliciting stimuli drops steadily the longer an instinctual behaviour-pattern is inactive. The stimulus may even drop to
zero; as when a hand-reared starling snapped at imaginary
flies. And if the eliciting stimuli do not appear for some time,
the organism is

> thrown into a state of general unrest and begins to search
> actively for the missing stimulus. In the simplest case, this
> 'search' consists only in an increase of random locomotion, in
> swimming or running round; in the most complicated, it may
> include the highest achievements of learning and insight.[13]

6   *Specifically moral and other-regarding dispositions also depend on
inherited instinct, and not merely on the inhibition of such instinct or its
restraint by reason.*

Now many, including some philosophers, appear to think that
all human behaviour which tends to promote the welfare of the
community, as opposed to that of the individual himself, is due
to imposed inhibition or rational reflection. On the contrary,
moral responsibility, and the feelings and emotions which
undergird it, could not have arisen unless men had been
members of structured communities before ever conceptual
thinking took place. If social customs did not develop this kind
of autonomous power, there would be no good faith and no law.
However much rational insight one may have into an action
and the maxim underlying it, there would be no imperative or
prohibition unless some emotional source of energy, which can
derive only from our instincts, supplied the motive. Men on the
whole behave well in difficult situations, so long as these are of a

kind which occurred often enough in palaeolithic times for social norms to have evolved for coping with them. This is as much as to say that there are some kinds of strain which people are genetically adapted to take. But in our predisposition to conform with social norms, we differ a great deal from one another. A man who is instinctively inclined to behave in a socially beneficial manner does not make many demands on his reserves of moral responsibility, and has them available for exceptional circumstances; whereas one who has to use all his reserves to curb day-to-day inclinations will be very likely to break down under additional stress.[14]

7   *The redirection of aggression outside one's community is a possible solution to the problem of discharging aggression.*

One form of social organisation in animals is characterised by collective hostility of one group against another. The malfunction of this form of aggression seems to be a model in which we can see some of the dangers threatening ourselves. Now jackdaws, geese and monkeys seem to know one another personally, rats and bees only as clan members or otherwise. This seems to be done by the sense of smell: a rat can become a hated stranger to other members of its clan if its smell is changed. Like the smell of rats, human 'good manners' – that is to say the manners of one's group – inhibit aggression and form bonds. To enter a room without various little appeasing rituals provokes anger, just as overt aggression does. Members of the Latin races are often considered 'unreliable' by Germans and Anglo-Saxons, just because their more pronounced gestures of conciliation lead the latter to expect more good will than is actually forthcoming. Little misunderstandings arising from this do much to contribute to hate between groups; one feels one has been deliberately cheated or wronged by the foreigner. The extreme expression of this tendency is those cases in which other groups are not considered to be human – as in some primitive tribes where the word meaning 'member of the tribe' is the same as that for 'man'.[15]

The most familiar symptom of solidarity with one's own group and opposition to others is the emotion of militant enthusiasm. The object defended by militant enthusiasm seems originally to have been the small community held together by personal acquaintance and friendship; later, as the social unit grew and the norms and rites which characterised it became the factors holding it together, these themselves became the focus of loyalty. It seems that we do not enjoy combativeness because we are split into such groups as political parties, but we are split into political parties and other mutually opposed groups because this is a satisfying way of arousing our militant enthusiasm.[16]

8   *With the invention of long-range weapons, the expression of man's aggressive impulses towards other members of his species has tended to become less compensated by corresponding inhibitions than formerly.*

As was stated above, it appears that there has been little pressure from natural selection since palaeolithic times to prevent men from killing their fellows; and now suddenly 'the equilibrium of killing potential and social inhibitions' has been upset by the invention of artificial weapons. All at once we became like pigeons who had abruptly acquired the beaks of ravens. 'One shudders at the thought of a creature as irascible as all primates are swinging a well-sharpened hand-axe.' It is the distance at which shooting-weapons take effect which prevents the inhibition of the assailant's urge to kill which would otherwise occur; the pity which would allow a well-beaten opponent to slink away has no chance to operate.[17]

9   *The conditions of modern life leave people with no adequate scope for the discharge of their aggressive impulses, and this is a prime cause of violence and neurosis.*

We have evolved, on the contrary, as has previously been said, to find a deep satisfaction in the state of war. Now if we want to control any instinctual behaviour-pattern, the first thing to find out is the situations which evoke it. The militant enthusiasm which is so fruitful a source of war and other conflict is fostered especially in the following circumstances:
(a) When the group with which the enthusiast identifies himself appears to be threatened from without. This group may be of any size from a family to a nation state; or it may be represented

by the ideals in relation to which the group is identified. So the response may be brought into action on behalf of the sports club or the country, or in the service of any ideal whatever, from that of the practice of the most absurd rituals and mannerisms to that of the pursuit of scientific truth or social justice.

(b) When there is an identifiable hostile group which is supposed to constitute a threat to the original group or its 'values'; this can be concrete or abstract, the Jews or the Boches on the one hand, or capitalism, fascism, bolshevism or any other sort of -ism on the other.

(c) When there is an inspiring leader. Even those groups which adhere to ideals one would have thought inimical to the cultivation of leader-figures cannot do without them, as is clear from the fact that political parties of all kinds display huge pictures of their leaders.

(d) When there are many other individuals who share the enthusiasm; the degree of excitation seems to grow in proportion to the number of individuals involved.[18]

Fortunately, aggression can be transferred to substitute objects much more easily than most other instincts. And the choice of objects is more amenable to reason than might appear at first sight. Even those violently irascible people who break crockery when they are in a temper, and appear to have lost all vestige of control over their actions, tend to choose cheap things to smash rather than really valuable ones. Sport is of the greatest importance not merely as an outlet for aggression, but as a school for the control of human fighting behaviour. (Sir Arthur Grimble says, in his book *A Pattern of Islands*, that some of the Gilbertese were quite conscious that cricket took the place of inter-tribal warfare.) Thus there is some ground for hope at least that we may manage to sublimate our excess of the warrior virtues and our innate disposition to admire them, into the more strenuous forms of sport, and perhaps outstandingly into braving the perils of space exploration. Another means of preventing the mutual group hatred which leads to war is personal acquaintance between members of different nations, since no one can wholeheartedly hate a nation among which he has several personal friends. We can learn a great deal on this matter from the demagogues who pursue exactly the opposite policy, since they know very well that any sort of fellow-feeling makes an obstacle to aggression.[19]

Natural selection seems to determine the fate of human cultures in rather the same way as it does that of species: the successful ones surviving, the unsuccessful perishing. Many superstitions get institutionalised; and this disposition to maintain patterns of behaviour which have got one by in the past is evidently of survival value short of discovery of anything better. There is a danger that valuable patterns of behaviour may be rejected when the role that they play is insufficiently appreciated; the legend of the tree of knowledge is perhaps a defence of sacred traditions against such premature displacement. Human cultures fortunately seem to have evolved a mechanism for gradual change. At about the age of puberty, human individuals tend to loosen their allegiance to the norms and values provided by their cultures, and to look around for other ideals.[20] If the older ideals seem inadequate under scrutiny, but none appear to take their place, it may be suspected that the aimlessness and boredom of the typical young delinquent are the natural consequence. Alternatively, the need to belong to a group fighting for ideals may be so strong that almost any ideals, however absurd in themselves, will serve the purpose. This seems to be the explanation of the formation of juvenile gangs, whose social structure is probably like that in very primitive human societies. Apparently this fixation is apt to happen only once in an individual's life;[21] once the allegiance to a cause or the embracing of new social norms is thoroughly established, it cannot be erased again, at least not so as to make room for another equally strong attachment.[22]

It may be objected that the ascription of love and friendship to geese and even fish, let alone of chivalry to lizards,[23] is excessively anthropomorphic. Now certainly human society, or some other society of equally intelligent and sensitive beings, is the necessary locus of love and friendship in the full sense of these terms; and it is deceptive to talk, when referring to animals other than man, as though this full context existed. Could the Egyptian goose, it might be asked, who makes certain gestures to her mate in the presence of an intruder, *really* mean 'Drive him off! Thrash him!'? The answer is surely that to say that this is the meaning of the gesture is to say that the gesture is as it were woven into the other actions and the total situation of the geese concerned, very much as the verbal expression is in the case of human beings.[24] Perhaps where some are in danger of excessive anthropomorphism in describing such a situation, others are in danger of not enough of it. It is no *more* misleading, on the face of it, to assume that there is among other animals the complex human situation which provides the paradigm occasion for the application of terms like 'love', 'hatred' and 'incitement', than to assume that there is nothing at all analogous to it. Particularly in cases like that of the greylag goose, in whose social behaviour there are so many striking parallels to that of human beings, it seems less arbitrary to make use of the equivalent human terms, at least when the appropriate qualifications are made or can be assumed, than to refuse to use them. Animals are not men; but, *pace* Descartes, they are not mere things either.

It might further be objected that the kind of argument which Lorenz uses, for instance, to show that a disposition to aggression is innate in man, can never amount to real proof. The question then arises of what would count as a compelling argument in such a context. In questions about biological evolution, crucial experiments are not possible; palaeontology, like history, does not conform, at least at all neatly, to the canons of scientific inquiry which have been laid down by, for instance, Sir Karl Popper. All that one can do is to provide hypotheses to fit the known facts – though it is important for their scientific status, certainly, that evidence *conceivably could* turn up which would tend to falsify them. Lorenz's account surely ought to be accepted until we have a better hypothesis to account for the existence of aggression and of love, and the particular relationship that is to be observed between them in so many kinds of animal. And this theory entails that the human predisposition to aggression is innate. The contrary thesis, that aggressive tendencies are only instilled by environment (which it is admitted on all hands can be shown to exacerbate or ameliorate them), not only is not capable of proof, but does not have a shred of evidence in support of it. The grounds for believing it are ideological, not scientific.[25]

The very widely held belief, that aggression between human beings is due only to environmental factors, is a fallacy confirmed by no evidence, but only by the fantasies of millenarians

and the sentimentality of educationists. If aggressive dispositions are innate in the vast majority of human beings, we
cannot, if we are to survive as a race, go on indulging ourselves
in the luxury of blaming the contingencies of social systems for
it. Bertrand Russell, when he tried running a school on the most
permissive principles possible, found that the children tended
all the same sometimes to hit one another. Evidently, he
concluded, his enlightened regime could not counteract the
harm done to the children by their parents. Russell's assumption here, that an aggressive disposition must be due entirely to
environmental and not at all to genetic factors, is a very
widespread one. Marxists and Western democrats are alike
predisposed to believe that we are born as *tabulae rasae* ready for
the imposition of characteristics, intellectual or moral or emotional, by our environment.[26] To deny this doctrine is unfortunately to set limits to the influence which can be exerted on
human behaviour by education. Apparently, each one of us is
born with certain latent capacities for behavioural development, which our environment, though it can as it were play one
of a huge number of variations on it, cannot modify to an
indefinite extent.

Certain potentialities for development, including more or
less aggression, are built into each individual at birth. These
cannot be altered radically short of destruction of the organism.
To believe otherwise is either to contest what appears incon-
testable, that many behavioural dispositions in animals are
innate and not learned; or to postulate a complete difference in
this respect between man and other animals. Intelligence and
reason certainly give us a degree of manoeuvrability in relation
to our instincts, such as other animals do not have; it would
indeed be self-destructive to deny this, as I have already
argued.[27]

It has been suggested that hard work may be a means of
sublimating aggressive tendencies, and hence that the slowing-
up of the pace of work might release aggression elsewhere in a
person's life.[28] ('In my young day, students and workers had too
much to do to be for ever protesting and striking. And one
notices in general that it's usually the arts students, who have
far more time on their hands than the scientists, who make most
of the trouble.') Now I understand that human work in general

is rather analogous to the non-human animal's hunt for food, and in the case of the predator to its killing of animals of *other* species, than to intra-specific aggression. However, intra-specific aggression may surely very readily be expressed incidentally in work. The fact that castigation of one's opponents seems to give additional zest to academic work might be taken as confirmation of this.

Lorenz's causal analysis of the obvious human tendency to form mutually opposed groups has some disquieting consequences. We tend to assume without question what we very properly feel *ought* to be the case, that the strength of our moral feelings is due to the moral turpitude of our enemy. Lorenz's arguments, like those of the psychoanalysts, insinuate the unpleasant suggestion that we often infer the badness of a group of persons or a set of ideas from the strength of the moral feelings we have against them.

Another reflection is perhaps a good deal more disquieting. It seems to be a corollary of Lorenz's theory that different races are liable to differ somewhat from one another in the average predispositions to behaviour of their members, since the palaeolothic inter-tribal struggle for survival would be liable to have affected the evolution of different human groups in somewhat different ways. Lorenz himself cites the example of the Ute Indians, who he claims are *as a race* especially prone to certain types of neurosis. This particular claim has been shown, by one of the more careful and well-informed of Lorenz's critics, to be at least highly questionable.[29] But even if it were shown to be false, the corollary to be deduced from Lorenz's theory is by no means disproved. I find its possible implications ideologically repulsive, but have not seen any convincing scientific objections to them. To be sure, I have seen emotional objections made by scientists in the name of science; but this is another matter. I do not think anyone could with any show of plausibility use evidence of the kind supplied by Lorenz to support any one of the varieties of racialism which have been influential up to now. (A case could surely be made for the view that the Caucasoid races have demonstrated, by their hideous record of bloodshed during the present century, that they are genetically unsuited to run their own affairs – let alone those of anyone else – and had better be governed by members of a race or races with a better record in this respect.) And I would have thought that the evidence so far obtained makes it very reasonable to suppose that genetic and environmental differences between individuals are more important factors in determining intelligence and character than are differences of race. Yet one central premiss of racialism, that human races as such differ in the normal predispositions to behaviour of their members, does find support in Lorenz's work.

It is, of course, true that there is a positive correlation between the degree to which many animals, including man, are frustrated, and how aggressive they are.[30] But this does not by any means imply that if there were never any frustration in the life of a human being, he would never be aggressive at all.[31] And even if it were granted that if a man were never frustrated, he would never be aggressive, it is surely almost inconceivable that the human environment could ever be organised in such a way that no one was *ever* frustrated in *any* way. Lorenz nowhere asserts that it is fruitless to inquire into how we may diminish and sublimate our aggressive dispositions, and how we may avoid the frustrations which exacerbate them; indeed, a great deal of the final part of *On Aggression* seems designed to impress upon the reader the urgency of just this kind of research. Lorenz's outlook on the future of man is in some ways alarming, but it is by no means hopeless; and even if it *were* hopeless, this would be no valid objection to the reasoning on which it is based.

Some human societies, though indeed all too few, show no disposition to attack their neighbours and little inclination for internal quarrelling. It would be useful if this singular lack of aggressiveness could be accounted for, and the moral applied two ourselves. Geoffrey Gorer has pointed out that a number of such tribes in New Guinea have two other characteristics in common: that their members show enormous gusto in concrete pleasures like eating, drinking, laughter and sexual intercourse; and that they make little distinction between their character ideals for men and women, and in particular cherish no ideal of brave, aggressive masculinity.[32] The first may amount to some indication that the slogan 'Make love not war' has some justification beneath its prima-facie absurdity; the second that the widespread contempt for womanish

characteristics in men and mannish characteristics in women
should at least be subjected to critical scrutiny.

It seems worthwhile to conclude this chapter with a comment on those who would object in principle to the use of
studies of animal behaviour to shed light on human moral and
social problems.[33]

(i) The grasping of analogies, of likeness in what is at first sight
unlike, would appear to be one of the most important of man's
mental characteristics. Without it, human knowledge would
never have advanced beyond the mere amassing of observable
data.

(ii) Not all analogies prove fruitful for the advance of knowledge. It is not enough to apprehend that there may be some
analogy between types of phenomena A and B (say, the movements of the moon and the fall of an apple). One has to work out
what *would* occur *if* A were similar to B in the relevant respect,
and then find out by observation or experiment whether it does
so or not. You cannot assume that *whatever* you find out about
the Trobriand islanders will apply to the bourgeoisie of Europe
or North America. But you may propound, test and possibly
even verify the hypothesis that *some* of the things you have found
out are so applicable.

General objections to the practice of applying studies of
animal behaviour to man seem characteristically to oscillate
between denial of (i), which would render science impossible;
and assertion of (ii), which is not relevant to the refutation of
such a case as is put forward by Lorenz. According to the
criterion alluded to at the end of (ii), the analogy between the
behaviour of other animals and that of men would appear to be
a fruitful one. For example, there is evidence, as I have said,
that young geese and monkeys deprived of a close relationship
with a mother or mother-substitute are apt to develop abnormalities in behaviour and show signs of distress; there is also
evidence that something similar applies in the case of human
children. It is not infrequently suggested that in the Ideal
Society of the Future, this inconvenient need by children for
parents or parent-substitutes, or at least for a small group of
regularly available and caring adults, would cease. The parallel with non-human animals would suggest that this is not the
case. That the typical expression of parental affection differs

somewhat between goose, monkey and man is not to the point. The moon is not all that like an apple.

That man's intelligence and reason give him a measure of freedom of manoeuvre in relation to his inheritance of instinct is certainly true, but by no means incompatible with what is argued by Lorenz. This freedom of manoeuvre is adequate to account, it seems to me, for the wide range of solutions provided by human cultures to the problems set by basic human instincts.[34]

What in general is to be learned from Lorenz on the central topic with which we are concerned? It is that certain basic predispositions, inherited from our animal ancestors, are part of our 'nature', in the sense that they have evolved along with the structure of our bodies and the chemical constitution of our internal organs. The result is that man cannot be treated, from an educational point of view, as though almost any overall pattern of behaviour was open to him. Important among man's inherited predispositions is a tendency to aggressiveness towards other members of his species. Education can indeed use, control and redirect this tendency; if it treats it as though it did not exist, the result is likely to be disastrous. It is important to bear in mind that Lorenz does not imply, in *On Aggression* at least, that man is *merely* an animal, in the sense that the exercise of intelligence and reason, and the culture which is its product, has no effect on his behaviour; only that he *is* an animal, and as such with predispositions for behaviour and social interaction, within which the intelligence and reason which seem specifically human give him *considerable* but by no means *indefinite* freedom of manoeuvre. The importance of this conclusion will appear very clearly during the subsequent chapters of this book.

4   Corrupt Society: Marx

No one would deny that the effect of the writings of Marx and of the great depth-psychologists, Freud and Jung, on people's conception of morality and the aims of human life, has been immense for better or worse. It therefore seems suitable to devote rather a large proportion of this book to an exegesis and criticism of their views. One principle which I tried to establish in the first chapter will constantly be applied to the criticism of their work: that any account of human beings, from which it can be inferred that they are incapable of cognitive and moral self-transcendence, of getting to know what is true independently of their material and social milieu and acting in accordance with that knowledge, is self-destructive. Now it will be found that there is possible a 'strong' and a 'weak' interpretation of the opinions of Marx and Freud on this matter, both of which may be supported by appeal to their writings. According to the 'strong' interpretation, human intelligence and reason are more or less a mere reflex of other factors: the economic and social environment on the one hand, and impulses of an organic nature on the other. Since this 'strong' interpretation rules out cognitive and moral self-transcendence, it is self-destructive, because one may deduce from it that no-one, including Freud or Marx, thinks or writes as he does because there is good reason for him to do so. According to the 'weak' interpretation, while human intelligence and reason are very strongly affected by organic and environmental factors, they are not wholly determined by them. There is excellent reason, as I shall try to bring out, for agreeing to a large extent both with Marx and with Freud on the 'weak' interpretation; and for holding that there is an immense amount to be learned from both of them as so interpreted about human morality and matters germane to it.

In this chapter, I shall expound and discuss Marx's views on a number of topics relevant to the central theme of this book.

The Materialist Conception of History

Marx's 'materialism' is to be contrasted sharply with 'mechanistic materialism'; he strongly criticised the eighteenth-century French materialists for leaving out of account what is specifically human. As he points out in the third of the *Theses on Feuerbach*,[1] while there is no doubt that circumstances influence men, it is no less true that men change circumstances. History is made by men, not just as they please, but in circumstances transmitted from the past and not chosen by themselves.[2]

In explaining human affairs and institutions, says Marx, one should not start from any arbitrary and abstract set of principles, but from real human individuals, their activities, and the material conditions within which they live. Thus the premisses for the reasoning involved can be obtained in a purely empirical way, without any idealisation or speculation. Men distinguish themselves from animals when they begin to *produce* their means of subsistence, their material life.[3] The animal, indeed, can be said to 'produce' in a limited and restricted sense; but it produces only what it needs immediately for itself or its offspring. 'It produces only under pressure of immediate physical need, whereas man produces free from physical need, and only truly produces when he is thus free.' The animal, again, only fashions things according to the standards and needs of its species; but man goes much further than this. He can, for example, fashion things according to the laws of beauty. ' . . . It is in the working over of the objective world that man first really affirms himself as species-being. This production is his active species-life. Through it nature appears as his work and his reality.'[4] Another feature of human labour which distinguishes it from animal activity, for example the work of the worst of architects from that of the best of bees, is that man assembles his product in imagination before he does so in reality. At the end of every human labour-process, we have what existed in the imagination of the labourer at the

beginning.[5] And this characteristic of man's productive activity
is the clue to what, at the deepest level, man *is*. 'As individuals
express their life, so they are. What they are, therefore, coincides with their production, both with *what* they produce and
how they produce. The nature of individuals thus depends on
the material conditions determining their productions.'[6]

This view, in contrast with all forms of idealism, remains on
the real ground of human history: 'it does not explain practice
from the idea but explains the formation of ideas from material
practice.' It is as a consequence of this that forms and products
of consciousness cannot be dissolved by mental criticism, but
only by the practical overthrow of the actual social relations
which give rise to them.[7] The social structure and the state
evolve continually out of the life process of individuals, not as
they appear to themselves and others, but

> as they are; i.e. as they operate, produce materially, and
> hence as they work under definite material limits, presup-
> positions, and conditions independent of their will ... Em-
> pirical observation must in each separate instance bring out
> empirically, and without any mystification and speculation,
> the connection of the social and political structure with
> production.[8]

The continuity in human history is due to the fact that each
generation finds itself in possession of the productive forces of
the previous generation, which serve it as raw material for new
production.[9] 'The development of science, of this ideal and at
the same time practical wealth, is ... only one aspect, one form,
of the development of human productive forces (i.e. wealth).'[10]

In production, men act not only on nature but on one
another; and their action upon nature, their production, takes
place only within these social connections and relations.[11]
Society is the product of man's reciprocal action; given a
certain state of production, and so of commerce and consumption, there will be a corresponding social constitution, family
structure and class organisation; in short, a corresponding civil
society.[12] The ultimately determining element in history is the
sum total of relations of production; these constitute the
economic structure and real foundation of society, 'on which

rises a legal and political superstructure and to which correspond definite forms of social consciousness'.[13] 'Ancient society,
feudal society, bourgeois society are such totalities of production relations, each of which at the same time denotes a special
stage of development in the history of mankind'.[14] Production
on the basis of exchange values at first brings about an alienation of the individual from himself and others. The individual
at an earlier stage of history seems more complete than at later
stages, since he has not elaborated the abundance of his
relationships or set them up as powers and autonomous social
relationships opposed to himself. However, it would be misguided either to hanker after the condition of primitive man as
such, or to maintain that the relative restriction of man in
present society was inevitable for him for all future time.

> It is as ridiculous to wish to return to that primitive abun-
> dance as it is to believe in the continuing necessity of its
> complete depletion. The bourgeois view has never got
> beyond opposition to this romantic outlook and thus will be
> accompanied by it, as a legitimate antithesis, right up to its
> blessed end.[15]

The doctrine, which seems central to Marx's thought, that
ideas are a direct reflection of the social and economic situation
of those who hold them, is not without ambiguity. It appears to
me that while there is a sense in which it is highly plausible that
ideas are a reflection of such circumstances, there is another
sense in which they *cannot* be *merely* so. Suppose that contemporary scientists believe that there is, and has been for many
millions of years, argon to the quantity of at least one per cent in
the atmosphere of the planet Mars. If they have 'ideas' to this
effect, and it really is the case, then their 'ideas' have reference
to a state of affairs which might well have obtained even if man
had never evolved at all, let alone acquired the means of
inquiring successfully into such recondite matters. Apparently
they can have 'ideas' of this kind, for all that they are men
whose thoughts and speech are embedded in twentieth-century
and specifically Western forms of social and economic life. The
same applies, of course, to knowledge by palaeontologists of the
remote past, and by anthropologists of the beliefs and institu-

tions of men of other cultures; for all that these specialists are as dependent as the rest of us on the contingencies of their material and social environment, they can apparently get to know what is or was so far beyond this environment, and might have been so even if the environment of the specialists concerned and the knowledge which is dependent upon it had never come into existence. Let us call this curious capacity which man appears to have – to know things which are quite independent of his social situation, to have 'ideas' within this situation which truly represent what is altogether outside it – 'cognitive self-transcendence'.[16] It is 'cognitive' in that it is a matter of knowledge, and 'self-transcendence' in that what is known does in a sense 'transcend' the knower and his social situation.

Now there may be distinguished two versions of that 'historical materialism' which stresses the dependence of human ideas on their material and social milieu; one of them having the consequence that cognitive self-transcendence is impossible; the other assuming its possibility and actuality, but quite properly stressing the material and social preconditions for its adequate development. Traces of both doctrines, which we may label the 'strong' and the 'weak' versions of historical materialism, are to be found in the works of Marx and his followers; the former when they are preoccupied with the association of human ideas with human practical activity (as notably in *The German Ideology*); the latter when they are emphasising that their views are scientific, and that science is the means of knowing the truth about the world (as, for example, in Engels's *Anti-Dühring*). The trouble with the 'strong' version is that it not only leads to wildly implausible consequences if applied consistently, but that it is actually self-destructive. Among the implausible consequences are that what scientists say about distant galaxies or long-extinct animal species can have no bearing on these matters themselves, but can only be a reflection of our present material circumstances, productive performances and social interactions. The self-destructiveness is due to the fact that what has just been said will apply, if historical materialism is carried through consistently, to historical materialism itself. If it is simply the expression of the practices and social interactions of one set of persons, why should others adopt it, or have any reason for thinking that it is true? If it represents, in a way that the accounts which contradict it do not, the truth about the matters with which it deals, this involves cognitive self-transcendence; those who hold to this particular set of ideas and opinions know what is so, and would have been so even if they had never come to know it. It may be concluded that the 'strong' version of historical materialism is impossible to accept, once its full implications are realised. It is quite a different matter with the 'weak' verson, which in my view is one of Marx's most permanent and significant contributions to human thought. This draws attention to the very large extent to which a man's physical environment, and the set of social relationships within which he exists as a member of his society and class, determine what he is liable to notice of the data available to his senses, the questions he is prepared to ask, the judgements and decisions which he can bring himself to make and so on.

A thoroughgoing opponent of historical materialism might urge that while the 'strong' version of historical materialism was self-destructive, the 'weak' was quite trivial. But this, I think, would be a mistake. Historians have as a matter of fact often overlooked or underestimated the influence of economic circumstances on the social relations characteristic of an epoch, and the effect of both on the ideas which were characteristic of it. At the very least, Marx has provided a much needed corrective to the tendency to envisage human ideas as though the milieu within which they flourished had nothing to do with them.

It may heartily be agreed that, short of appropriate material and social circumstances, ideas are apt to be ineffective. But, given the appropriate circumstances, ideas can surely be very effective indeed. The whole literary activity of Marx, and its phenomenal ultimate success, presupposes and demonstrates that persons in appropriate circumstances can be induced to act through being convinced, by argument, that such action is morally right and likely to be successful.[17] The limits which circumstances can impose on the nature and effectiveness of ideas are what give historical materialism its evident plausibility and at least partial truth. It seems plain, when one reflects on the matter, first, that material and social circumstances set limits on what men can achieve and indelibly stamp the nature of their achievement; second, that features of a man's material environment and his day-to-day activity within it are apt to suggest to him some ideas rather than others; third, that social pressures may make some ideas difficult or even dangerous to entertain, and may make acceptance of a socially convenient falsehood a condition of good reputation, physical comfort or even survival. At least in all these ways, our thoughts and our actions, and the framework of ideas – our law, our science and our religion – which are involved in them, are thus subject to material and social influences. It is one of Marx's great merits to have pointed out the absurdities which ensue from neglect of these limits on the range and effectiveness of human ideas. For ideas to be effective, men must at least entertain them; short of favourable circumstances they will scarcely do so at all nor, even if they do so, put them into effect with a favourable result.

That circumstances have a very great influence on ideas, then, is true and important. The pressure of war stimulates inventions which are useful for the purpose of making weapons; and it must be a matter of distress to the high-minded how great an effect interest in gambling had on the development of probability theory. Yet a certain detachment of ideas from immediate circumstances, such as is consistent at best with a rather weak version of historical materialism, seems difficult to deny. The mathematics of conic sections was developed by the Greeks more than a millennium before any application for it was found. In the sciences, the truth of theory and the effectiveness of immediate practice certainly have a great deal to do with one another, but are by no means to be too closely confused, unless indeed cognitive self-transcendence is to be denied. One of the tests, sure enough, of whether a scientific theory is true, is whether it has practical results which can be relied upon. And yet, except on a very paradoxical interpretation, in grasping that a typical scientific theory is true, one comes to know something that would have been the case even if one had never existed at all, let alone propounded and tested the theory or come to believe it on the testimony of others.

It is of course a cardinal doctrine of Marx's historical materialism that the moral, political, and religious ideas of a people are utterly dependent on the prevailing mode of production and the social relations based upon it. It is interesting to pursue the question of how far this applies to their scientific ideas as well. So far as it does not, one may wonder why this particular class of ideas is exempt from the influences which control the others. So far as it does, it may be asked for what reason one ought to take scientific doctrines seriously as stating what is really the case, but not, for example, religious doctrines. Marx is right to say that man makes religion, and he regards this as of prime importance for the criticism of religion;[18] but man also makes science and this does not show, at least on Marx's view, that science is merely part of an ideological superstructure which cannot show us how things really are. In his earlier writings particularly, Marx seems to expound the view that truly scientific discourse may be distinguished from ideological illusion in treating strictly of what can be directly and 'empirically' perceived.[19] This was untrue then, and is more obviously untrue now, when scientists speak in terms of theoretical constructs which are not and cannot be directly observed, for all that their existence and occurrence may be *verified* in observation. In any case, Marx had definitely abandoned this view by the time he wrote *Capital*.[20] To meet this objection, one might protest that even if such entities cannot be observed, at least their effects can be. But if one thus relaxes the appeal to experience in order to accommodate the more sophisticated developments of science, it is by no means obvious that religious belief is excluded. Many theists would maintain that it is reasonable to assert God's existence in order to account for some features of the world which we observe.[21]

It might be argued, following some hints from Marx,[22] that scientific doctrines have a pragmatic justification such as religious and other ideological beliefs do not. Religious beliefs, Marx maintains, tend to shrivel and constrict man, to make him deny himself; whereas scientific beliefs are means by which man can fulfil his nature through acting upon his environment.[23] I have already argued that such a reduction of the question of truth to the question of the practical has consequences which are impractically paradoxical. That religious belief has often tended to stultify and diminish man may be conceded to Marx; whether it always has done so, and whether it must do so by its very nature, will be briefly considered later.[24]

What I have said about self-transcendence in relation to judgements of fact would appear to apply equally to judgements of value. We may, for example, have good grounds for judging that one particular human action as opposed to another, or one particular social or political programme as opposed to another, will tend to foster general happiness and fulfilment and diminish general misery and frustration. Once again, in the matter of judgements of value as well as of fact, there appears to be an oscillation between two different and indeed incompatible accounts in the works of Marx and his followers. On the 'strong' view, all a man's particular value-judgements and all the general principles by which he justifies them are merely a reflection of his class position. One man will work for the revolution, if that is in the interests of his class; another will oppose it, if that is in the interests of *his* class; and there is no objective and overriding practical or moral value in accordance with which one is right, the other wrong, or each partly right and partly wrong. According to the 'weak' version, however great the influence of a man's material and social environment on his moral and political attitudes, some degree of transcendence of it, such as to make possible knowledge of what is the case and what ought to be done, is possible – as Marx himself at times clearly conceded. Thus he commended such classical economists as Ricardo, and the British factory inspectors, for achieving an objective view of some matters in spite of their class position.[25] On this interpretation of Marx, one general course of action, that of advancing the revolution, may be justified by the overriding moral principle that the happiness and fulfilment of the vast majority of human beings ought to be maximised, their suffering and frustration minimised. In one passage Marx speaks of the 'hired' labour of capitalist society as 'inferior' to the 'associated' labour which will characterise future society;[26] and the sense in which he supposes it to be 'inferior' is quite clear. It is not just earlier in time, but such that less real productivity and less intrinsic satisfaction is to be got out of it.

It seems evident that to come to a justified true judgement on what course of action will tend to the betterment of mankind in the sense given, and to act accordingly, rather than just repeat-ing and living by the prejudices expressive of one's own self-esteem and that of one's group, demands cognitive self-transcendence in the sense described earlier. Let us call cogni-tive self-transcendence in the sphere of morals and politics, together with the disposition to act upon it, 'moral self-transcendence'.[27] When Marx speaks of the 'communist con-sciousness' as belonging not only to members of the working class, but to certain others through contemplation of the plight of the working class,[28] he is in effect alluding to moral self-transcendence and implicitly acknowledging its possibility. And there can be few more striking expressions of moral self-transcendence than Marx's own description of the effort involved in completing the first part of *Capital*. 'I have sac-rificed health, happiness and family . . . I laugh at so-called "practical" men and their wisdom. If one were willing to be an ox, one could naturally turn one's back on human suffering and look after one's own skin.'[29]

Marx mentions, as a consequence of the materialist concep-tion of history, that it is of no use trying to dissolve the products of consciousness by mere criticism, and that one rather has to overthrow the social situation which gives rise to them.[30] But presumably, in such cases, the judgement that the prevalent social situation and system of ideas is relatively unsatisfactory, and that there is a more satisfactory social situation and set of ideas with which they ought to be replaced, can be justified by good reasons and is not a mere reflex of the fact that one belongs to an underprivileged section of society. Unless this were so, it would seem to be just as irrational and irresponsible to commit oneself to the cause of revolution as to that of reaction and oppression. At least that there is something unsatisfactory about capitalism, that it ought to be changed, and in which direction it ought to be changed, are matters that have to be argued for, to be justified in terms of 'ideas'. Thus, once again, the 'weak' form of historical materialism would seem to be the only one acceptable; in the long run the revolution ought only to be fostered, if it ought to be fostered at all, *because* this is the reasonable and responsible thing to do; and that ideas can have this degree of influence on action is consistent only with a relatively 'weak' version of historical materialism. However, its

truth in this 'weak' version is by no means a trivial matter, since
it is always to be remembered that, even if the overthrow of the
privileged class is in itself justified by argument, it remains that
mere argument will not persuade people to reject beliefs which
have an important function in maintaining their privileged
social and economic position.

Such beliefs are of course what are referred to by Marx and
his followers as 'ideology'.[31] A certain ambiguity in the meaning
of this term is worth mentioning. In one use the term is merely
descriptive; in another, which I think is more characteristic of
Marx himself, it is pejorative as well. In the purely descriptive
sense, an ideology is a set of ideas which gives a group of people
a direction for their lives and heartens them in the following of
this direction. In this sense there can be and ought to be a
working-class as well as a bourgeois ideology, a communist as
well as a capitalist one. In the pejorative sense, an ideology is a
set of ideas which gives direction to living only at the cost of
restricting cognitive and moral transcendence in favour of
personal or group illusions or hatreds. In the former sense,
Marxism presents itself as the 'ideology' of the working class; in
the latter sense, it presents itself as the opponent of all 'ideology' in the name of science. It does not seem to me very
important whether one uses the term in the one sense or the
other; what *does* seem very important is that the senses should
be distinguished clearly from one another. Otherwise, a belief
which has been shown to be 'ideological' in the purely descriptive sense, the one in which everyone has and ought to have an
'ideology', may be assumed without ado to be 'ideological' also
in the narrower and pejorative sense; or one may merely use the
term 'ideology' as a term of abuse for all ideologies which
happen to be opposed to one's own, while appearing to make a
point against them in doing so.

The distinction between these two senses of ideology enables
one to articulate fairly sharply the difference between what
Marx calls 'moralising criticism' and the 'critical morality'
which he opposes to it.[32] It is characteristic of 'moralising
criticism' to strain at gnats and swallow camels; to affect deep
sensitivity on trivial issues, and to allow crying evils like those
endured by the factory workers described in the first volume of
Capital to go unnoticed and unremedied. It is plain that

'moralising criticism' is an attitude which is ideological in the abusive sense, since it diverts attention from the greater evil to the lesser out of class interest; while a genuinely 'critical morality' is ideological only in the broader and more neutral sense. Marx's contribution to our understanding of 'ideology' in the narrower sense, to the manner in which a dominant class adverts and allows others to advert only to those facts which seem to justify its privileges, and suppresses those which tend to indicate that those privileges are excessive, is surely one of his most important and permanent achievements.

Present and Future Society

Man in bourgeois society is the victim, on Marx's account, of alienation.[33] Basically, alienation is a state in which man is aware that things and other people are against him, oppress him, obstruct his short-term satisfaction and long-term happiness; when they might be at his disposal, and for his enjoyment and the general enhancement of his life. The insight into the nature of this alienation characteristic of man in modern society, and the delineation of the circumstances which contribute to it, seem to me among the most important lessons to be learnt from Marx.

The alienated worker under capitalism

does not confirm himself in his work, he denies himself, feels miserable instead of happy, deploys no free physical and intellectual energy, but mortifies his body and ruins his mind. Thus the worker only feels at home outside his work and in his work he feels a stranger . . . His labour is . . . not voluntary but compulsory, forced labour. It is therefore not the satisfaction of a need but only a means to satisfy needs outside itself . . . The external character of labour shows itself in the fact that it is not his own but someone else's, . . . that he does not belong to himself in his labour but to someone else.

The analogy with religion, in which man makes over to God what really belongs to himself, is clear enough.[34] As the division of labour increases, work becomes increasingly simplified, the special skill of the labourer becomes worthless and he is transformed into a simple, monotonous productive force that has no use for highly developed faculties of body or mind. Another effect of the division of labour is that one man is enabled to do the work of five, ten or twenty, and competition between workers is increased accordingly. Thus work becomes ever more repulsive, as competition increases and wages decrease, the latter because each worker, driven by want, undersells the others. Machinery intensifies the process, replacing skilled labour by unskilled, men by women, adults by children.[35]

Members of the propertied class as well as workers are subject to alienation; but while the worker feels ruined by it and by the actuality of an inhuman existence, the propertied class feels quite comfortable in its alienation, retaining as it does some semblance of a human life.[36] The worker is superior to the capitalist in that he *feels* enslaved by the alienation of which he is the victim, whereas the capitalist is rooted in it in such a way that he is quite content with it. In that the miserly aim of financial profit is the supreme and dominating aim of the capitalist, he is in just as slavish a relation to capital, in his own way, as is the worker.[37] Fortunately, developments in modern industry itself will compel society, if it is to survive at all, to dispense with the detail worker of today, who is diminished to a mere fragment of himself by the repetition throughout his life of one trivial operation, and to replace him with the fully developed man fit for a variety of labours, to whom his different functions are so many ways of giving free rein to his own natural and acquired powers.[38] As a result of this development, we may expect a society where there is 'free individuality, which is founded on the universal development of individuals and the domination of their communal and social productivity'.[39]

In the case of religious alienation, man's place is usurped by God, while the illusory hopes of religion at once compensate man for his sufferings and express his deepest desires. The abolition of religion as the illusory happiness of the people is in effect a demand for their real happiness. In the case of political alienation, the state appears as a coercive power over and above society, in such a way as in fact fosters the interests of the class in power against those of everyone else. 'Atheism is humanism mediated with itself through the supersession of religion, and communism is humanism mediated with itself through the supersession of private property.' But, as may easily be inferred from the materialist view of history, economic alienation is basic, and its end with the abolition of private property will bring about the end of the other kinds of alienation as well.[40]

As to the nature of the society which he envisaged for the future, Marx did not on the whole go into details, declining, as he put it, to write 'recipes for the cookshops of the future'.[41] And he often took issue, as for example in the *Communist Manifesto*, with more utopian socialists for their idealistic forecasts. Such forecasts naturally ran counter to a basic tenet of historical materialism, that all ideas are a product of contemporary social reality and practice, and lack adequate grounding if extrapolated far beyond this. But the broad lines of what he expected seem clear enough.[42]

Marx was influenced in this matter by Saint-Simon, who had looked forward to a time when government of people would have been succeeded by administration of things. Once class distinctions had disappeared, according to Marx, and production was controlled by 'a vast association of the whole nation', public power would cease to be truly political, 'political power, properly so-called', being 'merely the organised power of one class for suppressing another'.[43] One result of this would be the disappearance of bureaucracy. There would still be public power of a kind in communist society; but 'when class rule will have disappeared there will no longer be any state in the present political sense of the word'.[44] In the place of bourgeois society, and the state which directs it in the interests of the bourgeois class, there will be an 'association in which the free development of each is the condition for the free development of all'[45] which 'excludes class division' and as a consequence of this 'will have no political power properly speaking'.[46]

The disappearance of the state must await the time when 'all the springs of co-operative wealth flow more abundantly',[47] and so there will be no call for political power in the strict sense to be exercised in response to economic pressures. The central government in the resulting 'association' would retain 'few but important functions';[48] but just *what* 'social functions, analogous to the functions now fulfilled by the State, will remain in a Communist society' could 'only be answered scientifically' (that is, I think, by investigation of the actual conditions then obtaining).[49] But at least it appears that force, as embodied in the institutions of army and police, would no longer be required. External force would be unnecessary, since the revolution would be nothing if not international; and internal force would be superfluous in that punishment would consist in 'the judgement of the criminal upon himself'.[50] Production would be communal and the social product distributed to each individual according to his need. The use of time would be planned in such a way that everyone would have as much time as possible to develop his manifold potentialities.[51]

Marx's most explicit statements about the nature of labour in future communist society are to be found in the *Grundrisse*, where he presents his position as midway between that of Adam Smith and that of Fourier. According to Adam Smith, labour is necessarily a burden, and rest a fitting state. At the other extreme, Fourier had claimed that in the ideal future work would be indistinguishable from amusement and play. Against the former view, Marx pointed out that a certain quantity of work is necessary for human well-being; labour of the right kind and in its proper place amounted to 'the self-realisation and objectification of the subject, therefore real freedom'. But in opposition to Fourier, he insisted that really free labour, for example musical composition, was an intensely serious and taxing business. 'The labour concerned with material production can only have this character if (1) it is of a social nature and (2) if it has a scientific character' (that is, I think, if the worker's mind is intensely engaged with what he is doing).[52] When Marx talks of 'abolishing' labour, as for example in the *German Ideology*,[53] it is evidently not labour of this kind that he has in mind, but alienated labour.

One of the main themes of the *Grundrisse* is that the development of machinery and automation will give people so much more free time that they will develop, in a communist society, many capacities at present stunted by work for long hours in an alienating situation. Technology will 'produce the material elements needed for the development of the rich individuality, which is just as universal in its production as consumption, and whose labour thus appears not to be labour any more but a full development of activity, in which the natural necessity has disappeared in its direct form'.[54] And *pari passu* with the nature of labour itself, the organisation of labour will be changed. 'The development of heavy industry means that the basis upon which it rests – the appropriation of the labour time of others – ceases to constitute or to create wealth.' At the same time, direct human labour ceases to be the basis of production, being transformed more and more into supervision and regulation; moreover, the product ceases to be made by individual direct labour, and is rather the result of social activity.[55] As to the present organisation of labour, 'like slave labour, like serf labour, hired labour is but a transitory and inferior form, destined to disappear before associated labour plying its toil with a willing hand, a ready mind, and a joyous heart'.[56] 'The liberation of labour', in fact, may be regarded as 'the fundamental and natural condition of individual and social life which only by usurpation, fraud and artifical contrivances can be shifted from the few upon the many'.[57]

, In *Capital*, Marx contrasts the realm of freedom with that of necessity. The former 'only begins . . . where that labour which is determined by need and external purposes ceases.' Even under communism, man's struggle with nature 'remains a realm of necessity. Beyond it begins that development of human potentiality for its own sake, the true realm of freedom, which however can only flourish upon that realm of necessity as its basis. The shortening of the working day is its fundamental prerequisite'.[58] But under communism both the division of labour, and the dichotomy between physical and mental labour, would be things of the past; the same person would be able (so to say) to hunt in the morning, fish in the afternoon, rear cattle in the evening and go in for criticism after dinner. The progress of technology and automation would permit rapid change from one kind of activity to another. 'In a communist society there are no painters but at most people who engage in painting among other activities';[59] the member of such a society would be the 'all-round man' of the *1844 Manuscripts* and the 'social individual' of the *Grundrisse*.[60]

Marx's account of the future seems based on the assumption that men tend naturally to co-operate in pursuit of the common good, except when material scarcity or social inequity frustrate this tendency; or at least that they *will* spontaneously so co-operate, when automation is sufficiently far advanced, and when the ownership of the means of production is no longer concentrated in the hands of a privileged few. He is surely quite correct in his opposition to the pessimistic Hobbist and Freudian view, represented for him by the writings of Max Stirner which he attacked in *The German Ideology*, that every man naturally seeks the fulfilment only of his own needs and desires, and can be induced to co-operate with his fellows only by external constraint. He also has the merit of having brought out with unprecedented clarity and force the manner in which social injustice and material want at least greatly increase whatever tendency there may be in human individuals and groups to seek their own satisfaction at the expense of that of other individuals and groups. But it does not follow, from the falsity of the view at the opposite extreme, that each man is naturally disposed to seek the common good above all else; or that he would do so as a matter of course even if social institutions were organised in such a way as to induce him so far as possible to do so. Both the study of actual human behaviour, and reflection on probable human evolution, tell rather heavily against all the following views: that each man is selfish by nature; that each man is devoted to the general good by nature; and that each man is a *tabula rasa* in this respect, open to an indefinite amount of conditioning in his desires and resulting behaviour.[61] Stirner seems to have fallen into the first error; Marx to be inclined to the latter two, the former in those early writings where he is inclined to talk of human nature or the human essence, the latter in those later writings where he avoids doing so.

Most human races have apparently evolved in rather small groups which survived by successful competition against other similar groups; and there is plenty of evidence in human behaviour here and now that we are predisposed, as one might expect from this, to find satisfaction in co-operation with our own group against others. Thus, as well as 'individual bias', there is always 'group bias' to be reckoned with as a force apt to operate against activity in the general interest.[62] The success of Marxists in promoting conscious opposition between classes could be taken as an illustration of the point. It looks, in fact, as though dissensions between groups are *exasperated* rather than *created* by economic and social inequalities; and as though, even in a society deliberately and artfully fashioned in order to encourage dedication to the general good, most people could only become committed to it as a result of rather arduous self-dedication.

In *The German Ideology*, it is true, Marx makes a distinction between human desires which are constant in that 'they exist under all circumstances, only their form and direction being changed by different social circumstances', of which he takes the desire to eat as an example, and relative desires 'which owe their origin merely to a particular form of society, to particular conditions of production and exchange'. In a communist society, he says, the former would be given the opportunity to develop in a natural and unrestricted way, while the latter would wither away, through being deprived of the conditions of their existence. Exactly which desires fall into which category 'can only be decided in a practical way, through the changing of real practical desires themselves, and not through historical comparisons with earlier historical circumstances'.[63] If I understand this passage rightly, its point is that, until we are actually in the situation envisaged, we will have insufficient data for an adequately grounded judgement on exactly which human desires and dispositions will remain, which not.

But the caution which seems implicit here is in marked contrast with other passages, where Marx's forecasts seem at once more confident and more optimistic. He usually seems to assume that all desires and dispositions tending to selfishness belong to the second category. One of his arguments against Max Stirner is an illustration of the point. 'Communists', he says, ' ... do not put egoism against self-sacrifice or self-sacrifice against egoism ... On the contrary, they demonstrate the material basis engendering it (egoism), with which it disappears of itself.'[64] But the crucial question is whether this 'material basis' is merely a particular range of possible economic and social orders, or whether it is partly the physical and psychical constitution with which human beings have evolved, and thus constituent of all possible human economic and social orders.

In *The Communist Manifesto*, he remarks how obvious is the thesis that man's consciousness changes with every change in the material and social conditions of man's life.[65] This last has immediate consequences for the conduct of human affairs. 'There is no need of any great penetration to see from the teaching of materialism on the original goodness and equal intellectual endowment of man,' on the omnipotence of experience and education, and on the influence on men of their environment, how necessarily materialism issues in communism and socialism. If man acquires all his knowledge from the senses, then his environment must be arranged in such a way that he is accustomed to what is truly human, and comes to experience himself really as man (as opposed to in dehumanising circumstances as at present). And 'if correctly understood interest is the principle of all morals, man's private interest must be made to coincide with the interest of humanity.' The individual who actually commits the crime must not be punished; rather the anti-social sources of crime should be stopped up and each man given scope for self-expression within society. In a nutshell, 'if man is shaped by his surroundings, his surroundings must be made human'.[66]

The bearing of these passages, with their certainty and optimism, seems very different from the agnosticism and caution which seemed implicit in those cited before. What seems to underlie them, as I have already suggested, is the assumption that, since selfishness and anti-social behaviour are exacerbated by economic factors and the social structures based upon them, they might be done away with altogether by the right kind of reconstitution of the framework of economy and society. But it should be stressed that, even if the optimism of the passages just cited seems excessive, this is by no means to impugn the truth and importance of Marx's insights on these matters on a more cautious interpretation. That tendencies to selfishness and crime are encouraged by economic and social inequities; and that social reconstruction ought to be aimed largely at ameliorating those factors which really compel some persons to be criminals, and increase the tendencies towards crime in others; these things remain true and of the utmost importance, and insight into them available now is due at least as much to Marx as to anyone else.

Evidence that man's evolutionary inheritance, as opposed to the contingencies of his present environment, may have far more influence on his behaviour than Marx appears to have supposed, is to be found in the work of the psychoanalysts, in animal studies, and elsewhere;[67] it is also strongly hinted at by the fact that art and literature from very different ages, cultures and economic circumstances remain sources of enjoyment and enlightenment to us. Marx touches on this point in the *Grundrisse*. He remarks that the view of nature and of social relations which shaped, for example, Greek art, is not possible in an age of automatic machinery, railways and telegraph. Why, then, it may be asked, does Greek art continue to appeal to us, and even in some respects constitute a model beyond our attainment? An analogy, he suggests, may shed light on the difficulty. We cannot *become* children again without being childish; but without becoming childish, we may still enjoy the artless ways of a child. Similarly, the childhood of human society, as reflected in its art, may exert a perennial charm, as of an age which will never return.[68]

A more plausible and convincing reason why art and literature of widely different backgrounds has an appeal for us is that human nature remains far more the same through the successive forms of society and prevailing ways of production than Marx will allow. It was not for nothing that Freud could allude to the Greek story of Oedipus in order to characterise rivalries which he thought were operative in every human family at all times. It is by no means any 'childlike' quality that explains the continuing appeal of, say, the *Oresteia* of Aeschylus; it is rather that Clytemnestra stalks the bingo halls of Pudsey as she did the royal palace of Argos. The same may be expected to apply to wider social as to close family relationships: comradeship in arms, as one can tell by comparing the *Iliad* with some accounts of modern war, has not all that different a flavour whether one is using bows and spears, or automatic rifles and three-inch mortars. The upshot is that a comprehensively critical theory of ethics will take seriously the possibility that there are rather complex predispositions to desire and to behaviour which come from man's evolutionary inheritance, as opposed to his immediate physical environment; and that these are liable to set limits on what can be done with human beings by arrangement of their economic and social circumstances in the present and the future.

Confidence in the potential unselfishness and co-operativeness of human beings, together with observation of the evident fact that they are not always ideally co-operative in the present scheme of things, inevitably tends to underestimation of those factors in present social arrangements which tend to promote such unselfishness and co-operation as do now exist. As Rousseau (of all people) wrote:

> I do not say that you should leave things as they are, but I say you should only change them with extreme circumspection. At present you are more struck by abuse than by advantages. I fear the time will come when you will be more conscious of the advantages, and unfortunately that will be when they have been lost.[69]

A revolutionary might ask whether the bringing into being of the classless society, a state of society where each exerts himself for the good of all and all for the good of each, is not worth a great deal of suffering and indeed of lying and deception here and now – especially when one bears in mind that the exploiting classes in any case lie and deceive and inflict suffering as a matter of course. But even if one concedes what is not indisputable, that the end would be worth the means, the question still arises of whether or how and in what circumstances, the means of revolution is likely to bring about such a desirable end. If one neglected Rousseau's warning, might not one find the resulting sum of misery and oppression actually worse than at present?

As Bakunin suggested, those who took power in the name of the workers might well cease to be workers after taking power, and run society, as earlier exploiting classes have done, largely in their own interests.[70] The revolutionary might protest that the economic and social conditions which will prevail ultimately as the result of revolution will be quite different from those which have obtained up to now, and so there is no basis for such a depressing forecast. But what is sauce for the goose is sauce for the gander; if it is conceded that past and present conditions provide no adequate basis for such forecasts, the revolutionary would have no better grounds for his optimism than others would have for their less sanguine forecasts. Following some hints in Marx, it might be claimed that all such extrapolations from the present to the post-revolutionary future are futile. But if this is taken seriously, there is removed the prime justification for revolutionary activity; unless there is some means here and now of determining the probable long-term effect of our actions, no one present political action with long-term consequences can reasonably be preferred to any other.

The state of society where the present grounds of selfishness and crime will *so far as possible* be abolished, and where work for the common good will be as little irksome as possible, does seem the ideal to aim at by all those who have the direction of society; one may share this ideal with Marx even if one does not hold, as he apparently does, that such a state of society is bound actually to come into being in future. On the question of labour in future society, it seems wise to temper some of Marx's more optimistic prognostications, which seem to imply that every sort of irksome work will be able to be done away with, with his more cautious remarks on the subject in the third volume of *Capital*. Here he admits that the realm of necessity, in which man has to struggle with nature, will always, even under communism, be a necessary precondition of the existence of a realm of freedom, in which man expresses and fulfils himself.[71] It would appear from this that the common good, by its very nature, would demand that a man had to perform tasks which, at least sometimes and to some extent, were irksome to him. That such tasks would be minimised in a really just and happy society, that they would be shared as far as possible, and that they would in general be allotted to those who found them least disagreeable, is not to be denied. The same again applies to the 'alienation' of man in his labour. There is a great deal of satisfaction to be got out of some kinds of work in most circumstances, and some kind of satisfaction to be got out of most kinds of work in some circumstances. Surely Marx is right that the present conditions of civilisation greatly impede the intrinsic satisfaction to be got out of work; and his analysis of how this comes about, by people carrying out on the orders of others repetitive and routine tasks which are meaningless in themselves, is masterly. A just and happy society would surely be organised in such a way that the intrinsic satisfaction available in work should be obtained as far as possible, and the disagreeable work that remained minimised, well compensated, and fairly shared.[72]

I have suggested that the strain of scepticism in Marx about forecasts for the future is at odds to some extent with his confidence that the future will inevitably be a vast improvement on the present in the respects described. It seems to me reasonable to combine a moderate form of the scepticism – though we should be cautious, we do have reasonable grounds for extrapolating from our knowledge of past and present to what is liable to happen in future – with a moderate form of the optimism – we know how the human lot would very probably be greatly improved, and the object of long-term political activity should be to bring such improvement about. But the gap between the ideal, and what is liable to be realised at any point in the future, entails that there is likely to be a permanent need in society for institutions which Marx thinks are in the long run dispensable, or at least for some analogue of them. This is the next topic to be considered.

Classes and the State

'The history of all hitherto existing societies is the history of class struggles'.[73] Obviously, classes are central on Marx's account for the understanding of history and human affairs in general.[74]

However, the concept of 'class' does seem to vary to some extent in meaning and application in Marx's writings.[75] The tripartite division of the society of his time into capitalists, proletariat and landowners is the one most usual for him.[76] Many of the groups he sometimes referred to as 'classes', like the petty bourgeoisie and the peasants, were on his account rapidly disappearing. Even the landowning class, according to him, will finally disappear into either the capitalist or the proletarian class;[77] 'society as a whole is more and more splitting up into two great hostile camps, into two great classes directly facing each other; bourgeoisie and proletariat'.[78]

There is a subjective element in class membership properly

speaking on Marx's account: that is to say, a class in the full sense only exists when fully conscious of itself as such, and as in common hostility to some other class or social group. Thus he sometimes hesitates as to whether even the capitalists form a class; once he said that they did so in as far as they carried out a common war against another class, but not in as far as they were hostile to one another as competitors.[79] Something similar applies to the proletariat: in *The Communist Manifesto*, he writes that the organisation of the proletariat into a class is constantly being upset by competition between the workers themselves.[80] He spoke of the International as an instrument for the organising of workers into a class.[81]

By the proletariat, Marx generally means just the mass of industrial workers, though sometimes he appears to include farm labourers, as when he states that the proletariat includes the vast majority of people in capitalist countries. Once he considered the possibility that the capitalist tenant would oust the peasant, and the tiller of the soil thus become just as much a proletarian, in the sense of wage worker, as the urban labourer, and so share interests with him.[82] But on the whole Marx regarded the peasants as a reactionary body of men, and was unwilling to group them with the proletariat. Another group Marx seems to have found difficulty in classifying was his own, the intelligentsia. He often referred to them as ideological representatives of the bourgeoisie; the perfecting of the illusion of that class about itself, he says, is their source of livelihood.[83] But he did consider that certain intellectuals could in some circumstances achieve an objective view of some aspects of society in spite of their class background; thus he credited the British factory inspectors, and some economists such as Ricardo, with such an objective view on some important matters.[84] However, the fact that just a few individuals in a class may be able to transcend its limited viewpoint on a particular matter has as little effect on the class struggle as a whole as the secession of a few nobles from their class in the period before its outbreak had on the course of the French Revolution.[85]

Apparently Marx has many criteria for applying the term 'class'; but the most important ones are a group's relationship to the prevalent means of production, and its self-consciousness and degree of political organisation. He disclaimed credit for discovering the existence of classes and of the class struggle; he thought his own original contribution was to point out the linking of classes to definite phases in the development of production, and the ultimate issue of the class struggle in the dictatorship of the proletariat and the classless society.[86] In general, one may say that classes for Marx are the social groups through whose conflict society developed in accordance with changes in its economic substructure.[87]

The state is analogous to religion in being at once a statement of man's ideal aims, and a compensation for their lack of realisation.[88] It is in opposition to the real interests of members of society, and constitutes an illusory community which screens the actual struggle between classes. Each mode of production gives rise to its characteristic form of political organisation, which is such as to further the interest of the dominant class.[89] Thus, in the case of the modern state, 'the executive . . . is but a committee for managing the common affairs of the whole bourgeoisie'.[90] The bourgeois state is an insurance pact of the bourgeois class both against the exploited class and against its own members as individuals. The disappearance of classes and their conflicts will automatically entail the end of any need for organised power wielded by one class for the suppression of another; hence the state will be abolished.[91] 'As soon as the goal of the proletarian movement, the abolition of class, shall have been reached, the power of the state, whose function is to keep the great majority of producers beneath the yoke of a small minority of exploiters, will disappear and governmental functions will be transformed into simple administrative functions'.[92] That the state will be abolished 'merely means: when class rule has disappeared, there will no longer be any state *in the present political sense of the word*'.[93]

Some idea of the shape of things to come had been provided by the Paris Commune of 1871. Not all of the Commune's proposals were approved of by Marx; but he certainly thought it had important potentialities.[94] The Commune represented

the reabsorption of the state power by society as its own living forces instead of as forces controlling and subduing it, by the popular masses themselves, forming their own force instead of the organised force of their suppression, the political form of their social emancipation instead of the artificial force ... of society wielded for their oppression by their enemies.

The general suffrage, which is commonly abused as a sanction for state power and as a plaything in the hands of the ruling class, and as a rule is 'only employed by the people to choose the instruments of parliamentary class rule once in so many years', was here adapted to its real purpose, the choosing by the people of their own administrative functionaries. Elsewhere, there had usually prevailed the delusion that administration and government were mysteries to be trusted only to a trained caste, who are state parasites, richly paid sycophants and sinecurists; this helps to keep the masses subjected to authority and to turn them against themselves. In the Paris Commune the state hierarchy was done away with altogether, and the haughty masters of the people were replaced by servants who could be removed from their positions at short notice. They thus had a real as opposed to a mock responsibility, working as they did under continuous public supervision.[95] The merely repressive aspects of the old government power were got rid of altogether, and its legitimate functions wrested from an authority usurping pre-eminence over society, and restored to society itself in the persons of its responsible agents.[96]

That the stage of the dictatorship of the proletariat was necessary, that state power as such would not disappear as an *immediate* consequence of the proletarian revolution, was emphasised particularly by Lenin in *The State and Revolution*. With the revolution, according to Lenin, the *bourgeois* state would be smashed and a *proletarian* state set up in its place. The state is necessarily an instrument by means of which one class suppresses another and thus 'the product and the manifestation of the irreconcilability of class antagonisms'; what would happen at the revolution would be that the state would be changed from a means of suppressing the proletariat, the 'millions of toilers', into a means whereby the proletariat may oppress the bourgeoisie, the 'handfuls of rich'. It is essential not to confuse the abolition of the bourgeois state with the abolition of the state as such, as demanded by anarchists. Engels's famous words about the state 'withering away' apply to the proletarian state after the revolution. For ultimately the proletariat will come to abolish all class antagonisms, the state as state, and itself as proletariat. Once the state becomes representative of the whole of society, it makes itself unnecessary.[97]

It has to be admitted that the account by Marx and Lenin of the relation of state power to class conflict is at least largely true as a matter of fact. And surely history does show, as Lenin says,[98] that the rich and fortunate minority will virtually stop at nothing to maintain its privileges. From a practical point of view, it might be asked, is there anything else to be done than simply adopting the viewpoint of the working class, and using every practical and theoretical means available to overthrow and oppress the former oppressors? And if a number of lies have to be told, or a number of injustices perpetrated, in the process, is this so very serious a matter? Are not such lies already told, and such injustices already perpetrated, and to a far greater degree, *against* the interests of the working class?

It seems to me that Marx and Lenin imply that what I have called moral self-transcendence, which would be potentially independent of any mere class interest, is at best not worth the effort and at worst impossible. Those who do see through the viewpoint of their own class, Marx seems to be saying,[99] merely adopt the viewpoint of another – as I suppose he and Engels had done. As Marx and Lenin see it, the immediate effect of a socialist revolution will be to replace the bourgeois state with a state which is a means of implementing proletarian rather than bourgeois interests; and the ultimate effect of this will be the establishment of a society where there will be no conflicting social interests at all.

Anyone who believes in the possibility of what I have called 'self-transcendence', whether cognitive or moral – and I have argued that disbelief in it is self-destructive – will be inclined to wonder why one should, in a pre-revolutionary situation, simply abet the interests of one class or another. He will wonder whether it is not in principle possible to set up or work towards setting up a state, or at least something analogous to a state – it would not be a state in exactly Marx's or Lenin's sense – whose function would be to foster the public interest as opposed to that of any one group against others, and which would be subject to constant criticism by those who use their capacity for cognitional and moral self-transcendence, so far as it falls short of this ideal, as it will probably be liable to do to a greater or lesser extent. Let us call this hypothetical state a 'state B' as opposed to a 'state A' which, being a state in the sense meant by Marx and Lenin, is by definition such as to implement the interests of one group against others. It must be conceded that once a 'state' really does tend to operate for the general good of society, as opposed to merely for some sectional interest, it will be very different from the vast majority of states which have existed up to now.

Our 'state B' would point to possibilities of and promote work towards reconciliation between conflicting groups within society – one should not say 'classes', since classes in the sense meant by Marx and Lenin are by their very nature irreconcilable; it would make sure, and if necessary exert force to make sure, that group differences did not become irreconcilable; and it would bring pressure to bear to stop injustices, and the misrepresentations which foster injustice, from mounting up. A primary function of political action, on this view, would be to do everything possible to ensure, by criticism and publicity in season and out of season, that the state becomes or remains a 'state B' as opposed to a 'state A'. In the case of *any* group of men, however righteous their cause, the questions have constantly to be asked: 'What is their story? What are they really up to? What are the differences?' That these questions have always to be asked in relation to every individual and group, and more especially in relation to oneself and the groups of which one is a member, is one of the principal assumptions of those who are aware of the implications of moral self-transcendence. Such persons have to learn to live with accusations of disloyalty, just because they will try to speak the truth as they see it, and because their slogan is not 'our party right or wrong', but 'our party because and in so far as it is a means of promoting justice and happiness, and of cherishing those elements in the present situation which work towards them, and acting against those which frustrate them'.

Even if I am right that the notion of a 'state B' has some sense and application, it is not difficult to see why Marx's assumption that *all* states, including that to be set up by the proletariat, must be of type 'state A' is plausible. Those who have the public interest at heart will at least tend to confirm the self-image of the oppressed and impugn that of their oppressors; and where, as in the case of the proletariat as conceived by Marx and described by him in detail in *Capital*, one group carries almost all the burdens of society and enjoys almost none of its available goods, they will tend to foster the interests of that group, and expose the mystifications of those who oppose it, in a quite systematic way.

Marx holds in effect that the complete identification by an individual with the interests of some class is inevitable *now*, but that all such bias will ultimately disappear in the classless society, so there will then be no need of any state to adjudicate between the interests of conflicting groups. Now there seems to be good reason, as I have said, to agree that the injustice and frustration consequent on the division of society into classes immensely *worsens* conflict within society; but I cannot find any reason, apart from unlimited confidence in the malleability of human behaviour, to believe that its removal would either in the short or in the long term eliminate such bias altogether. Given that it will not – that tendencies to individual and group bias would remain even in a society deliberately organised with a view to overall justice and happiness – it would thus seem that organisations of the kind that I have described as 'state B' will always be necessary.

On this account, the business of conscientious citizens or those who strive to attain and implement moral self-transcendence is not, as on Marx's or Lenin's view, to maintain their sectional interest or to replace one sectional interest with another, but to mount a continuous campaign against sectional interest so far as it excludes or impugns the general interest. To be sure, the effect of this will be to foster the interests of the most victimised elements of society against those who take advantage of them. It might be argued that, if this is so, the distinction which I have drawn is of no practical importance. But I think it can easily be shown that *failure* to make the distinction will inevitably lead to systematic injustice and distortion of truth.[100] The fact is that every group whatever has motives for distorting the truth, even that group whose interests most closely coincide with overall social justice, as in the case of the proletariat. In the case of any state of affairs whatever, the questions, 'What is it in the interest of my group to maintain and allow others to maintain about this?' and 'What would one say about this as the result of a thoroughly intelligent and reasonable assessment of all the available evidence?' have to be distinguished sharply from one another.

Lenin had a way of referring to intellectuals as 'insects',[101] and then as now, I am sure, they often richly deserved the epithet. They deserved it so far as they were indifferent to, or even actively abetted, the frustration and suffering of the great mass of ordinary people. However, Lenin's contempt may not have been altogether unmotivated by the fact[102] that intellectuals have a tendency to point out what is true or right when this does not correspond to the group bias of the proletariat, or rather, in the light of the point which Bakunin made against Marx,[103] to the group bias of those who speak in the name of the proletariat. In a revolutionary or near-revolutionary situation, intellectuals may ask questions which are awkward for reasons other than mere bourgeois counter-revolutionary bias. At least when they are doing their job properly, when they are trying to achieve and implement cognitive and moral self-transcendence, they are apt to resist confusion of the questions 'What is the situation? What ought to be done about it?' with the questions 'What statements suit the aims and self-image of our class? What actions will further its purposes?' and the dismissal of all opposed statements or proposals as merely the propaganda of opposed groups or classes.

The fact is that intellectuals are liable to *spoil*, by their awkward questions, the self-righteous discharge of pent-up aggression between individuals and groups. But unless such questions are asked and attended to, there cannot but ensue an epidemic of unjust arrests, imprisonments and executions. Even so august a body of men as Lenin's 'self-acting armed organisation of the population'[104] might occasionally make mistakes of this kind; and then, like other groups of men, take more or less ruthless steps to cover them up. You put one man away on a false charge; and you have to put away ten more who would otherwise embarrass you with adverse publicity.

There is a strong tendency with Marx to confuse the question of what is true with that of what is apparent from the viewpoint

that suits the interests of a particular social group; this is one of
the results of his insistence on 'the unity of theory and
practice',[105] and his dismissal as 'scholastic' of the 'dispute over
the reality or non-reality of thinking that is isolated from
practice'.[106] It seems to me true and important that an oppressed class will have less motive for concealing the facts of
oppression than will its oppressors; what ought however to be
added is that they are liable to have strong motives for exaggerating them. The actual record of Marxist states in relation to
their own history may be thought sufficiently to show the
dangers of this tendency. What went on in the Ukraine in the
nineteen-thirties is something which can only be discovered by
diligent examination and comparison, carefully and deliberately 'isolated from practice' whether bourgeois or communist, of documents and the reports of eye-witnesses; there is
no more certainty that what comes out of such a process will
suit the self-image or the policies of revolutionaries than that it
will support the self-image or the policies of counter-
revolutionaries. Any cause, however good – except the unremitting pursuit of truth as such – may be assisted, people being
what they are, by judicious falsifications.

The proletarian has been shamefully exploited and de-
graded; there seems something peculiarly mean about the
suggestion that he might, on gaining power, behave much in
the same kind of way as other human beings in power have
done. There is thus no doubt that the thesis that he will not so
behave has an emotional appeal such as is peculiarly calculated
to strike the man of good will. And if, when the revolution has
occurred or is supposed to have occurred, the new leaders
apparently turn out to further their own interests and those of
their friends in the usual way rather than working for the
general good, is there not an overwhelming temptation either to
suppress consciousness of the fact; or to attribute it entirely and
unquestioningly to the lurking influence of dispossessed classes
or outsiders, or to the continuing effects of pre-revolutionary
modes of education, or to the fact that the *real* revolution has not
yet come about? All these moves may be attributed to Marxists;
very often they are largely justified, and perhaps at times
wholly so; the point here is merely that there may be sometimes
some crucial contributory factor, some predisposition which

belongs to human nature over all changes in economy and society, which they leave out of account.

If what we have called 'state B' is possible and desirable, the army and the police[107] would be likely to remain as its instruments in the restraining of powerful groups which, at the national or international level, tend to act against the general interest. They will in one sense be 'alienated'[108] from the general body of citizens, in that they each constitute a special group with a special task, which at best occasionally includes coercion of other citizens. But they need not be 'alienated' in that they may be clear-sightedly and gratefully accepted by the average citizen as preserving him from the effects of individual and group selfishness on the part of others. As to abuses in the army or the police which, on the view of human nature suggested here, can and always will be prone to occur, it is the business of the conscientious citizen to expose these institutions so far as the necessary power invested in them is used for themselves or in the interest of more powerful elements in society.

Similar considerations apply to bureaucracy: an elaborate administrative machinery will be an element of state B as of state A, but state B will always be on the look-out for its abuses, amusingly described by Marx. The bureaucracy, he says, consitutes an imaginary state beside the real state, and counts in its own eyes as the final aim of the state. It is a hierarchy, and has a hierarchy of knowledge, the apex entrusting the lower strata with knowledge of the particular, while the lower strata leave knowledge of the universal to the apex. There results a system of mutual deception. Each thing is treated not as it really is, but according to its bureaucratic essence (that is, so far as I can see, as it appears to such narrow and corrupt interests and concerns). The whole spirit of bureaucracy is secretive and mysterious, guarded as a closed corporation from without and by hierarchy within. The aim of the state becomes the aim of the bureaucrat, a matter of careerism and the struggle for higher posts.[109] It may be objected that, in a technologically sophisticated society, it is difficult to see how the variously specialised administrative machinery which is apt to give rise to the abuses of bureaucracy could ever disappear. But at least it can and ought to be subjected to constant criticism, on a basis of coherent and articulate moral principle, by those capable of cognitive and moral self-transcendence. It is the business of the conscientious citizen to attend to the question of how far, on the evidence available to him, the specialist knowledge and career structure of administrative organisations contributes to the general benefit, and in particular the efficient production and fair circulation of goods, and how far they favour their members or other privileged groups in society in despite of this.[110]

Writing in similar vein to Marx on bureaucracy, Lenin is justifiably hard on petty state officials and functionaries, who have to make up for their lack of personal worth with a lot of artificial marks of dignity on which, as everyone knows by experience, they are neurotically insistent.[111] But there seems reason to doubt whether, in any society more elaborate than a primitive tribe, at least where the special situation of revolutionary conflict is absent, there is not liable to be a recurrent gap between the authority which is due to some individual in the interests of the ordering of society for the common good, and the authority which he can exercise by his real merit and the sheer force of his personality. This difficulty is just one aspect of that fundamental dilemma, of how the benefits of belonging to an intimate community may be preserved in a highly organised modern technological society, which has perplexed so many of the great social scientists.[112] I think that the doctrines which Lenin took over from Marx and Engels, and the situation in which he lived and acted to such extraordinary effect, prevented him from adverting to the dilemma, or at least tended to convince him that it applied only to pre-revolutionary and perhaps immediately post-revolutionary society.[113]

There are signs in Marx's own writings that such a notion as our 'state B', which included an army, a police and a bureaucracy subject to constant criticism in the interests of the common good, might not have been regarded as entirely chimerical by him. The suggestion which he made in opposition to Bakunin, that some of the functions of the present state would be liable to remain in a future society, would seem to be a gesture in this direction. He appears to admit exceptions to his general account of the state simply as an instrument of class domination – as in *The Class Struggles in France* and *The Eight-*

eenth Brumaire.[114] And in relatively backward countries, where classes were not fully developed as such, he thought that the state could play a relatively independent role – as it had, for instance, in the transition between feudal and bourgeois forms of society. In fact, he held that the state *simply* as the instrument for the domination of society by a class was to be found only in North America, 'where the state, unlike all other national structures, was from the first subordinated to bourgeois society and bourgeois production'.[115] These facts, at least when taken together, suggest that the distinction we have made between two kinds of state, or two possible functions of the state, may not be wholly incompatible with Marx's views. But the general possibility and usefulness of the distinction depends on a view of permanent factors in human nature, and of the possibility and desirability of the transcendence of the point of view of any 'class' whatever, which is certainly against the general tenor of Marx's writings.

Revolution and Party

At certain stages of their development, according to Marx, the material forces of production come into conflict with the existing relations of production. They turn from forms of expression of these forces into their fetters. Then there follows a period of social revolution.[116] Now all previous revolutions, up to and including the bourgeois revolution, have been carried out either *by* minorities or *in the interests of* minorities. But the proletarian revolution will be at once *of* the vast majority and *in the interests of* the vast majority. Thus the proletariat cannot stir without the whole superincumbent official society, organised as it is by the few for the sake of the few, 'being exploded into the air'.[117] The radical nature of this revolution is due to the nature of the class carrying it out; the situation facing the proletariat being one in which class antagonisms have been simplified and sharpened to such a degree as to permit their abolition.[118] A class has been brought into existence 'which has to bear all the burdens of society without enjoying its advantages', and which is thus forced into decided antagonism with all other classes. It is formed by the majority of members of society, and from it 'emanates the consciousness of the necessity of a fundamental revolution, the communist consciousness, which may, of course, arise among the other classes too through the contemplation of this class'.[119]

Marx emphasised that the revolution would not be a merely mechanical result of the conflict of economic forces; that it had to be brought about by the deliberate activity of human beings. The revolutionary class, he said, so far from being merely passive in relation to the forces of production, is itself the greatest of productive forces.[120] The proletariat would change itself in bringing about the revolution; which indeed would itself not merely be a matter of the proletariat overthrowing the ruling class, but of its fitting itself to get rid of the muck of ages and to found society anew. 'In revolutionary activity, the changing of oneself coincides with the changing of circumstances'.[121] However, the right economic and social situation for revolution does have to obtain for it to be practicable; those who aspire to bring about revolution when it does not obtain – as though the successful outcome depended on nothing but their own efforts or powers of organisation – are mere speculators, comparable to alchemists as opposed to genuine scientists of revolution.[122]

Where landowning peasants form a sizeable proportion of the population, they are inclined to hinder the workers' revolution. If the workers should be able to seize power all the same in such a situation, they will be well advised to avoid confrontation with the peasantry which will inevitably ensue if, for example, inheritance and private property are abolished forthwith. The workers should rather first win the peasants to the revolutionary cause by improving their general condition; this will in the long run facilitate the necessary transition from private to collective ownership of land. However, the abolition of property and inheritance will be welcomed in those cases where the capitalist landlord has already expropriated the peasant and turned him into an agricultural wage labourer with the same basic interest as the city worker.[123]

Marx thought that in some relatively advanced countries, like America, England and Holland, revolution might come about peacefully;[124] he suggested that workers in the two former countries might gain a majority in parliament or Congress and by legal means set aside the obstacles that stood in their way.

On the other hand, he always thought that force would be necessary in the majority of cases; and he blamed the Paris commune for being unwilling to start a civil war.[125] 'We must make it clear to the governments, we know that you are the armed power that is directed against the proletariat, we will proceed against you by peaceful means where that is possible and with arms when it is necessary.' But he disapproved of revolutionary terror, regarding it as due to weakness and immaturity, and as a sign that the attempt was being made to impose by sheer force what was not yet latent in the economic and social situation. Physical force, as opposed to terror, was justifiable so far as this situation made it likely to be successful.[126]

The Communist Manifesto says that it is the business of the party, as distinct from other working-class organisations, to point out and lay emphasis on the common interest of the proletariat in its struggles in each separate country, and to represent the interests of the whole working class in the various stages of its struggle against the bourgeoisie. The party has a theoretical understanding of the line of advance of the whole movement, and its claim to be the vanguard of the working class is not based on interests separate from those of the proletariat as a whole, or on any sectarian principles.[127] When the First International was founded in 1864, Marx insisted that it must avoid sectarianism. The general aims of the working class, he said, derive from the real conditions in which it finds itself, conditions present in the whole class, but reflected in the heads of its members in widely different forms, some more or less imaginary, some more or less in accordance with the conditions themselves. Those who best understood the real meaning of the class struggle, the Communists, are the last to promote sectarianism.[128] Sectarian movements are characteristic of the earlier stages of the proletariat's struggle against the bourgeoisie, before it is sufficiently developed to act as a class; 'this is the infancy of the proletarian movement, as astronomy and alchemy are the infancy of science'.[129]

Marx's insistence on the identity of the party's interest with that of the proletariat as a whole can be taken in two ways, one of them salutary, the other by no means so. Its effect is excellent so far as it causes party leaders and functionaries to feel that they are not properly to be called 'communists' unless they are really acting in the public interest, or at least in the interest of that vast majority of people which constitutes the working class. Its effect is very different, however, so far as it may be used as a pretext for party members not attending to the question of whether they are really so acting. If I am recognised – and who would dare to say inappropriately? – as leader of a communist party running a socialist society, my real commitment to the interests of the vast majority can perhaps too readily be taken for granted. And given the power and influence, I can always ensure that those who ask awkward questions about the matter can be threatened into silence, or put away if unduly persistent. The fact is that the statement that the party's interests are identical with those of the working class as a whole is crucially ambiguous, on one interpretation being such as to invite constant self-criticism by those who regard themselves as its members, on another encouraging complacency and self-deception. The practical effects of the ambiguity may well be felt to be abundantly exemplified, whether one is a Marxist or not, by the history of the communist movement.

calls 'sectarianism'. Given that the fundamental unity in policy and in theory which is the opposite of 'sectarianism' is desirable, there are at least two ways in which this might be achieved. In cases of disagreement, the disputants might be at pains to scrutinise the evidence against their own point of view, and for the points of view of their opponents, in as unprejudiced a way as possible, in order that all concerned could arrive at a combination of the best insights of each. But, on the contrary, a powerful group might find a convenient pretext for ruling out all dissent from its own point of view, on the ground that this was mere 'sectarianism'.

The aim of the party, of course, and the justification for its existence, is bringing about and directing the course of the revolution. Now there are at least two aims to be understood by revolution, according to Marx and his followers; what is to be gained by distinguishing them depends on facts about human nature. One aim of the revolution is the overthrow of the bourgeoisie and the establishment of the dictatorship of the proletariat. The less immediate aim is the inauguration of the state of affairs in which each will gladly and spontaneously work for the good of all, and all for the good of each – when there will be no more individual or group selfishness. One of the theses most characteristic of Marx and his followers is that the former state of affairs will at least in the long run lead to the latter; but it seems germane to ask, if one is more impressed with the sceptical than with the optimistic streak in Marx,[130] what evidence there is that it will do so. I heartily agree with him that the ideal constitution of society would be one in which action for the general good would be made satisfying to the individual *so far as possible*. But I look for evidence that the prima-facie tension between self-interest, group interest and the general interest would be altogether done away with in any possible social order, given the predispositions to behaviour which men have inherited along with their bodily structure; or that consistent application of oneself to the general good would not always involve some self-denial. Marx did say that the task of the proletariat was not only to overthrow their oppressors, but to fit themselves to found society anew.[131] The possibility that they would do the first, and fail to do the second, seems here at least to be left open; and a less optimistic person, particularly after reflecting on the actual history of Marxist socialism, might be disposed to emphasise this possibility rather more strongly than did Marx himself.

The question of what Marxism really is, and what it entails on this or that particular issue, is one over which rivers of ink have flowed. It is, I believe, unanswerable; this is because of an ambiguity in Marx's position on a number of fundamental issues. Preoccupation with the question, furthermore, tends to deflect people from asking what is ultimately a more important question, that of which propositions attributable to Marx are likely to be true and which are likely to be false. Of each of the following pairs of theses, representing respectively a 'strong' (a) and a 'weak' (b) interpretation of Marx, the argument of this book would tend to show that the first is false, the second true.

I (a) Human behaviour can be modified to an (almost) un-limited extent by environment; there are (almost) no inherited predispositions to behaviour.

(b) While basic predispositions to behaviour, evolved over millennia, remain relatively constant in the human species, human behaviour can be very largely shaped by environment.

II (a) Human thought is fitted only to cope with present problems and cannot effectively extrapolate to states of affairs in the remote future when circumstances will be different.

(b) An overall conception of human good may be articulated which is independent of particular material circumstances, but its detailed application to any particular set of circumstances can hardly be worked out until this obtains, or nearly does so.

III (a) Truth and morality are entirely relative to class interest.

(b) Group bias due to economic and social class very largely condition what people believe on matters of fact and value.

IV (a) 'What is to be done' is to identify oneself with the interest of the working class and to use every means at one's disposal to further that interest.

(b) 'What is to be done' is clearly to conceive and pursue a general good which transcends the restricted interest of any class, but which tends in a situation of social injustice to coincide with the interest of the most oppressed classes.

V (a) The social and economic state of affairs, not obtaining at present, which is the end in relation to which 'what is to be done' is to be determined, is not an ideal; it is something bound to come about, at least in the long run, as a working-out of processes at work in the economy and society of the present.

(b) The state of affairs in relation to which 'what is to be done' is to be determined is an ideal which may never be realised, owing to dispositions innate to man; but all the same it may and should provide effective norms for political and social policy.

VI (a) All sacrifice of the individual for the common good, and all labour of an irksome kind, will be done away with in the society of the future.

(b) Self-sacrifice and irksome labour, while they would still exist, would be minimised and fairly distributed in the kind of just and technologically sophisticated society which we may hope to attain in the future.

VII (a) All (or almost all) tendencies to selfishness in human individuals and groups are bound up with capitalism and earlier modes of production and will disappear once socialism is fully established.

(b) A relatively just ordering of society, which can be put into effect in the foreseeable future, will encourage tendencies to individual and group selfishness far less, and co-operation for the common good far more, than have the general run of early industrial societies.

With regard to my earlier suggestion that Marx's views on a 'strong' interpretation are self-destructive, it will be noted that II (a) (together perhaps with III (a)) on the one hand, and VI (a) and VII (a) on the other, are not really compatible.

5 The Corrupt Individual Consciousness: Freud and Jung

The writings of Freud appear to be applications of two basic principles of explanation. The first is a generalisation of our usual manner of explaining human actions and policies, in terms of the motives and intentions of their agents, to account for behaviour in cases where the agents themselves cannot thus account for it; where these motives and intentions are thus 'unconscious', but still supposed to exist and to operate. The second is a kind of reductionism which at times presupposes, and at times tries to demonstrate, that thinking is *really* only an indirect route to pleasure, and pleasure *really* only a matter of the release of tensions which have built up in the organs of the body. In terms of the distinction I suggested earlier,[1] the first principle is a matter of extending B explanation to phenomena to which it had not previously been applied; the second of reducing B explanation to A explanation. The first principle surely represents one of the most important discoveries ever made in the human sciences. The second seems, on the contrary, for reasons which I have already given,[1] to be almost entirely superstitious; due to an attempt to reconcile a great discovery with erroneous beliefs about the nature and implications of scientific explanation.

It will be convenient to use Freud's theory of the unconscious to illustrate the application of the first principle; and his account of instinct to bring out the nature of the second.

The Unconscious

In the 1880s Freud's colleague Josef Breuer discovered that, in the case of hysterical patients, there were forgotten events of their past lives such that, when these were brought to the patient's remembrance and there was an appropriate discharge of emotion, the pathological symptoms tended to disappear. Some of the cures effected in this way were very sensational; occasionally paralysed limbs, where there was no organic lesion to account for the paralysis, were completely cured from the time that memory of the 'traumatic' event was recovered. Doctors before that time had found their knowledge of man as a physical organism of no use in treating such hysterical conditions, alarming as their symptoms often were.[2]

The point of the techniques evolved by Breuer and Freud was and is to recover the memory of the traumatic event or events. The fact that patients could be induced, by however indirect means, to recover such 'memories', and the fact that this recovery had the remarkable effects which it did, together seemed to indicate that there were parts of the mind which, although not open to conscious reflection, yet had an important effect upon behaviour. It is these parts or aspects which are referred to by the term 'the unconscious'. The technique used by Breuer to recover these memories, which owing to their painful nature had been (to use another famous and much abused Freudian term) 'repressed', was that of hypnosis. Under hypnosis, the patient would tell Breuer about the traumatic event; Breuer would then wake the patient from his trance and tell him in his turn. Freud was dissatisfied with hypnosis for two main reasons: first, that he himself was not very good at it (as he admits with the admirable frankness characteristic of him); and second, that the cures achieved by means of it, though sometimes very sensational, were not as lasting as those achieved by means of another method which he himself practised with his patients. This was the method of free association. In following this method, the therapist takes some significant word or idea – typically, from one of the patient's dreams – and gets the patient to declare with complete frankness whatever ideas emerge in connection with it. When at length there comes a halt in the flow of ideas, it is a sign that one is getting close to the trauma (that, as one might say, the therapist and the patient, in their joint efforts to bring the trauma to light, are getting 'warm').[3]

What applies to the causes and cure of hysteria applies also to other neurotic ailments. The neurotic suffers from uncon-

scious memories, that is to say, from the effect on him of events
in his past which can be recalled with the help of techniques
such as those described, but hardly otherwise. These express
themselves in terms of a kind of counter-will, or tendency to act
in marked contrast, in certain significant circumstances, with
what might be expected to be in conformity with his explicit
motives and intentions. The distortion of the patient's memory,
his tendency to erase or transform real occasions in his past life,
and to substitute unreal ones, is in proportion to the mental
energy required to repress from consciousness the traumatic
memory or memories. The aim of the treatment is at once to
remove symptoms and replace them by conscious thoughts,
and to repair the damage in the patient's memory; both
destinations being reached by the same route.[4]

It was not until later in his life that Freud made the famous
tripartite division of the psyche into id, ego and superego.[5]
When someone says, of a sudden impulse, '*It* was too much for
me', he is referring to his id, which he thus in effect distinguishes from his conscious self or ego. The id consists of needs
derived from our biological nature striving, in a completely
unco-ordinated and uncircumspect way, for satisfaction. There
is no recognition in the id of the passage of time; impressions
and wishful impulses decades old, sunk into the id beneath the
weight of repression, affect the person's thought and behaviour
as though they had only just occurred. Only by being made
conscious can they be deprived of their energy. The ego tries to
co-ordinate the drives constituting the id, and to take account
of the inconveniences and dangers usually attendant upon their
immediate satisfaction; it is the façade between the (rest of the)
id and reality. (Freud sometimes writes of the ego and the id as
contrasted and opposed to one another; but sometimes as
though the id were the psyche as a whole, and the ego a part of
it. I shall argue later that this ambiguity is of some
importance.)[6]

In so far as the ego controls and tames the id's impulses in the
manner described, 'it replaces the pleasure principle, which
was formerly alone decisive, by what is known as the "reality
principle", which though it pursues the same ultimate aims,
takes into account the conditions imposed by the real external
world'. Short of the ego, which is nothing other than that aspect
of the id 'that has been expediently modified by the external

world with its threat of danger', survival would be impossible. Freud adopted his new terminology on the ground that parts of the ego, defined as that which co-ordinates the disparate impulses of the id and suppresses some of them, are by no means all immediately available for conscious inspection. For example, repression itself, and unconscious resistance to analysis, are activities due to the ego of which the subject is not conscious; and it is the relationship between the ego and id as they have just been described, rather than between those parts of the psyche which are conscious and those which are unconscious, which is of primary importance for psychoanalysis. This leaves open the important theoretical possibility that portions of the ego are unconscious without possessing the primitive and irrational nature of the id. And indeed the interpretation of dreams indicates that rather complicated mental acts may be performed unconsciously.[7]

There remains the superego, which is roughly equivalent to conscience. It often treats the ego very harshly, particularly in neurotics; it is as important for mental health that the ego should be on good terms with the superego as that it should be in control of the id. Now if one throws a crystal to the ground, it does not shatter haphazardly, but breaks along lines determined by the crystal's structure. Insane persons may be regarded as rather similar broken structures, whose shape shows the underlying form of the normal human mind. Some such people have the delusion of being observed, and of hearing reports of their own doings. 'How would it be if these people were right, if in each of us there was present in his ego an agency like this which observes and threatens to punish, and which in them has merely become sharply divided from their ego and mistakenly displaced into external reality?' Indeed, in the case of normal people, there is hardly anything that they so regularly separate from and set over against themselves as their conscience. The mental disease of melancholia is characterised by a peculiar cruelty and severity in this agency. One may say that the division between ego and superego is the most delicate, and phylogenetically speaking the latest, of the divisions within the psyche.[8]

Anxiety[9] is the ego's admission of its own weakness. Three kinds of anxiety may be distinguished; *realistic* anxiety in relation to the external world, *moral* anxiety in relation to the superego, and *neurotic* anxiety in relation to the impulses of the id. The ego exercises influence over the id by putting into operation the pleasure-unpleasure principle, which alone has any influence over the id, through the medium of anxiety; and so the impulse is repressed. However, this is but an equivocal show of strength on the part of the ego, for by the act of repression it drives the impulse out of the range of its influence.[10]

It is neither unusual, nor in my opinion quite inappropriate, to regard Freud's theories and therapeutic practice as a sustained application of Socrates' injunction, 'know yourself'. There is nothing new in the acknowledgment that there is great danger in refusal to be conscious of one's disagreeable emotions and disreputable impulses, or to admit them for what they are. What is perhaps most significant in Freud is his detailed articulation of how this failure of consciousness may issue in uncontrollable behaviour, sudden slips in speech and action,[11] and even in apparent symptoms of severe physical disease; and of how an individual's increase in consciousness may result in his greater freedom of action and self-disposability. On these matters at least, it is striking that none of the theorists and practitioners of depth psychology and psychotherapy, for all their disagreements with Freud and with one another, have gone against him. 'Where id was, there ego shall be' – where previously there were ungovernable impulses followed by reasonable regrets or by agonies of conscience, there will be deliberate, consistent and satisfying speech and action – is surely the effective maxim of all psychotherapy, whether the terminology is accepted or not. Freud's tripartite division of the psyche into ego, id and superego, though more controversial, corresponds very well with our ordinary conceptions of and language about ourselves, as well as accounting rather neatly for certain types of mental disorder. But Freud himself would have been dissatisfied with this view of his achievement, and with the assessment of his theory and practice as a mere application in a new way of ancient philosophical and religious wisdom. He thought of himself as a scientist and had a particular view of the requirements of scientific explanation. Of central importance for Freud's attempted reduction of B explanation to A explanation – which he seems to have assumed was of the essence of science – was his theory of instinct, and particularly the account of sexuality which he derived from it.

Instincts and Sexuality

Freud remarks that people are inclined to assume the existence of just as many 'instincts' as happen to suit their immediate point of view. He himself distinguished two principal instincts or groups of instincts to correspond with the two great biological needs, the preservation of the individual and the preservation of the species – hunger and love. Defence of the independence of psychology from the other sciences, important as it is, should not make one forget 'the unshakeable biological fact that the living individual organism is at the command of two intentions, self-preservation and the preservation of the species, which seem to be independent of each other, which, so far as we know at present, have no common origin and whose interests are often in conflict in animal life'. In analysing the nature of an instinct, one has to distinguish its *source*, its *aim* and its *object*. The source is a state of excitation in the body, the aim the removal of that excitation, the object that towards which it may be directed in the fulfilment of the aim. (Thus the source of hunger would be an abnormal state of the stomach, the aim of hunger the alteration of this state to the normal one, the object the food by means of which the organism could fulfil the aim.) It is 'on its path from its source to its aim' that 'an instinct becomes operative psychically'. The relations of an instinct to its aim and its object are subject to alteration; it is on this fact that all the achievements of human thought and culture depend. That kind of alteration of object or aim on which society sets a high value is what is known as 'sublimation'; here the aim and object of instinct are transferred to politics, administration, science, the arts or other socially acceptable ends. Sometimes an instinct which is quite unambiguous as to its aim comes to a stop on the way to satisfaction. 'Such ... is the relation of tenderness, which undoubtedly originates from the sources of sexual need and invariably renounces its satisfaction.' The sexual instinct, in fact, is particularly notable for its capacity for alteration of aim, its ability to allow satisfaction to be deferred, and its general plasticity. It is owing to this that it has proved capable of contributing 'invaluably to the highest cultural, artistic, and social achievements of the human mind'; and on the other hand of playing a uniquely large part in the causation of mental and nervous disorders.[12]

The self-preserving instincts, apart from hunger and thirst, are also flexible. The aggressive instinct or group of instincts has an importance rivalling even that of sexuality. It goes without saying that the assumption of an aggressive instinct runs counter to religious beliefs and social conventions which are very precious to mankind. However, history and day-to-day experience combine to show that the conviction that human nature is basically good is itself an evil illusion, supposed to make our lives easier and more beautiful, but in fact only causing untold damage. It was sadism and masochism which both convinced Freud of a basic aggressive instinct in man, and provided him with a model of its relationship with the sexual instinct. Every instinctive impulse, when examined, seemed to consist of a fusion or alloy of the two classes of instinct, similar to that found in sadism and masochism. Now it appears to be the case that the destructive instinct as well as the sexual was originally contained within the ego, or rather in the id, the whole person. (This would fit in with the doctrine previously mentioned, that the source of an instinct is a state of excitation within the body, its aim the removal of that state.) It would seem to follow that masochism is older than sadism; and that aggression against others is really a self-destructive impulse, a death-wish, turned outwards. We have apparently to destroy something else in order to avoid destroying ourselves; a sad conclusion, Freud remarks, from the point of view of moralists, who will doubtless console themselves for some time to come with the alleged improbability of his speculations. But the fact is that the trend towards self-destruction has all too many manifestations in human living. Some people repeat fatally the same reactions to events, or seem dogged through their lives by a relentless fate. Again, it is characteristic of patients undergoing psychoanalysis that they resist cure without knowing that they are doing so; indeed, 'it seems that an unconscious need for punishment has a share in every neurotic illness'. The problems which the unconscious sense of guilt, which seems to be an aspect of this self-destructive tendency, has opened up, and its connection with morality, education, crime, and delinquency, have proved a happy hunting-ground for psychoanalytic workers and theorists. The instinct for self-destruction also has important consequences for the conception of the superego. This, once instituted, employs against the impulses of the id the latent aggression which the child had harboured against his parents but could not discharge, both for fear of retribution and because the aggression was tinged with erotic elements.[13]

The sexual instinct itself, Freud claimed, was complex in nature and origin. He did not recognise a single instinct which is from the first an urge towards the sexual function itself, with its goal the union of two sex-cells. What actually had to be taken into account were a number of component instincts, each of which are liable in time to play a part in the sexual function proper; these arise from regions in the body which Freud calls 'erotogenic' zones. 'An erotogenic zone . . . is a part of the skin or mucous membrane in which stimuli of a certain sort evoke a feeling of pleasure possessing a particular quality.' An infantile sexual manifestation has three characteristics. 'At its origin it attaches itself to one of the vital somatic functions; it has as yet no sexual object, and is thus auto-erotic; and its sexual aim is dominated by an erotogenic zone.' These component instincts strive for satisfaction through the build-up and release of tension, at first more or less in isolation from one another; and they are not all taken up into the final organisation of the sexual function. Some are set aside as unserviceable, by repression or by some other means. A few are diverted from their aim in the ways described earlier, and used to strengthen other impulses. Some persist in minor roles, to provide fore-pleasure in acts introductory to sexual intercourse proper. In the long development of the sexual function, several preliminary phases of organisation are to be recognised, and one may account for its aberrations by its fixation at one or other of them. The first of these phases is known as the *oral*, since, in consequence of the way in which the infant is fed, 'the erotogenic zone of the mouth dominates what may be called the sexual activity of that period'. Next the *anal* zone and its impulses come to the fore;

undoubtedly this is in connection with a general strengthening of the muscles, and in particular the control of the sphincter and its functions. Two stages in this phase have been distinguished, the first characterised by the destructive trends of annihilating and losing, the second by trends friendly towards objects, of keeping and possessing. 'It is in the middle of this phase that consideration for the object makes its first appearance.' Similarly, it is possible to distinguish two stages in the first or oral phase, the first of oral incorporation, in which there is no ambivalence towards the mother's breast; the second, the oral-biting or oral-sadistic stage, where there is a powerful ambivalence which increases with the sadism characteristic of the anal phase. After the anal comes the *phallic* phase, during which the male organ and its equivalent in girls is at the centre of interest; then begins the period of *latency* which lasts until puberty. The term *genital* phase should be reserved for the definitive sexual organisation established at last, in normal cases, after puberty.[14]

Regression to earlier stages of sexual organisation often occurs under pathological conditions. Each type of mental illness is characterised by its own form of regression, and it appears that those with psychotic conditions have regressed to an earlier stage than have neurotics. If 'sexual' gratification, in the comparatively narrow sense of pleasure derived from stimulation of the erotogenic zones, is not stimulated at puberty to reproduction, some form of perversion ensues. In the sexual act proper, a distinction is to be made between the *fore-pleasure* which consists in the excitation of erotogenic zones, and the *end-pleasure* which comes about at the climax of sexual intercourse. There is danger of perversion if at any point the immediate pleasure in what should have been mere fore-pleasure is too great, and tension towards the normal kind of sexual climax not great enough. This is apt to happen when, at some point in the past, one of the component instincts of sexuality has contributed an excessive amount of pleasure. It is to be remembered, however, that no normal person fails to make some addition which might be called perverse to the normal sexual aim; for example, by looking and gazing. It is only when such additions actually supplant the normal aim, rather than forming a prelude of accompaniment to it, that one should speak of a pathological aberration. Children who have been especially assiduous thumb-suckers will be likely, when grown-up, to become

> epicures in kissing, will be inclined to perverse kissing, or, if males, will have a powerful motive for drinking and smoking. If, however, repression ensues, they will feel disgust at food and produce hysterical vomiting. The repression extends to the nutritional zone owing to the dual purpose served by the labial zone. Many of my women patients who suffer from disturbances of eating ... constriction of the throat and vomiting, have indulged energetically in sucking during their childhood.[15]

The cash value of Freud's theory of instinct appears to be to the effect that, where a drive in human beings is not directly a matter of the build-up and release of tension in a bodily organ, it is not instinctual in the sense of basic or inherited, but must be the result of the effect of environment on such instinct. Now hunger and thirst and their satisfaction are plainly somatic states, and so also is the build-up and release of tension in the 'erotogenic' zones which for Freud is the essence of sexuality. It seems clear enough that, as Freud says, hunger and thirst are states the nature of whose satisfaction is more or less unequivocal; a hungry or thirsty man eats or drinks, or he is not satisfied. But apparently, as he rightly insists, the sexual instinct may much more readily be satisfied in ways which are oblique and indirect. However universal the sexual instinct may be, many find at least a degree of satisfaction in life without engaging in behaviour which is 'sexual' in any ordinary sense. Given the premisses that the sexual instinct exhibits such flexibility and that all instinct is fundamentally a matter of the build-up and release of tension in bodily organs, there follows almost inevitably Freud's notorious conclusion that a vast range of desires and satisfactions which are not at first sight of a somatic nature at all are *really* sexual. It is also easy to see why Freud thought that his emphasis on sexuality was essential to the status of psychoanalysis as a science. As Stuart Hampshire has written: 'The theory holds together as a whole only so long as the apparent over-emphasis on sexuality preserves the necessary link with biology, which he calls [in one of his letters to Jung] "the organic foundation without which a medical man can only feel ill at ease in the life of the psyche"'.[16]

Freud is surely on the right lines when he suggests that, given the truth of the theory of evolution, one should in the study of instinct look for enlightenment to those characteristics which man shares with other animals. When the question is asked of the nature and complexity of the predispositions to behaviour[17] innate in animals and men, three general possibilities suggest themselves: (i) simple urges of a somatic nature are all that is innate in either animals or men, and any desires or needs which are of a more complex nature are simply due to the influence of environment; (ii) complex predispositions to behaviour, in relation either to conspecifics or to the rest of the environment or both, are innate in other animals but not in man; (iii) complex predispositions of these kinds are innate both in other animals and in man. Freud's account of instinct seems to assume the truth of the first thesis; but the evidence against it which is to be found from the study of animal behaviour, some of which I mentioned in connection with Konrad Lorenz, is overwhelming. It would be at least rather curious if the second thesis were true; that man alone among the higher animals was without inherited dispositions to behaviour which were not simply a matter of build-up and release of tension in bodily organs. One could hardly defend it short of an appeal to something like special creation, or some other doctrine which implied that we did not inherit the structure of our central nervous system from creatures very like the surviving higher animals usually supposed to be most closely related to us. Thus the falsification of the first thesis, and the obvious implausibility of the second, seem to leave us only with the third. And this is to the effect that man, in common with the other higher animals, inherits an elaborate set of predispositions to behaviour along with his bodily structure.

To take one example of what is at issue, it seems clear that many mammals and birds inherit a strong predisposition to curiosity;[18] if this is granted, it does seem very strange to regard human curiosity as determined by 'sexuality', however broadly this term is understood, to the degree that Freud does.[19] That the child's attention to the erotogenic zones of his body, and his parents' attitude to this, may have a great deal of effect on his later curiosity about other matters, need by no means be denied. But it is one thing to try to determine the nature and degree of this effect by empirical methods, another thing to maintain it on the basis of assumptions about how psychology will have to be related to biology in order to be scientifically respectable. The relation between the child's interest in his bodily functions, and his parents' attitude to this, on the one hand, and the overall development of curiosity in him on the other, is something well worth empirical investigation. It is not the least of Freud's merits to have suggested that the relation between the one and the other is probably much closer than is usually supposed. But however close the relation were found to be, it could hardly be sufficient to establish that curiosity was basically or even primarily sexual.

In general, it has to be said that Freud's reduction of thought about what is so, the 'reality principle', to the pleasure principle, is not compatible with what we have called 'cognitional self-transcendence', with the capacity of human beings to get so far beyond their activities and their immediate or even long-term desires as to find out what actually is so. And I have already argued that denial of cognitive self-transcendence is self-destructive.[20] If it is really true that, as one author put it,[21] Freud showed the human mind to be no more suited to discovering the truth than a pig's snout, then this is of course totally destructive of all human claims to knowledge, including those of Freud himself.

To say that the reality principle cannot really be a mere adaptation of the pleasure principle is as much as to say that the ego cannot be a part of the id. I have already said that Freud usually speaks of the ego and id as though they were essentially contrasted with one another; but sometimes he says that the ego is a part of the id.[22] The former account of their relation, it may be inferred, is the only one that makes sense in the last analysis; the latter being due to those reductionist prejudices of Freud alluded to earlier. The ego, in the sense of the human subject questioning, judging, deliberating and acting in accordance with the reality principle, is essentially contrasted with the id, in the sense of those repressed impulses and unadmitted motives and strategies which disrupt reasonable thinking and smooth performance.

Freud's theory of instinct throws light on his reasons for holding one of his most controversial views, which has largely been rejected even by the most orthodox of his followers: that man had a fundamental death-wish.[23] Towards the end of his life, Freud came to acknowledge that aggression was as basic an ingredient of human nature as was sexuality.[24] A true instinct, on his account, has its source and aim in the organism itself; its object is only incidental, a means of fulfilling the aim. It seems to follow that aggression, if it is really a basic human instinct, primarily is aimed inwards, and only incidentally and derivatively is directed to an external object. What applies to the sexual origin of curiosity seems also to apply to the death-wish; one has to consider how far its existence is postulated to account for evidence, and how far as a consequence of erroneous assumptions about the nature of explanation. That some people perversely seek out suffering, and others are intent on self-destruction, does appear to be the case, however one accounts for it.

Freud's theory of instinct is one indication of his speculative genius; but it seems quite inconsistent with the existence of those 'innate releaser mechanisms' and that capacity for 'imprinting' which have been discovered by research into the behaviour of the higher animals, and which there is every reason to suppose are characteristic of man as well.[25] The intricacy of inherited behaviour patterns among non-human animals is sometimes perfectly astounding; as in the case of migratory birds which can follow a route covering thousands of miles to their winter quarters, when they themselves have never travelled along the route, and in some cases are unaccompanied by other members of the species which have done so. Freud is surely quite right in saying that a theory of human instinct should be based on animal biology; and also that it should be sufficiently rigorous and systematic to prevent those concerned with the explanation of behaviour from postulating a separate and autonomous 'instinct' every time it suits them to do so.[26] However, to seek some satisfactory basis for the theory of instinct is not necessarily to attempt to relate it to 'organ pleasure' or anything else of the kind. It is rather to ask how the behaviour observed as characteristic of a species would tend to foster the survival of that species; then to find out by observation or experiment to what extent each item of behaviour is controlled by innate factors and to what extent by environmental ones;[27] and finally to determine how that particular innate or 'instinctive' organisation of behaviour might have evolved step by step from an organisation of behaviour deemed to be more primitive.[28] Freud appears to hold that all concern by an individual human being for the good of another must be due to some kind of diversion of the sexual instinct from its normal aim and object; but given the spontaneous parental behaviour of many mammals and birds, and the tendency even in insects, let alone in the higher animals, for individuals to expose themselves to danger or death on behalf of the group, this seems very arbitrary. Would Freud have wished to maintain that the tendency of many animals to sacrifice themselves for the life of their young was due to a diversion of the sexual instinct? But if he denied that this applied in the case of other animals, on what ground could he have supposed that it applied in the case of man?

Freud said that whenever he was assailed by doubt as to the truth of his fundamental theories, he recalled how strongly they were vindicated by the study of dreams.[29] It therefore seems appropriate to consider next Freud's account of dreams and their interpretation.

Dreams and Symbolism

In the cure of neurotics, and in the bringing to light of the traumatic events of their past, dreams prove of the greatest importance. 'In every dream an instinctual wish has to be represented as fulfilled.' There is a regression to primitive mental mechanisms, as a result of which 'ideas are transformed . . . into visual pictures', and thus 'the latent dream-thoughts . . . are dramatised and illustrated'. It is remarkable that just the same mechanisms are to be found in the construction of neurotic symptoms from unconscious wishes and memories as in the construction of the manifest dream out of the latent dream-thoughts.[30]

Now it is notable that small children dream explicitly of wishes which have been aroused shortly before the time of the dream but left unsatisfied. The same really applies to the dreams of adults, but the situation is complicated by the fact that their dreams are not, as in the case of children, a matter of *explicit* satisfaction of *conscious* wishes, but of the *disguised* fulfilment of *repressed* wishes. 'The dream . . . is one of the détours by which repression can be evaded; it is one of the principal means employed by what is known as the indirect method of representation in the mind.' In order to find out the inner meaning of a dream, the dreamer must engage in 'free association' from each element of it; that is to say, he must state, without holding anything back, everything that occurs to him in connection with it. The associations turn out to be a very varied collection, and to include memories of the day before and of long ago. Some of this material the patient pours out; some is forthcoming only after he has been held up for a while. Mostly it is clearly connected with the elements of the manifest dream; but every now and then the patient interjects something which occurs to him, but which appears to him to have no connection with the dream. 'If one listens to these copious associations, one soon notices that they have more in common with the content of the dream than their starting-points alone. They throw a surprising light on all the different parts of the dream, fill in gaps between them, and make their strange juxtapositions intelligible.' Whatever consecutiveness there may be in the succession of dream-events is quite unimportant from the point of view of analysis. It is merely one more way, besides the transformation of the elements themselves, in which the unconscious thoughts can be disguised in such a way as to get past the repressive agency in the mind, which is called 'the censor'.

> In a line of associations ambiguous words, or, as we may call them, 'switch-words', act like points at a junction. If the points are switched away from the position in which they appear to be in the dream, then we find ourselves on another set of rails, and along this second track run the thoughts which we are in search of but which still lie concealed behind the dream.

In respect to its connection with the dreamer's life, the dream stands on two legs, one of which links it up with the exciting cause of the dream in the dreamer's recent experience, the other of which connects it with some momentous childhood event.[31]

The changes effected by what is called 'the dream work' between the dream-thoughts and the manifest dream, which are demanded both by the archaic regression of the mental apparatus and by the requirements of the censorship, are of the following kinds: there is *condensation*, as the result of which one element in the manifest dream may correspond to numerous elements in the dream-thoughts; there is also *displacement*, through which ideas are separated from the emotions originally attached to them, and the emphasis is transferred from important to indifferent elements. It is displacement above all which renders the dream strange and incomprehensible to the dreamer himself. Parallels may be found in waking experience to the manner in which the dream-work substitutes concrete images for thoughts. H. Silberer noticed that when he tried to do intellectually exacting work in a drowsy state, a thought would often be replaced by a visual image. For example, he thought of having to revise an uneven passage in an essay and saw himself planing a piece of wood.[32]

It is easy to find superficial objections to the view that dreams are the fulfilment of wishes. People are aware that they themselves have had dreams in which the principal emotion was one of agonising dread; and they ask how these can possibly be maintained to fit such an interpretation. It must however be borne in mind that in these cases the wishes which gave rise to the dream have been prohibited and rejected by the censor; one must not expect, in general, to understand how any dream fulfils a wish until the dream has been interpreted. It may happen that the dream-work is not wholly successful in creating a wish-fulfilment, so that part of the painful feeling within the latent dream-thoughts is carried over into the manifest dream. Also, the dream-work may succeed in transforming the painful *content* of the dream-thoughts into a wish-fulfilment, while the painful *emotion* remains unchanged. Again, it is to be noted that 'the attitude of the dreamer towards his wishes is a peculiar one; he rejects them, censors them, in short, he will have none of them'. Their fulfilment then can afford him no pleasure, rather the opposite – and the opposite characteristically takes the form of anxiety or dread. Even punishment-dreams are wishes; though in this case the wishes are not those of the instinctual impulses, but of the critical, censoring superego. A real limitation to the theory of dreams as wish-fulfilments, it must be admitted, is to be found in the case of the dreams characteristic of traumatic hysteria, where the situation which precipitated the condition is re-enacted. For example, someone who has been all but run over by a car will dream over and over again of the circumstances which led up to this. It is interesting that this does not seem to occur when the accident has actually happened, with the result, for example, of the breaking of a limb and the attendant physical pain. Here the dreamer's unconscious seems to be attempting by means of such repetition to master the traumatic situation.[33]

A train of association often comes to a halt just before it reaches the dream-thought, and makes contact with it only by way of an allusion. Here the analyst has to fill in gaps and draw conclusions himself. How then can one be sure that he is not reading something into the associations rather than genuinely interpreting them? The legitimacy of the procedure is impossible to bring out in an abstract way; the honest doubter will be convinced, however, if he carries out a dream-analysis himself, or studies one in the literature on the subject. The symbolism of which dreams make use is partly peculiar to each dreamer, partly more or less communal. It is a consequence of this that though it is to some extent helpful to assign particular meanings to particular symbols, no dream can be understood at all thoroughly except in relation to the life and problems of the individual dreamer. The number of things that are represented by more or less universal symbols is not very great. The human body, parents, children, brothers and sisters, birth, death, nakedness and sexual organs and activities more or less complete the list. The only typical and recurring symbol of the body as a whole is a house. Parents are apt to appear as kings and queens, children as little animals; birth is usually signified by some reference to water. A journey means death, and clothes and uniforms are allusions to nakedness.[34]

However, 'an overwhelming majority of symbols in dreams are sexual symbols'. The number three, so redolent with sacred associations, signifies the complete male genital apparatus, with its threefold appearance. The penis is represented by sticks, umbrellas, trees and poles; also by penetrating and injurious objects such as pointed weapons and firearms. Yet other symbols for the penis are objects capable of raising themselves in defiance of the laws of gravity, such as balloons and aeroplanes. Somewhat less obviously appropriate symbols are certain reptiles and fishes, and above all snakes. The imposing mechanism of the male genitals as a whole may be represented by any kind of machinery, while the female genitals may be referred to by anything which encloses a space, such as a room of a house or a jewel case. Fruit may stand for breasts or buttocks, woods and thickets for pubic hair. The complicated topography of the female sexual organs seems to account for their representation as a landscape. Wild animals signify human beings whose senses are excited, and hence evil impulses or passions.[35]

How do we arrive at the meanings of these symbols, when dreamers themselves can give us no direct help in the matter? Many sources provide us with clues, such as jokes, myths, fairy-stories, and poetic or colloquial uses of language. Everywhere there is encountered the same symbolism, which is convincing confirmation of the interpretations suggested where dreams are concerned. It seems that every human being has this symbolism as his birthright, whether he is conscious of the fact or not − a conclusion remarkable enough. It is certainly rather hard to account for the fact that, while these symbols have a wider range of meaning in the other contexts mentioned, in dreams the meaning is entirely sexual. It seems that what has happened in these other contexts is that a primarily sexual meaning has undergone a secondary adaptation. One may take as an example of this adaptation the symbol of a bridge. This primarily signifies the male organ, in its role of joining the parents together:

> but afterwards it develops further meanings which are derived from the first one. In so far as it is thanks to the male organ that we are able to come into the world at all, out of the amniotic fluid, a bridge becomes the crossing from the other world (the unborn state, the womb) to this world (life); and since men also picture death as a return to the womb (to the water), a bridge also acquires the meaning of something that leads to death, and finally, at a further remove from its original sense, it stands for transitions or changes in condition generally.[36]

The story of Theseus finding his way through the labyrinth is a representation of anal birth, with the twisting paths in place of the bowels and Ariadne's thread standing for the umbilical cord. The dying and rising phoenix probably represented the penis recovering after collapse rather than, or at least earlier than, the sun setting in the evening and rising again in the morning. The story of Prometheus' liver being repeatedly consumed by a vulture, but always growing again, has a similar significance, and describes 'the revival of libidinal desires after they have been quenched through being sated'.[37]

The dream is a pathological product, in the same class as hysterical symptoms, obsessions and delusions; it is distinguished from the others by its transience, and the fact that it occurs under conditions which are a part of normal life. In psychosis, loss of reality seems to occur for one of two general reasons: either the repressed unconscious has become so strong as to overwhelm the conscious mind, or reality has become so distressing that the ego as it were throws itself into the arms of the unconscious. In the 'harmless dream-psychosis' withdrawal is only temporary. It has already been mentioned that just the same processes are involved in the construction of neurotic symptoms as in that of dreams; and it is found that, just as in the case of dreams, neurotic symptoms have a connection with events of early childhood.

> In every one of our patients we learn through analysis that the symptoms and their effects have set the sufferer back into some past period of his life. In the majority of cases it is actually a very early phase of the life-history which has been thus selected, a period in childhood, even, absurd as it may sound, the period of existence as a suckling infant.[38]

In spite of Freud's own conviction that it was above all dreams and their interpretation which vindicated his fundamental theories, it does seem clear that a great many of his insights into dreams may be salvaged even if his theory of instincts, and the stress on sexuality which is its corollary, is abandoned. That there is a *meaning* in some sense, even if not known to the subject himself, in such phenomena as dreams, neurotic symptoms, and sequences of moods and images, has

been described as Freud's greatest discovery; but there seems
no prima-facie reason why acceptance of its validity should
entail acceptance of Freud's theory of instinct, and as a matter
of fact many have embraced the former and not the latter. It
might be objected that every hypothesis in psychoanalysis is
confirmed in the analysis of patients; and that in particular the
stress on sexuality in psychoanalytic theory is due only to what
has been found by research into the patients' past, and what
patients themselves tell their therapists about their early experiences. But on Freud's own account, the basic and universal
symbolism which he discovered in dreams, and which he says
has a largely sexual reference, is *not* spontaneously associated
with sexuality by patients.[39] On the contrary, he says the fact
that this symbolism has a sexual reference is something of
which the doctor has to inform the patient.

Freud admits that the universal and apparently inherited
symbolism which we find in dreams as a matter of fact has or
comes to have reference to many aspects of human life and fate
which are not sexual in any ordinary sense. In that case, one
may ask how far it is even *meaningful* to insist that the symbolism
is *primarily* sexual, and only derivatively associated with other
significant aspects of human experience and development. In
confirmation of his view of this matter, Freud cites the example
of sufferers from a certain type of psychosis, who, when they are
told something of a sexual nature and are asked to repeat it,
spontaneously translate it into the symbolism in question.[40] But
it seems to me that this phenomenon is at least as consistent
with the view that the symbolism which we inherit is from the
first, as it has been expressed, 'multivalent'.[41] The artificiality
of Freud's insistence that the symbolism is primarily sexual
comes out with especial clarity in his discussion, derived from
his friend and disciple Ferenczi, of the symbolic significance of
bridges.[42] It may be wondered what is the cash value of the
claim that a bridge *primarily* signifies the male organ linking the
parents together – and *by derivation from this* the passage from
pre-natal to post-natal existence and by further derivation
transitions between stages of life in general – once it is admitted
that there is an elaborate symbolism which is independent of
culture and which as a matter of fact has reference to many
fundamental aspects of life.

Part of the attraction of Freud's sexual theory is that it appears, at first sight, to restrict the significance of dreams to the past and present life of the dreamer himself. But in fact there are a large number of concessions in Freud's writings to the view that the material of our dreams and fantasies is of a 'collective' rather than a merely 'individual' nature. The existence of a detailed inherited sexual symbolism is one such concession; another even more striking example is the thesis put forward in *Totem and Taboo* and other writings, to the effect that events in the remote historical past, such as parricide and the castration of young boys, have been somehow repressed by the race with effects on present human behaviour just like those of repression on the part of individuals.[43] These concessions suggest, and the parallels in animal behaviour strongly confirm,[44] that human beings are born with a set of very general predispositions to act and to develop relationships, and to change these habits and relationships at more or less definite periods of their lives; and that failure by an individual to conform to this pattern – for example when he does not for some reason establish something approaching normal relationships with parental figures or with a peer group, or if he cannot break out of his initial set of relationships to form new ones when he reaches maturity – is liable to lead to maladjustments which will be felt as distressing both by the individual himself and those who have anything to do with him. If this account of the matter is at all on the right lines, then Freud's stress on the sexual significance of dreams, fantasies, neurotic behaviour, and so on, must be either erroneous or misleading. It will be erroneous, in the light of Freud's own concessions, if taken to imply that nearly all maladjustments in personal relationships and so on are really either sexual in the ordinary sense, or are ultimately derived from abnormalities in the build-up and release of tension in the 'erotogenic' zones of the body. It will be misleading, if one merely means by 'sexual' whatever pertains to the infant's relationships with parents and siblings and the rest of the environment. It seems both more plausible and more economical to suppose that neurosis and psychosis are due to violation of basic predispositions to behave and to relate to people with which each individual is born, some of which are due to be exercised comparatively early, some comparatively late in life.

Neurosis and the Development of Personality

According to Freud, the childhood wishes which result in susceptibility to later traumas are *invariably* sexual. The fact is, he says, that even very young children have wishes, especially in regard to their immediate family, which may best be described as 'sexual', though it is to be admitted that this is to employ the term in a rather broad sense. This does not matter, provided the terminology makes one see the origin of neurosis and perversion where they belong – in the experiences of very young children. The son of the family wishes to take his father's place, the daughter her mother's; this is the well-known 'Oedipus complex', named after the figure in Greek legend who killed his father and married his mother. From it there result frustrated desires and tensions between parents and children, brothers and sisters. From these frustrations and tensions, it may be surmised, every neurosis ultimately derives. The barrier against incest, which is such a striking feature of cultures throughout the world, is a reflection of the repudiation of these infantile wishes.[45]

The childhood traits which cannot be continued into adult civilised life are, if all goes well, diverted or 'sublimated' to cultural ends. The desire for looking or gazing at a sexual object develops into curiosity, and so ultimately in a few cases into the kind of disposition suitable for the acquisition of scientific knowledge; the desire for being looked at or gazed at into theatrical and artistic display. Curiosity 'cannot be counted among the elementary instinctual components, nor can it be classed as exclusively belonging to sexuality. Its activity corresponds on the one hand to a sublimated manner of obtaining mastery, while on the other hand it makes use of the energy of scopophilia [desire for gazing]'. As to other character traits, it is possible to trace a connection between some of the more salient of them and particular erotogenic components. 'Thus, obstinacy, thrift and orderliness arise from an exploitation of anal erotism, while ambition is determined by a strong urethral-erotic disposition.' The value once possessed by faeces passes over into the value of gifts. Faeces are the child's first gift, given out of love for the person who is looking after him; from a high valuation of faeces there is later derived a high valuation of gold and money in general.[46]

Even if conscience is a power which works within us, it has not been so from the first. In this it differs fundamentally from sexuality, which was present from the beginning. Very small children are quite amoral, without any inhibitions against the gratification of their impulses. The part later played by the superego is at first played by the external power of parental authority. Only later does the secondary situation develop, this one we are too apt to regard as 'normal', in which there is a superego which observes, directs and threatens the ego just as the parents did. Contrary to what one might have supposed, the superego can be relentlessly severe even where parents and teachers have been mild and kindly. As it develops, the superego takes on the influence of those who have stepped into the place of the parents, such as schoolmasters and educators, and those chosen by the subject as models. Parents and school-masters are apt to be excessively severe, forgetting the difficul-ties of their own childhood, and the final result is that the child's superego comes to reflect rather the parents' superego than the parents themselves. Thus the superego 'becomes the vehicle of tradition and of all the time-resisting judgements of value which have propagated themselves . . . from generation to generation.' So-called 'materialist' views of history are in-clined to underestimate this factor and to imply that ideologies are nothing but the product of prevailing economic and social conditions. This point of view is worthy of respect, but is not the whole truth; men never live entirely in the present. The superego also has important bearings on group psychology; it seems that groups with leaders 'have introduced the same person into their superego and, on the basis of this common element, have identified with one another in their ego'.[47]

If our early life has made us at loggerheads with reality – and the requirements of civilisation are such that there is no one of us who is not so to a greater or lesser extent – we may be unable to attain satisfaction in ways deemed to be normal, and have to resort to neurosis instead.

If we survey the whole situation we arrive at a simple formula for the origin of a neurosis: the ego has made an attempt to suppress portions of the id in an inappropriate manner; this attempt has failed, and the id has taken its revenge. A neurosis is thus the result of a conflict between the ego and the id, upon which the ego has embarked because ... it wishes at all costs to retain its adaptability in relation to the real external world.

Neurotic illness is however rather an escape from than a solution of such a conflict; the patient 'seeks to evade' the actual issue 'by transforming his libidinal impulses into symptoms'. Some otherwise predisposed to neurosis may avoid it after all by the use of a creative or artistic gift, which is such as to enable them to transform their fantasies into artistic creations as opposed to symptoms. Indeed, 'the deeper you penetrate into the pathogenesis of nervous illness, the more you will find revealed the connexion between the neuroses and other productions of the human mind, including the most valuable'.[48]

It is to be noted that psychoanalysis is *not* committed to the denial of any innate or hereditary factors predisposing to neurosis. One may indeed state with confidence that hereditary sexual constitution provides a great variety of degrees of predisposition, according to the manner in which this or that component impulse of sexuality is particularly strongly accentuated. There seems to be a remarkable correlation, again, between severe neurosis and parental syphilis; one finds that often in families where there is syphilis in the parents, the male children will be perverts and the female hysterics. Psychoanalysts do not mention such innate factors much because they are emphasised enough or too much in other quarters, and psychoanalysts have nothing of moment to add.[49]

It has been said already that the libido of the neurotic is fixated on his infantile experiences. But the odd thing is that these 'experiences' – of which typical examples are observation of the parents' sexual intercourse, seduction by an adult, and the threat of castration – often did not occur at all. In most accounts which patients under analysis give of their infancy, truth and falsehood are mixed up. But this does not matter, since, so far as neurosis and its cure are concerned, it is *psychical reality* rather than *material reality* which is the deciding factor; and fantasies about one's past have just as much psychical reality as do genuine memories of it.[50]

The fixation of libido on an early stage is the predisposing

internal factor, a particular external frustration the immediate
and accidental factor, in the aetiology of neurosis. In some
cases the former predominates, in others the latter, and there is
a continuous gradation between the two extremes.

> At one end of the series stand those . . . cases of whom one can
> say: These people would have fallen ill whatever happened
> . . . however merciful life had been to them, because of their
> anomalous libido development. At the other end stand cases
> which call forth the opposite verdict – they would have
> undoubtedly have escaped illness if life had not put such
> burdens upon them.

If the environment denies satisfaction to the libido, even when
it is prepared to accept another object than the one denied to it,
it is compelled to regress to an earlier phase of sexual organisation. A good example of such regression, in this case to the oral
phase, is the fear of being poisoned, which may be a symptom of
paranoia and is probably connected with withdrawal of the
mother's breast. It is worth remarking in this connection that,
among primitive peoples, children are fed at the breast for two
or even three years. If the regressions are not prohibited by the
ego, they will result in sexual perversion; if they are so prohibited, a conflict is set up which is likely to be the basis of the
neurotic symptom. It consorts well with this that neurosis may
well replace perversion in the history of a single individual – as
the saying goes, 'Young whore, old nun'. The relation of the
symptom to the repressed wish is just the same as that of the
element in the manifest dream to the dream-thought; 'the
symptom . . . comes into being as a derivative, distorted in
manifold ways, of the unconscious libidinal wish-fulfilment, as
a cleverly chosen ambiguity with two completely contradictory
significations.' Thus it is that a compromise is achieved between the conflicting demands of the id and the ego. Hysterical
symptoms seem to need some 'somatic compliance', either in a
normal or in a pathological process in a bodily organ. Short of
this, there tends to occur an entirely psychical symptom such as
a phobia or obsession.[51]
    A fear which is very productive of male neurosis is that of
being castrated; the little boy fears this will be the penalty for

being in love with his mother, and it naturally is a major source of anxiety to him. It is to be suspected (Freud says) that during the primeval period of the history of the human family castration was actually carried out by jealous and cruel fathers on growing boys; circumcision, which plays a part in the puberty rites of many primitive peoples, seems a clearly recognisable relic of this. In women, fear of the loss of love takes the place of fear of castration, and this kind of fear is a continuation of the infant's anxiety at its mother's absence. It may even reflect the original experience of anxiety at birth, which after all is itself an example of separation from the mother. Some analysts would add the fear of castration itself to this series, on the ground that loss of the male organ is loss of the ability to unite once more with the mother, or her substitute, in the sexual act. It is to the credit of Otto Rank that he has called attention to the significance of the event of birth; but his extreme view, that experience of anxiety at birth provides the model for apprehension by a person of all later situations of danger, has not generally commended itself.[52]

In considering the salient differences between men and women in character and development, one must certainly beware of underestimating those social influences which tend to force women into passive roles. Yet there do seem to be overall differences which are not dependent upon the contingencies of particular social systems. The development of the baby girl into the normal woman involves two extra tasks, as compared with the development of the baby boy into a man. She has to change her dominant erotogenic zone from clitoris into vagina, her object from mother to father. As one might expect, the constitution will not adapt itself without a struggle, and in the case of women the adaptation is especially complicated and difficult. One might have supposed that there would have been some lag in aggressiveness during the sadistic-anal phase in girls as compared with boys; but such is not the case, as may readily be discovered by analysis of children and their play. On entry into the phallic phase the little girl, so far as her psyche is concerned, is to all intents and purposes a little boy. The girl's special attachment to her mother lasts, in some cases, beyond the fourth year of life, and while it lasts the father is little more than a troublesome rival. The phallic phase in the

girl is characterised by sexual wishes directed towards her
mother, and the phantasy of seduction in this phase is regularly
directed towards her. And there is some truth at the basis of
this, so far as in seeing to the little girl's bodily hygiene the
mother will be liable to stimulate pleasure in her genital
organs.[53]

Nearly all women patients claim to have been seduced by
their fathers. At length it was realised by psychoanalysts that
this is not usually the memory of a real occurrence, but a
fantasy expressing the typical turning-away from the mother
and attachment to the father. This turning-away is accom-
panied by hostility, which may become very striking and last all
through life, or be over-compensated later on. The analyst
hears a string of accusations supposed to justify the hostile
feelings, some of them obvious rationalisations. A special feature accounting for girls turning away from their mothers is
that they hold them responsible for their lack of a penis. The
wish to get a penis in spite of everything may drive a mature
woman to undergo analysis; and 'what she may reasonably
expect from analysis – a capacity, for instance, to carry on an
intellectual profession – may often be recognised as a modification of this repressed wish.' Alternatively, the wish to have a
penis may find its fulfilment in giving birth to a baby, in
accordance with a widely established symbolical equivalence.[54]
Envy and jealousy seem to play an even greater part in the
mental life of the average woman than they do in that of the
average man, and it is penis envy which may be held to account
for this. It must be admitted that some psychoanalysts somewhat depreciate the importance of penis envy in the phallic
phase and believe that what we find of this in older women 'has
come about on the occasion of later conflicts by regression to
this early infantile impulse'. But, in the case of penis envy,
Freud himself would be inclined to lay particular emphasis on
the infantile causal factor.[55]

In the boy, the Oedipus complex – sexual desire of the
mother coupled with rivalry towards the father – develops
directly out of the sexuality of the phallic phase; and it is usually
abandoned owing to the threat of castration, to be succeeded by
the setting-up of a severe superego. But girls are apt to remain
in their Oedipus conflict for an indeterminate length of time,

and to surmount it incompletely and late. So the formation of the superego suffers; 'feminists are not pleased when we point out to them the effects of this fact upon the average feminine character'.[56] Women have on average not so great a sense of justice as men, owing to the strength of their envy; also they tend to be 'weaker in their social interests' and to have 'less capacity for sublimating their instincts than men'. On the other hand, it is to be noted that the development of sexual inhibitions, and consequently of such reactions as shame, disgust and pity, occurs earlier and meets less resistance in girls than in boys. All these factors help to explain the greater proneness of women as compared to men to neurosis and particularly hysteria. It may finally be remarked that while a man of thirty often seems youthful and unformed, a woman of the same age frequently gives the impression of an alarming psychic rigidity, with the libido already having taken up its final positions, as though 'the difficult development to femininity had exhausted the possibilities of the person concerned.' This is not to imply, fortunately, that the conflicts of such a woman are quite beyond help by analysis.[57]

In the cure of neurosis by psychoanalysis, the personal relationship which is established between the patient and the analyst proves of fundamental importance. There comes a time in the treatment when certain subtle changes take place. If the patient is a girl and the analyst a fairly young man, it will be as though the patient were falling in love with the analyst; if the analyst is much older, as though she were adopting him as a father. Even if the patient and the analyst are of the same sex, there will be a similar attachment on the part of the patient, along with an overestimation of the analyst's qualities, and jealousy of those around him. In male patients, negative feelings are more frequently bound up with the positive ones. It may be suspected that this complex of attitudes is already formed within the patient, and is 'transferred' on to the analyst; and this is why this phenomenon is known as the 'transference'. (The archaic and infantile attitudes which the patient once adopted to his parents, and which he has failed to get over in the course of growing up, are transferred to the analyst; then the patient can be made conscious of them and ultimately deal with them.) 'The therapeutic work falls into two phases; in the first all the libido is forced away from the symptoms into the transference and there concentrated, in the second the battle rages round this new object and the libido is made free from it.' One overcomes the transference by showing the patient that his feelings do not originate in the present situation, and that they do not really relate to his therapist; that he is reproducing a relationship which occurred long ago.[58]

There are a number of factors which make the neurotic resistant to cure. One is a feeling of guilt, which convinces him that he does not deserve to be other than he is. Again, there is a certain 'gain from illness' which accrues to him in social, professional and family life. (This is, of course, a matter of common experience; there are very many people for whom 'allowances' have to be made for fear that they may be 'upset', and it is not altogether inconvenient to be such a person.) Also, the attitude of the patient's family may be highly equivocal; and less interest may appear in the cure of the patient than in keeping him as he is. It may be wondered why psychoanalytic theory does not lay more emphasis upon present factors in the patient's situation in the causation of his neurosis, and less on his infantile past. The answer is that these present factors, for all their *practical* importance, are of little *theoretical* significance.[59]

Civilisation and Suppression

Freud's view of civilisation, as is well known, is a rather gloomy one. It is not that he fails to set a high value on civilisation, or that he advocates a return to barbarism; but he does hold that civilisation subsists and cannot but subsist at the price of renunciation of a large number of instinctual gratifications, for which everyone more or less consciously hankers. The fact is that modern man has bartered many of his chances of happiness for the sake of security. (If it were not for our inhibitions, our lives would be at least intermittently delightful, but they would also be dangerous and short.) We cannot live without some compensations for the frustration of our desires, and we may list the possible compensations under three heads: diversions of interest, which make us forget our misery; substitute gratifications, which diminish it; and intoxicants, which lower our sensitivity. Art is only a mild narcotic, and quite inadequate to distract us when we are really unhappy. Religion is a particularly crude way of bamboozling ourselves into believing that reality is in the last resort in conformity with our wishes; it derives from childish helplessness and longing for a father, and the more sophisticated forms of it merely substitute sententious humbug for crude wish-fulfilment.[60]

Freud always maintained that civilisation was built up at the cost of renunciation of *sexual* desires, and that this constituted a heavy burden. But late in life he came to believe that the same applied, even more strongly, to our *aggressive* tendencies. 'It is they above all that make human life difficult and threaten its survival. Restriction of the individual's aggressiveness is the first and perhaps the severest sacrifice which society requires of him.' The love of one's fellows, and the relative stability within society which is its result, is achieved only by dint of latent aggression being turned elsewhere. 'One . . . wonders . . . how the Soviets will manage when they have exterminated their bourgeois entirely.' The superego serves as it were as a garrison introduced into the individual psyche, taking over some of the dangerous aggression and turning it against the individual's own unruly impulses. However, the ego is not happy in being thus sacrificed to the needs of society, in having itself to submit to the aggressiveness it would be only too glad to turn against others. It is fortunate that the aggressive instincts are always alloyed with erotic tendencies, which 'have much to mitigate and much to avert under the conditions of the civilisation which mankind has created'.[61]

Freud realised that his estimate of human life and its possibilities is somewhat austere, and he knew that people would hold this against him. Frenzied revolutionaries and pious believers are alike in demanding consolation, and he had none to offer.[62] The world-view of which psychoanalysis forms a part, as Freud sees it, which it presupposes and towards which it tends, is simply the scientific world-view. This may be characterised primarily in a negative way, as implying 'that there are no sources of knowledge of the universe other than the intellectual working-over of carefully scrutinised observations'. When persons who like to think of themselves as broad-minded suggest that religion and philosophy are equal in value to science, and that science has no business to interfere with them, one can only reply that the urge to truth is by its very nature intolerant, that it admits of no compromise or limitation and must regard every human sphere as belonging to it. There are three powers which may conceivably dispute the position and ambition of science: art, philosophy and religion. Of these, only the third is necessarily an enemy. Art is in general harmless and beneficent, since it makes no other claim than to be a traffic in illusion. So far as philosophy sets up any opposition to science, it is ineffective, and soon collapses; in any case, it has no influence on the mass of mankind. But religion 'is an immense power which has the strongest emotions of human beings in its service'. Science has nothing to offer in place of the comfort which religion affords in the difficulties of life, or the assurance which it provides of a happy issue to all human affliction. However, science has long been by its very essence hostile to the religious world view, and psychoanalysis has added the final touch to its case 'by showing how religion originated from the helplessness of children and by tracing its contents to the survival into maturity of the wishes and needs of childhood'.[63]

But whatever the value and importance of religion were, it would have no right to restrict thought, even in application to itself. And the prohibition of thought by religion can be shown to be full of danger both for individuals and for society: psychoanalysis shows how this tendency is apt to widen its range to cover all sorts of different things, for example when women are prevented from even thinking about their sexuality. Some have made the suggestion that religion would do well to give up its claim to 'truth' in the ordinary sense, and frankly offer mere uplift and consolation. However, religion cannot take such a step 'because it would involve its forfeiting all its influence on the mass of mankind. The ordinary man knows only one kind of truth . . . and he cannot join in the leap from the beautiful to the true. Perhaps you will think as I do that he is right in this.' As to the future, our best hope is that the intellect may establish a dictatorship in the mental life of man; once it has achieved supremacy there, it will not fail afterwards to give the emotions the place that they need and deserve. This dictatorship of the intellect will ultimately prove to be the strongest possible uniting bond among men.[64]

In opposition to Marx and his followers, Freud believes that the class structure of society originates in the opposition between neighbouring human clans or races. But he agrees with them that the influence of men's material circumstances on their intellectual, ethical and artistic attitudes is very great. However, economic motives cannot be assumed to be the only or even the primary ones determining the behaviour of individuals in relation to their fellows. Whatever the material circumstances of their lives, 'men can only bring their original instinctual impulses into play – their self-preservative instinct, their aggressiveness, their need to be loved, their drive towards obtaining pleasure and avoiding unpleasure.' And the superego, with its tendency to cleave to the moral ideals of the past, always resists, for a while at least, adaptation to a new environmental situation.

If anyone were in a position to show in detail the way in which these different factors – the general inherited human disposition, its racial variations and cultural transformations – inhibit and promote one another under the conditions of social rank, profession and earning capacity . . . he would have supplemented Marxism so that it was made into a genuine social science.

It is a blot on Marxism that it has come to prohibit thought in just the same way as religion has done; indeed, it is remarkable how Marx's writings have come to be treated very much like the Bible and the Koran, though they are no more free of contradictions. And however mercilessly Marxists have set themselves to destroy the illusions of others, they have developed no less potent ones of their own. Marxists hope in a few generations to alter human nature to such an extent that men will live together virtually without conflict in a new social order, and that they will then undertake socially necessary duties without any compulsion being required. Meanwhile, Communist authorities employ various devices to divert attention from evidence which is such as to suggest that instinctual restrictions are absolutely necessary for human society. They channel outside those aggressive tendencies which would

otherwise tend to disrupt the community, finding support for
this in the natural hostility which the poor feel against the rich,
and those who were once powerless against their former oppressors. Still, the great experiment being carried out by
Communism, however disagreeable in its details, seems a
forecast of a better future when great nations still officially
announce that they expect salvation through Christian piety.[65]

    To reject Freud's 'sexual' theory as very misleading or false,[66]
is by no means to imply that his whole account of the development of character and the causation of psychic disorder is based
on a mistake. That habits of action and relationship formed in
early infancy are liable to leave a permanent trace seems
plausible and, if true, of very great importance; and another
corollary of the 'sexual' theory, which seems at least worth
investigating, is that each crucial stage in the development of
the individual corresponds with the tendency to gain pleasure
from a particular organ of the body.[67] To regard scientific
curiosity, for example, as *merely* a deflected pursuit of organ-
pleasure is to fall foul of the paradoxes alluded to above which
are the consequence of the attempt to replace B explanation
with A explanation. But it is by no means implausible or
unlikely that a natural tendency in man to use intelligence and
reason to find out what is true may be reinforced or discouraged
by its association with the pleasure or pain, the satisfaction or
anxiety, characteristic of each stage of development.[68] The
researches of Freud and his disciples have been of the utmost
importance in demonstrating both that this is so of human
characteristics in general, and how it comes about in particular
instances.
    Freud's views on the 'superego' seem ambiguous in at least
one crucial respect: some of his remarks seem to imply that it is
simply imposed upon the individual by his environment, others
that it is the result of a latent predisposition which environment
can more or less encourage. That a severe superego may not be
a reflection of real severity in an individual's parents or guar-
dians, as is admitted by Freud,[69] seems to confirm the latter
opinion. Dogs and other animals seem to have evolved not only
with instinctual impulses of a sexual or aggressive nature, but

with tendencies to inhibit these in certain circumstances; it would be curious, as I have already argued,[70] if the same did not, in some way at least, apply to man. The capacity for moral self-transcendence, or the ability to conceive and implement a long-term and overall good rather than merely reacting to particular selfish or immediate impulses, presupposes both impartial curiosity and the operation of the superego; the reasons for holding that they are innate would apply to the capacity for moral self-transcendence as well.

That Freud may be prone at times to exaggerate the causal significance of infantile experience in the development of neurosis and the formation of character is strongly suggested by his admission that many of his patients' 'memories', for example of being seduced as children, are of events which did not really happen.[71] That these memories have all the same a psychic reality for the patient is not relevant to the issue; the crucial question is whether it is some real event in the patient's infancy, and not rather, for example, a strategy for coping with his present environment, which is the more important factor in explaining this present psychic reality. It seems to me that it is largely the mistaken impulse to reduce all B explanation to A explanation which makes Freud insist that the 'gain from illness' accruing to the patient at present, for all its *practical* importance, had little theoretical significance.[72]

If the superego and the capacity to exercise moral self-transcendence are both latent for genetic reasons in the individual psyche itself, and not merely imposed by the environment, it seems to follow that it is reasonable to take a less gloomy view of civilisation than Freud does. We are genetically disposed not only to exercise, but also to restrain, impulses of sexuality and aggression; this is because we have evolved to live in communities, and if tendencies to selfishness are inborn, tendencies to co-operation with one's fellows are no less so. In this matter, Marx and Freud seem a good corrective to one another; while Marx, as we have seen, tends to exaggerate, Freud appears to underestimate, the human predisposition to co-operate for the general good. Freud's view of Marxism will be discussed in a later chapter, where a brief comment on his aspersions on religion will also be in place.[73]

Many of the oversights which I have attributed to Freud were pointed out by Jung, whose theories of human nature and development so far as they are relevant to morality, have next to be summarised. On Jung's account, man has evolved with a certain very general range of instincts, dispositions and capacities for relating to his fellows. Now the individual, particularly when he is a member of a very civilised society, is apt to develop in a very one-sided way, leaving an 'unconscious' aspect of himself which reveals itself in dreams and in tendencies to feel and to behave which, characteristically, he does not acknowledge. This one-sidedness, and the corresponding build-up of corrective tendencies in the unconscious, is increased when decisions are shirked and necessary adaptations avoided. The ideal union of conscious and unconscious, the realisation of which is a sort of built-in aim of human life, is what Jung calls the 'self', as contrasted with the 'ego' or conscious personality. When the conscious and the unconscious are locked in a conflict of a kind which precludes fruitful development, there is neurosis; the task of the therapist is to reconcile and unite the opposed aspects of the personality. In extreme instances, when the conscious mind is totally cut off from its unconscious roots, pressure builds up to such an extent that the barrier between the two breaks down, and the conscious mind is deluged with the raw material of fantasy at the expense of external reality. This is the state of schizophrenia, or madness in the conventional sense. The myths and religions evolved by mankind are all means of dealing with the unconscious, of harnessing its energies so that the conscious person and his society may develop and flourish. There are found to be recurrent figures and motifs in dreams, myths, fantasies, religious systems and the delusions of schizophrenics; these are the 'archetypes', shared by mankind at large, together constituting the 'collective unconscious', which correspond to the instinctive patterns of behaviour which are a part of man's evolutionary inheritance.

There follows an account, summarised from Jung's works, of 1, the nature of man's instinctual energy or libido; 2, its expression in normal living and its aberrations in neurosis and psychosis; 3, the role of dreams, myths and religions in expressing and controlling libido; and 4, the nature of the 'collective unconscious' and the 'archetypes' of which it consists.

1   *Libido*

Libido is 'the energy which manifests itself in the life-process and is perceived subjectively as conation and desire'. From the genetic point of view, it is derived from bodily needs like hunger, thirst, sleep and sex, and emotional states. This instinctual energy is what we try to divert into the channels of civilised living. Against Freud's emphasis on sexuality, Jung objects that there are many basic instincts with which men have to come to terms, of which sex is only one of the most important. Freud's usage either posits an unnecessarily narrow basis for our psychic life, or expands the concept 'sex' until it has little connection with the normal meaning of the word. What is required in psychology is a neutral term for a psychic energy which can be apparent in various forms, rather as the 'energy' postulated by the physicist is convertible into heat, sound, kinetic energy, and so on. To say that all or most psychic energy is 'really' sexual is rather like saying that all or most physical energy is 'really' sound; if not downright false, it is at least very misleading.[74]

According to Freud, our dreams and our myths, our art and our literature, play the part that they do in our lives largely because the elements of which they are made up remind us of the organs of sex, or of the persons with whom, particularly in our early childhood, we have had 'sexual' relations in Freud's rather broad sense.[75] These persons are our parents and siblings, or those who have played the part of these in our infantile environment. Now it is true, and indeed very important, that there *is* an element in the infant's relationship to its parents that is 'sexual' in that it foreshadows sexuality in the ordinary sense. Freud's mistake was that this fact, along with the frequent neurotic tendency to suffuse early memories with a tinge deriving from mature sexuality, led him to overestimate the place of sex in the psychic life in general, and to think that the symbols and analogies of which dreams and myths are made up largely signifies sexual organs and relations. Jung holds that they refer rather to that undifferentiated psychic energy which is libido in his sense of the term, and which is as closely related to hunger, thirst and the desire to sleep as it is to sex. The libido of the young child is directed to the nutritive function and progresses to the sexual function by natural stages. In addition to this, Jung objects to the importance that Freud attributes to early infancy in the aetiology and treatment of the neuroses. To appeal to one's infantile past, or to sex, may itself suit the neurotic only too well – since it is liable to divert his attention from his present situation, and from his present responsibility for it which is itself likely to be the principal aetiological factor.[75]

On Jung's account, mental health is the result of a successful attempt, mental illness the result of a failure, to come to terms with this instinctual or psychic energy which he calls 'libido'. Myths, rituals and religions are attempts to conceptualise, and so to control and sublimate, this 'libido'; without such control and sublimation civilisation, science and technology would be impossible.

2   *The expression of libido in normal living and its aberrations in mental illness*

The aim of psychic development is often described in terms of achievement of 'balance', and quite rightly so, according to Jung; what is implied by this is worth considering. There is a strong tendency for each person, out of self-esteem or cowardice or the demands of public life, to take account of only one side of his character at the expense of the rest. For example, a man may reckon himself to be of an industrious, thorough and painstaking character – not adverting to the fact that he has recently allowed several letters to remain unanswered, and failed to bring home a book for his wife of which he could easily have made a note. He thinks he is a loyal citizen – but it so happens that he has failed to declare the whole of his income to the tax authorities. He would say that he was quite without superstition – however, he noted with misgivings that he had made a business deal on Friday the thirteenth. Unconscious virtues compensate for conscious vices, as well as vice versa; vice as well as virtue may represent an exaggerated attitude, virtue as well as vice be repressed. We tend to think of 'man as he really is' as discontented, anarchic and rapacious; but his noble, dignified and orderly tendencies are really just as central and inalienable. The colossal feasts of decadent Rome were indeed a substitute, but hardly for repressed sexuality; they were rather a substitute for repressed moral functions. When such an exaggerated attitude, with which one falsifies one's latent normality and complexity, makes development too one-sided, unconscious elements break through and disturb one's adaptation to the external world. In most people self-criticism, and the wish to keep up tolerable relations with other members of society, prevent things from coming to such a pass that the compensatory influences of the unconscious are entirely without effect. Steady neglect of such influences only leads to their increase, and ultimately to neurosis. 'The therapist therefore confronts the opposites with one another and aims at uniting them permanently.'[75]

It is of course extremely important not to confuse repression with suppression. Suppression comes about as a result of conscious moral choice; I experience and acknowledge my unjustified anger or my disorderly sexual desire, but refrain from acting according to its dictates. Repression, on the other hand, is a matter of failing to acknowledge these feelings and motives to oneself; it is thus 'a rather immoral "penchant" for getting rid of disagreeable decisions. Suppression may cause worry, conflict, and suffering, but it never causes a neurosis. Neurosis is always a substitute for legitimate suffering.' Unfortunately getting to know oneself, ceasing to see oneself in terms of the usual agreeable and largely fictitious picture, is an arduous and painful process; each of us carries a shadow, and is liable to project that shadow on to others, proclaiming that it is all *their* fault, that to put things right is up to *them*. Anyone with the courage to withdraw his projections has done something to shoulder the immense burden of evil in the world, which is as heavy as it is largely because of such projections and avoidances of responsibility.[76]

The more a person shrinks from adapting himself to reality, whether the outer reality of the external world or the inner reality of his unconscious, the greater the fear that besets his path through life. The reasons are projected outside himself –

the fault lies with external circumstances, or it is his family that is responsible. In many cases, the 'trauma' which is 'remembered' from the patient's infancy turns out to be a fantasy. 'It often looks as if the patient were really using his previous history only to prove that he cannot act reasonably'. The fact is that the libido which cannot or will not adapt to the present invests aspects of the past with a spurious vitality; the subject may come to live almost wholly in the past, battling with its difficulties and worried by its anxieties. Among the most significant objects of such preoccupations are the personalities of the parents: 'the patient's love, admiration, resistance, hatred and rebelliousness still cling to their effigies, transfigured by affection or distorted by envy, and often bearing little resemblance to the erstwhile reality.' Sometimes, it is true, the parents' own contradictory nature has made them treat their children so unreasonably that later illness is more or less unavoidable by the children; but this is by no means the rule in the development of neurosis.[77]

It may be asked how, if it is true that childhood experience is significant for neurosis only when activated by regressive libido, the regression itself is to be accounted for. The following analogy may be helpful. A man is trying to climb a mountain, and in the course of doing so meets an obstacle which makes him abandon the attempt. Suppose the obstacle was not really insurmountable, but he has shirked it out of cowardice. In this case, he has two alternatives, when he reflects on the matter afterwards: first, to admit his cowardice; second, to tell himself that the object really was insurmountable, though he knows that in fact it was not. The latter case, in which he deceives himself, pushing away the thought of his own inadequacy because of its disagreeable character, is the analogue of the neurotic's situation. 'Now the realisation of his cowardice gains the upper hand, now defiance and pride . . . His libido becomes engaged in a useless civil war, and the man becomes incapable of any new enterprise'. The prime questions for the therapist are 'What is the task which the patient does not want to fulfil? What difficulty is he trying to avoid?' It must be conceded that the neurotic's refusal to face a particular issue does not generally come out of the blue, that it does as a rule have a history; bondage to fantasies is apt to develop as a gradually acquired habit, out of innumerable shyings-away from obstacles from early childhood onwards. One may well get used to leading what is in general a lazy and inactive life, but pay for it by becoming prone to fears, compulsions and involuntary constraints. 'Non-employment of the libido makes it ungovernable.' However, it is to be noted that mere activity, which fails to take account of the natural direction of one's libido, is unavailing.[78]

The unmasking of the truth about oneself, which is the only way to psychic wholeness, is difficult and often dangerous: it is soon found to be the way of the cross. The illusions would be neither so common nor so persistent if they did not serve some purpose. We all have a very deep aversion from looking through the fog of our projections and recognising our own nature. One can indeed achieve a limited insight by shutting out any moral criterion, by repressing the moral shock of self-recognition through a timely appeal to 'scientific' objectivity. 'The result of this deception is that the insight is robbed of its efficacy, since the moral reaction is missing'. That we need to be born again is, of course, a central doctrine of many religions; the words of Jesus to Nicodemus in the third chapter of John's gospel are typical in this respect. The 'ego', or conscious personality, is to be contrasted with the 'self', that ideal possibility latent in each person, towards which he progresses so far as he faces honestly his own depths; that into which he is 'reborn', to the degree that his conscious psyche becomes integrated with his unconscious. The 'self' in this sense corresponds closely to the *purusha-atman* conception in Indian, and the *chen-yen* in Chinese philosophy.[79]

Rebirth is to be found not by a return to the mother herself, but by a return to her symbolical equivalent, the collective unconscious. It is of the utmost importance, in fact, that childish dependence is precisely *not* what is needed. Not to advance from the womb-state, to cling to the family or its later equivalent when the time has come to break away, is to court mental illness. Freud found, in the universal prohibition of incest, an important clue for the understanding of man's psychic life. But according to Jung, the incest prohibition is symbolic of a more fundamental desire and fear: that of a return to the womb-state in which we did not have to struggle to survive and prosper, and its analogue the oneness of nature which civilised man has renounced for self-consciousness. The incest taboo is a sign that the grown man is cut off from childish security, and a deep resentment remains in our breast against the law which thus separates us. However, 'the natural course of life demands that the young person should sacrifice his childhood and childish dependence on the physical parents, lest he remain caught body and soul in the bonds of unconscious incest.' The incest prohibition represents that tendency which, by keeping the libido away from childish dependence on the mother, forces one into maturity and independence, along 'the path of life's biological aim'. There is a vast difference between that kind of withdrawal to one's inner life which is a mere flight from reality, and that which is practical and purposive. The point is precisely not to be coddled and cherished; it is not for nothing that solitude and fasting have from time immemorial been regarded by men as the best way of strengthening and intensifying the meditation which may bring about the renewal of life. From the most ancient times, 'the great psychotherapeutic systems which we know as the religions' have opposed the morbid kind of regression, and have supported that which leads to health and the enlargement of personality. In general, sacrifice in religion is symbolic of the giving-up of infantile wishes.[80]

Our unconscious is the great source both of danger and of opportunity. Whenever a person has to accomplish something important, and he recoils in doubt of his strength for the task, libido streams back into its fountainhead; this is the crucial moment, when the issue hangs between dissolution and new life. Either the subject gets stuck in the wonderland of fantasy, or he is reborn to greater energy and fruitfulness. The loss of balance which obtrudes itself more and more on a life based on an unsatisfactory consciousness is biologically purposive. It may compel a person to co-operate with his unconscious in arranging his life on a more satisfactory basis. This will in fact come about if the conscious mind can assimilate the contents of the unconscious, understanding and as it were digesting them. 'If the unconscious simply rides roughshod over the conscious mind, a psychotic condition develops. If it can neither prevail nor yet be understood, the result is a conflict that cripples all further advance.' The positive potentialities latent in neurosis, however, ought to be emphasised. Of course there are millions of people who are profoundly ignorant of themselves, and yet never come near a serious neurosis. Neurotics have the distinction that their condition shows that their nature is of too high a calibre to tolerate in the long run the intellectual and moral torpor of their lives. So a surplus of energy builds up in the unconscious, and in time bursts out in the form of a more or less acute neurosis.[81]

Identification with a social role is a particularly fruitful source of neurosis. 'A man cannot get rid of himself in favour of an artificial personality without punishment. Even the attempt to do so brings on, in all ordinary cases, unconscious reactions in the form of bad moods, affects, phobias, compulsive ideas, backslidings, vices, etc.' Often the social model is something very different in his private life;

> his public discipline (which he demands quite particularly of others) goes miserably to pieces in private. His 'happiness in his work' assumes a woeful countenance at home; his 'spotless' public morality looks strange indeed behind the mask ... the wives of such men would have a pretty tale to tell. As to his altruism, his children have decided views about that.[82]

(One is reminded of Mrs Jellyby in Dickens's *Bleak House*, who neglects her children because she cannot spare time from her charitable activities on behalf of the natives of Borriaboola Gha.)

Neurotic fantasy can be understood in terms of the actions and reactions of the individual; there is hardly a trace of the archaic and bizarre material found in schizophrenia, where the reality of the external world may virtually disappear for the individual. Even in the most extravagant instances of neurosis, the subject may be detected at work arranging a little sentimental drama, tactfully directed for his own convenience; in schizophrenia, such drama as there is is far beyond the understanding of the subject himself. Here the conscious mind is, as it were, flooded with the raw materials of the unconscious. Psychic conflict is the common lot of man; it may be surmised that schizophrenics are congenitally disposed to experience

these conflicts with peculiar intensity, and hence to be unable
to deal with them by means of reason, distraction, or self-
control. At length the dreaming and myth-making aspects of
the personality usurp the functions of the conscious life in
which they have been denied adequate expression; 'I often had
the illusion', said one investigator, 'that the patients might
simply be the victims of a deep-rooted folk superstition'.[83]

People in general may be classified into two general *attitude
types*, introverted and extroverted; and four *function types*, according to whether intellect, feeling, sensation or intuition
plays the principal role in their orientation to life. These types
seem to override sexual distinctions, and to have a random
distribution between the classes of society. Thus types seem to
be a matter of innate predisposition rather than influence of
environment, since children show the typical attitude early,
and children of the same parents may be of opposite type,
without there being many differences in the discernible attitude
to them of their parents. The falsification of one's attitude or
function type leads to neurosis, which is cured by development
of the natural attitude or function. The extraverted type fits
very well, sometimes only too well, into locally or temporarily
abnormal conditions, and will thrive until he is destroyed along
with them. He is prone to sacrifice himself and his inner needs
to 'objective' claims, like the extension of his business or his
social influence; whereas the introvert is apt to do just the
opposite. In general, extroverts are better adapted to coping
with the first, introverts with the second half of life. There is a
rather similar polarisation of functions as of attitudes; thus, as
is notorious, intellectual types are particularly inclined to
repress feelings, and so feelings of a primitive or childish nature
may burst out and make a fool of them.[84] (It is remarkable that
Jung's distinction between 'introverts' and 'extroverts' has
been very widely accepted among psychologists, even those
who, like the behaviourist H. J. Eysenck, have no sympathy
whatever with his general views; while his distinction between
'function' types, though it may be suggestive in many cases, has
seemed about the least viable of all his central ideas.)[85]

The whole business of blending conscious and unconscious,
of integrating the personality, is termed by Jung 'the individuation process'. He cites the early Christian writer Origen to the

effect that the bad man 'seems to have as many personalities as he has moods', while those who 'come to perfection' are characterised by unity and changelessness. He suggests that the work of the alchemists in Europe takes on a wholly new complexion when one sees in it not merely a precursor of chemistry, but a preoccupation with this same individuation process. Many alchemists were more or less consciously seeking for what would heal the disharmony both of the world and of the human soul.[86]

3   The Role of Dreams, Myths and Religion in Controlling and Canalising Libido

Dreams and myths cope with libido by means of symbolism; there is an analogy between their typical elements and libido. The role of analogy in dreams and myths was one of Freud's great discoveries, but he insisted that what the analogues had in common was more often than not a sexual reference. Jung holds rather that they symbolise libido, in the sense of an instinctual energy of which sex is only one manifestation. 'The libido is fertile like the bull, dangerous like the lion or boar (because of the fury of its passion), and lustful like the ever-rutting ass, and so on.' Or it may be 'characterised by its instrument or something analogous to it, e.g. the phallus or its analogue, the snake'. It is health-giving as the sun, destructive as fire. By symbolising our libido, by naming it or picturing it as something outside ourselves, we gain mastery of it, and canalise its energy into civilised aims and activities. By making a picture or telling a story about the conflicts within us, we can get to grips with them; when we signally fail to do so, there result outbreaks of violence or mental illness.[87]

According to Freud, dreams are almost always to be construed as the fulfilment of wishes; Jung says that they are better regarded as compensations for one-sided conscious attitudes, and he emphasises their teleological significance. He records that he once undervalued a patient, only to dream about her perched on the topmost tower of a castle built on a cliff. The dream suggested a 'higher' estimation of her than that accorded by his conscious mind. To take a contrasted example:

a young woman who clung to her mother in an extremely
sentimental way, always had very sinister dreams about her.
She appeared in the dreams as a witch, as a ghost, as a
pursuing demon. The mother had spoilt her beyond reason
and had so blinded her by tenderness that the daughter had
no conscious idea of her mother's harmful influence. Hence
the compensatory criticism exercised by the unconscious.

A son idealises his father – and dreams of him behaving in a
drunken and disorderly fashion. A mild and inoffensive person
may have dreams of violence, an ascetic of sexual orgies.[88]
(Examples like the last, of course, fit neatly into the Freudian
scheme of wish-fulfilment; but it seems unnatural to force all
the dreams described into conformity with this.)

The criterion of correct dream interpretation is whether the
dreamer ultimately feels rewarded and enriched by the explanation; not, of course, whether it flatters him, but whether it
comes home to him with conviction as promoting a grasp and
understanding of his problems and difficulties.

If we have made a wrong interpretation, or if it is somehow
incomplete, we may be able to see it from the next dream.
Thus, for example, the earlier motif will be repeated in
clearer form, or our interpretation may be deflated by some
ironic paraphrase, or it may meet with straightforward
violent opposition . . . Just as the reward of a correct interpretation is an uprush of life, so an incorrect one dooms itself to
deadlock, resistance, doubt . . .

What applies in literary criticism applies in dream-
interpretation: the interpreter may be able to apprehend more
of the real significance of the product than can the producer
himself. In general, literary criticism and dream interpretation
are closely comparable, and the criteria of validity for the one
are much the same as the criteria of validity for the other.[89]

Some elements in dreams have an interpretation which is
more or less universal, and independent of the past experience
of the particular dreamer. Water is the commonest symbol of
the unconscious. 'All the lions, bulls, dogs and snakes that
populate our dreams represent an undifferentiated and as yet

untamed libido.' Snakes signify a threatening aspect of the conflict between instinct and the conscious mind; in general they are a fear-symbol. Sometimes the numbers three and four, representing three relatively conscious and one unconscious function,[90] play an important part in dreams; one dreams about three men and a woman, or three people and a dog, or vice versa. The odd fourth in the dream is always particularly instructive; it soon gets incompatible, disagreeable and frightening, representing as it does the function in each of us which 'has the strongest tendency to be infantile, banal, primitive, and archaic', and which is apt to make the worst fools out of those who have the highest opinion of themselves. Of course the same pattern of three, pitted against an incompatible fourth, appears in countless fairy-stories. 'The Trinity represents the most perfect form of the archetype in question', with the devil as the very different and incompatible fourth.[91]

Dreams are of two main types. Those of the first type 'have a personal character and conform to the rules of a personalistic psychology'; those of the second type have a collective character, inasmuch as they contain peculiarly mythological, legendary, or generally archaic material. Dreams of this kind impress a feeling of their importance upon the dreamer himself; in ancient Athens or Rome they might have been reported to the Areopagus or the Senate. They are prone to occur at decisive moments or stages in the dreamer's life. Dream-language is naturally very dependent on environment; but in dreams of the kind being discussed one only has to substitute, for example, 'eagle' for 'aeroplane', 'dragon' for 'car' or 'train', 'snakebite' for 'injection', and so on, in order to get back to the language and symbolism of myths. Dreaming and schizophrenia are so alike that one may actually say 'that the dreamer is normally insane, or that insanity is a dream which has replaced normal consciousness'. However, in schizophrenia, as opposed to the ordinary dream at least, archaic and collective material predominates.[92]

'The protective circle, the mandala, is the traditional antidote for chaotic states of mind'.[93] It is curious how often patients dream about mandalas, or produce paintings and drawings of them, in the course of getting well. The basic motif of these pictures seems to be 'the premonition of a centre of personality, a kind of central point within the psyche, to which everything is related, by which everything is arranged, and which is itself a source of energy.' Mandalas mostly turn up in connection with confused states of the psyche, with disorientation or panic. They have the effect of reducing these states to order, and patients are wont to emphasise their soothing and beneficial effect. In general, the making of pictures is useful to mental patients and others seeking psychic integration; such pictures are 'as it were self-delineations of dimly-sensed changes going on in the background, which are perceived by the "reversed eye" and rendered visible with pencil and brush'. Literary composition may be helpful in just the same kind of way.[94]

Dreams are part of the natural process by which transformation is achieved. It may also be assisted by such artificial means as yoga, or by religious practices. One may well seek transformation *in* a group; but it is of great importance not to confuse this with mere identification *with* a group. In a large crowd, the collective psyche is liable to be more bestial than human; as member of a mob, an individual may perpetrate acts of violence or cruelty which he would never contemplate on his own. Unlike real transformation, the effects of such identification are both short-lived and easily come by. There is some danger in the fact that this kind of experience brings with it a heightened sense of life which may prove fatally attractive. One good effect of ritual is that it has the effect of counteracting these tendencies in religious groups; while the individual's attention is engaged by the ritual, he is less liable to be overwhelmed by unconscious forces. In some religions, typified by Christianity, transformation is to be achieved through identification with a cult-hero. The Christian is to be reborn, with the Church at once the grave of his old personality and the womb of his new. Christ, like the Buddha for many Buddhists, is the symbol of the self, of the whole, transformed and complete man whose realisation is the goal of human living; men strive to attain this state through identification with him through the rites of the Church. Thus 'the mystery of the Eucharist transforms the soul of the empirical man, who is only a part of himself, into his totality, symbolically expressed by Christ.' A study of the history of religions reveals the Eucharist to be the quintessence and summation of a development lasting many thousands of years, by which the isolated experience of gifted individuals has been made the common property of a larger group.[95]

It might be objected that to regard religion in this way is to treat it as a mere tool which man can use for his own purposes. But this would be a mistake; religious persons have direct experience of a terrifying power which works upon *them* to transform them, so far from them manipulating *it* for their own purposes. It may also be objected that, even if it is granted that the practice of a religion may be psychically beneficial, this has no bearing on the question of whether it is *true*. Is not a man better left with an honest neurosis than taken in by the swindle of religious belief? But this is to neglect the important fact that the believer does not merely take on trust, but has direct experience of, that with which he has to do in his religion. Admittedly nothing 'metaphysical' is proved by this. However, no one can know what the ultimate things are; and if a person's life is richer and more fulfilled, and more beneficial to others, through his participation in religion, it does not seem unreasonable to speak of the grace of God as at work in him.

> We must confess . . . that religious experience is . . . subjective, and liable to boundless error. Yet . . . there would seem to be good reasons for thinking that even the Boundless is pervaded by psychic laws, which no man invented, but of which he has 'gnosis' in the symbolism of Christian dogma. Only heedless fools will wish to destroy this; the lover of the soul, never.

It goes without saying that, for the educated modern man, mere submission to religious authority is not enough; he must understand religion in its psychological bearings.[96]

4 Archetypes and the Collective Unconscious

Early in his career, Jung constructed a word-association test, in which the subject is presented with a succession of words, and is asked to say in response to each the first thing he can think of. If he hesitates longer than usual, or shows signs of emotion, this reveals that the word forms part of a *complex* in his psyche. A complex is a group of related feelings, thoughts and memories within the unconscious. Complexes behave like separate and split-off personalities, operating against the apparent wishes or acknowledged interests of the person who has them. They are more likely to be apparent to those who have anything to do with the person concerned, than to the person himself. For example, one with a mother complex may be abnormally sensitive to what Mother says, imitate slavishly her manner and opinions, and drag her into conversation in season and out of season. A main aim of therapy is to dissolve complexes, at least so far as they interfere with reasonably happy and useful living. Departing in this matter from the opinion of Freud, Jung thought there was good reason to suppose that some complexes derived not merely from childhood experiences, but rather from hereditary factors which reached far back into the history of the race. Such complexes were called by Jung 'archetypes', which together made up the 'collective unconscious' as opposed to the 'individual unconscious' of the subject's personal memories.[97]

For all that the common charge against Jung, that he has renounced science for mystagogy, centres largely round his notion of 'archetypes', there is nothing particularly mysterious about it. An archetype is simply a group of ideas and images which the human mind is found recurrently to throw up in dreams, fantasies, artistic creations, myths, schizophrenic delusions, and so on. They are not a matter of 'inherited ideas, but of a functional disposition to produce the same, or very similar, ideas'. The psyche's dependence on the human brain might have led one to expect what appears to be the case, that mankind has in common certain very general dispositions to behave, and to have feelings and ideas accordingly. The collective unconscious is an image of the world and of human life which has taken aeons to evolve; the archetypes are 'images of the dominant laws and principles' of things, 'and of typical, regularly occurring events in the soul's cycle of experience'. One would hardly expect the psyche of the new-born child to be a complete *tabula rasa*; after all, it meets sensory stimuli with specific aptitudes. The changes which befall a person during the course of his life are not indefinitely various; they are all variations of a limited number of types, with which our species has evolved with latent abilities to cope. When a difficult or distressing situation confronts anyone, the corresponding archetype tends to be precipitated in his unconscious; it will then attract conscious ideas, which are such as to render it perceptible and capable of realisation.[98]

The existence of the collective unconscious and of the archetypes of which it consists seems a matter which is easily confirmed by observation; Jung wonders how his many opponents would set about characterising the material in question. It must be admitted, of course, that the verbal and pictorial forms in which the archetypes appear to differ greatly according to the spirit of the times, even though they themselves hardly change in thousands of years. They generally appear in projection on persons in one's environment, mostly in the form of blatant 'over- or under-valuations which provoke misunderstandings, quarrels, fanaticisms, and follies of every description. Thus we say, "He makes a god of so-and-so", or, "So-and-so is Mr. X's *bête-noire*". In this way, too, there grow up modern myth-formations, i.e., fantastic rumours, suspicions, prejudices.' Archetypal motifs also appear, with the special impressiveness characteristic of them, in the dreams of normal people:

mainly in situations that somehow threaten the very foundations of the individual's existence, for instance in moments of mortal danger, before or after accidents, severe illnesses, operations, etc., or when psychic problems are developing which might give his life a catastrophic turn, or in the critical periods of life when a modification of his previous psychic attitudes forces itself peremptorily upon him, or before, during, and after radical changes in his immediate or general surroundings.[99]

The 'anima', the 'animus' and the 'shadow' are perhaps the most striking archetypal figures; the 'hero' and 'wise old man' are others which have been conspicuous in myth and literature. As to the anima, every man carries a feminine image within him, 'a deposit, as it were, of all the impressions ever made by women . . . since this image is unconscious it is always unconsciously projected upon the person of the beloved, and is one of the chief reasons for passionate attraction or aversion'. And there is a feminine side to every man, and a masculine side to every woman, which must be expressed in conscious thought and action if the subject is to be fully balanced and integrated. Unfortunately, in Western society at least, femininity in men and masculinity in women are usually disparaged; and this is apt to lead to rebellion and over-compensation. To put in a nutshell the difference between animus and anima, so long as they remain unconscious complexes, 'as the anima produces *moods*, so the animus produces *opinions*'. Being partial personalities, they are respectively like an inferior woman and an inferior man; this is why they irritate to the extent that they do. They may cause a great many difficulties in a marriage; since a man possessed or dominated by his anima is all the more acutely conscious of the animus-possession of his wife, and vice versa. As in the case of other archetypes, possession may range in degree all the way from mere odd moods and ideas to full-blown psychosis. In an extreme case of anima-possession, where the archetype is out of conscious control altogether, 'the patient will want to change himself into a woman through self-castration, or he is afraid that something of the sort will be done to him by force'.[100]

The 'shadow' represents those aspects of the psyche which have barely left the animal level, and stands in complementary relation to the ego-personality. Our instinctual nature has to be controlled for civilisation; but if it is entirely suppressed, creativity and spontaneity go by the board. And in any case, if adequate outlets are not provided for the part of our nature represented by the shadow, disaster sooner or later ensues. The animal within us only becomes more insistent when repressed; possibly this is why no religion is so defiled with the shedding of blood as is Christianity, and why the wars waged by Christian nations have been so peculiarly bloody. The telling of stories about a character representing the shadow brings about a therapeutic anamnesis of contents which should not be allowed to remain unconscious for too long. The Winnebago Indians enjoy telling stories about their 'trickster' figure; this is a way of 'keeping the shadow ... conscious and subjecting it to conscious criticism'. (The kind of farce in which we recognise inferior aspects of ourselves seems to fulfil much the same function with us.)[101] One tends to project one's repressed shadow on other members of one's own sex; this accounts for a great deal of bad feeling between men, and between women.[102]

The myth of the 'hero', culminating in some kind of death and rebirth, is almost world-wide. In typical examples, the protagonist will take a journey by ship, or have to cross a ford; he fights a sea-monster, is swallowed by it, struggles not to be bitten or crushed, and at last manages to destroy a vital organ. The monster dies and drifts to land, and the hero sees light again. He is helped in his adventure by birds and other animals; these seem to represent stirrings of the unconscious. The hanging-up of the hero, his 'suspense', is a symbol of intense expectation; 'Christ, Odin, Attis and others all hung upon trees'. As a child, the hero is commonly an abandoned foundling, threatened by extraordinary dangers. For example, in the Finnish myth, we are told that of the tribe of Kalervo only his young pregnant wife is left alive. When the child Kullervo is born, his enemies try to get rid of him by putting him to sea in a barrel, burning him, and hanging him up in an oak tree. These events seem to symbolise the dangers for nascent consciousness which lurk in the unconscious. The fateful transformations of the hero, especially his death and rebirth, are shared by the initiate who takes part in the corresponding religious rite.

The 'wise old man', as one finds from dreams and fairy-tales, tends to turn up when the hero is in a desperate plight from which only deep reflection or a lucky idea can deliver him. He often asks the hero who he is, where he comes from and whither he goes. He is apt to provide a magic talisman, and to use animals, especially birds, to provide the information that the hero needs. As well as being full of insight, he has moral qualities – not always excluding something of a wicked streak.

> In the Estonian tale . . . about the hired boy who lost the cow, there is the suspicion that the helpful old man who happened to be on the spot so opportunely had surreptitiously made away with the cow beforehand in order to give his protégé an excellent reason for flight. This may very well be, for every-day experience shows that it is quite possible for a superior, though subliminal, foreknowledge of fate to contrive some annoying incident for the sole purpose of bullying our Simple Simon of an ego-consciousness into the way he should go, which for sheer stupidity he would never have found by himself.

The wise old man is sage, magician or king, or a mixture of these.[103] (Prospero in Shakespeare's *The Tempest*, Sarastro in Mozart's *The Magic Flute*, and Zoroastro in Handel's *Orlando*, are outstanding examples of the wise old man.)

It is worth noting that most of the points which were made about Freud's limitations, in the discussion of his position earlier in this chapter, were made by Jung. The principal points of agreement and of disagreement between Freud and Jung may now be summarised.

(a) Jung is in agreement with Freud in seeing dreams, neurotic symptoms, and so on, as *meaningful*. As Jung puts it, 'Freud applies to the dream the same principle that we always instinctively use, when inquiring into the causes of human actions';[104] and Jung's whole output illustrates his following of Freud's lead in the matter.

(b) They agree both on the existence of the unconscious mind, and on the manner in which its existence is known. The unconscious, for both, betrays itself in dreams, moods, errors, slips of the tongue, and patterns of behaviour which run counter to the apparent wishes and goals of the conscious individual.

(c) They agree that the cure of neurosis is a matter of the integration of conscious and unconscious, and the consequent removal of the mistakes, disturbances and annoying accidents, which incommode or at worst entirely incapacitate the conscious person in his attempt to live in a manner reasonably satisfying to himself and others. For both, the cure is largely a matter of becoming clear and honest with oneself about one's feelings, moods, ideas and attitudes; of passing, to put it briefly, from self-ignorance and self-deception to self-knowledge.

(d) Jung disagrees with Freud not so much in maintaining the existence in the unconscious of collective elements, as well as those deriving from repression in the individual, as in drawing the full consequences of this. Freud admitted the existence of what amounted to an inherited symbolism, which he held to be more or less exclusively related to sexuality.[105] But this surely amounts to conceding the existence of what Jung would call a collective unconscious, and the insistence that this symbolism is exclusively or primarily of a sexual nature seems curiously forced, especially if one admits, as Freud did,[106] that the symbols can as a matter of fact, by reason of secondary developments, be interpreted in other ways. It seems simpler, more economical and more plausible, if one admits the existence of collective elements in the unconscious at all, to envisage them as originally open to a range of applications to situations and relations in human life, of which sexual situations and relations are merely among the more important.

(e) Jung disagrees with Freud over the importance that the latter attributes to sexuality. Sexuality was crucial for Freud's theories, in that it secured the link with animal biology, and provided an interpretation of such symbols as might most readily suggest the existence of a full-blown collective unconscious in Jung's sense. Freud's claim that there were in man inherited memories of a sexual nature, for example of castration and parricide, is in fact very difficult to square with the theory of evolution as generally understood; whereas Jung's alternative view that man has inherited a set of very general predispositions to behave in the basic situations characteristic of human life, and to have feelings and ideas to match, as the psychical equivalent to the differentiation of the human brain, seems perfectly in accord with it.[106]

(f) Jung differs from Freud in stressing that the human psyche has what amounts to an inbuilt aim. Here again, it seems that Jung was merely drawing out in a consistent fashion conclusions which were implicit in some of Freud's discoveries. Freudian psychoanalysis itself assumes that there are patterns of behaviour which the neurotic sufferer tends to miss; which he may be brought to attain through the replacement of 'id' by 'ego', by the substitution of deliberate, consistent and satisfying patterns of thought and behaviour for states in which he is either being ridden by ungovernable thoughts and impulses, or in the grip of agonising feelings of guilt. One corollary of Jung's finalism is his stress on the theoretical as well as practical importance of the present strategies of the neurotic, as opposed to what happened to him in his early life, in the explanation of his illness.[107] Freud's understanding of dreams and neurotic symptoms in terms of meaning is in fact the employment of what we have called B explanation; but his deference to the pseudo-scientific principle, that B explanation ought always in principle to be replaceable by A explanation, prevents him from following through the consequences of his discovery. One of these is that the causation of neurosis may in the last analysis be a matter of B explanation, of the patient's judgements and decisions here and now, admittedly facilitated by dispositions to judge and to decide which he has established since childhood, and not primarily of determination by events in his infantile past. Freud's admission that the crucial events in question often have not really happened[108] in effect concedes to Jung the crucial point at issue.

(g) Jung states clearly and consistently what is only intermittently and inconsistently recognised by Freud, that quite complicated mental acts, and not merely the psychic equivalent of impulses of an organic nature, may be repressed.[109] Jung insists that human instinct and the unconscious do not consist merely of simple and unco-ordinated impulses; one consequence of this being that an innate predisposition to control our immediate drives of sexuality or aggression, and not only these impulses themselves, may be repressed.

(h) The most notorious difference between Freud and Jung is probably that of their estimation of religion. While acknowledging that religion has played an important role in the development of culture, Freud regarded it as essentially the most blatant expression of the human tendency to envisage reality according to what one might wish rather than according to the available evidence. Science, as the result of a following-through of the 'reality-principle' as opposed to the 'pleasure-principle', and as a matter of pursuing reason and evidence wherever they may lead, is thus according to him inevitably destructive of religion, at least in the long run.[110]. Jung regards the religions as by no means a matter of flight from reality; they are for him means, on the contrary, by which the individual can to some extent understand and cope with his unconscious, and so achieve balance and come to fulfilment. He does not see scientific method as so unequivocally opposed to religious belief as Freud does; but while he affirms the psychological importance of religious belief, he is agnostic about the 'truth' of such belief in any other but such a 'psychological' sense.[111] To discuss the issue at length is not an object of the present book; something brief will be said about it in the final chapter.

In discussing the respective merits of Freud and Jung, J. A. C. Brown suggests that one is probably born either a Freudian or a Jungian.[112] Where issues of truth and falsity are concerned, as seems the case here, this really does seem a counsel of despair. If my arguments in this chapter have been at all on the right lines, there are good reasons for agreeing with Jung against Freud on most of the matters about which they disagree. On matters about which Freud appears more 'scientific' than Jung – for example in his attempt to reduce all thought to organic states, and all effort to find the truth on any matter to an indirect route to gaining pleasure – I have tried to show that the appearance is an illusory one.[113]

From cases described by Konrad Lorenz in his *Studies in Human and Animal Behaviour*, it appears that domesticated animals often lose the more elaborate patterns of behaviour characteristic of each species in the wild state, and in general become more sexy and aggressive.[114] This seems to throw a great deal of light on the disputed issue of the place of sexuality in the mental life of man. If it is so, and applies to man as to other animals, it is easy to see why it is that the Freudian view, that more sophisticated types of human behaviour are all along *really* sublimated or repressed sexuality or aggression, should seem so plausible to many. Indeed, one might say that the more sophisticated types of behaviour are *potentially* sexual or aggressive, in that they tend to become so when the general environmental situation with which they have evolved to cope no longer obtains. But this is not to imply that they arose in the first place simply through the influence of the environment on predispositions which were in the first place merely sexual or aggressive.

The relating of the theories of Freud and Jung to other accounts of man, and of the manner in which he may attain or fail to attain satisfaction and effective freedom, will be taken up in the final chapter. But first there have to be dealt with a number of issues in moral philosophy which have been left in abeyance since the end of chapter 1.

6 The Objectivity of Value-Judgements

In the first chapter, I set out an assumption, that what is good in human action and disposition has a great deal to do with what contributes to human happiness and fulfilment, and tends to minimise human misery and frustration.[1] The arguments of the intervening chapters have largely depended on this assumption, which will now be justified in the face of some sophisticated philosophical objections which have been raised against it. The principal objection may be summarised as follows. To say that an action or disposition tends to promote happiness or to minimise misery is to make a judgement of fact about it; to say that it is good or bad is to make a value-judgement. But there is no valid inference from any set of merely factual judgements to any judgement of value.

It used to be widely accepted that the logical gulf between statements of fact and judgements of value, between descriptive statements on the one hand and prescriptions or expressions of emotion or what you will on the other hand, had been proved once and for all. Recently there has been a good deal of dissent from this view, expressed in a number of books and articles; but, so far as I know, the arguments which constitute the alleged proof have not been attacked by anyone else in quite the way that I propose here. I shall try to show, in effect, that the fact-value dichotomy is founded on a series of arguments which are based in turn on a certain theory of meaning; that this theory of meaning has been widely discredited, but the arguments, and the theory of the nature of value-judgements founded on them, has survived somehow just the same.

The objections to deducing statements about value from statements which are merely factual depend on well-known arguments of David Hume and G. E. Moore.[2] The more detailed argument propounded by Moore seems to me, as it does to most contemporary philosophers, to demonstrate that to say that anything is good is not to imply that it has *any one kind* of property or effect, unless one is to count 'goodness' itself. But what seems to be false is the conclusion that he and others have drawn from this; that to say that anything is good is not to imply that it has *a selection from any one range of* such properties and effects. Both Moore himself, who concluded that goodness was a simple and unanalysable property, and the emotivists and prescriptivists who used his arguments in their own way, inferring that 'goodness' was not really a property at all, drew this conclusion. Now in the polemical sections of *Principia Ethica*, Moore considers one by one the definitions of good which are usually offered; like Napoleon, he prudently engages the enemy forces severally, rather than attacking them all together in combination. Had he done the latter, I believe that the outcome of his argument would have been different. It makes sense, to be sure, to claim that an action (let us say) is good, though it is likely to contribute to the happiness of no one; or that another action is good, though it makes no positive contribution to man's evolutionary progress (however this is conceived); or that another action is good though it is intuitively approved by no one; or that yet another is good though it is against the revealed will of God. Such statements certainly make sense, and, as Moore rightly argued from this, a definition of good in terms of *any single one* of these characteristics *taken by itself* is thereby invalidated. But suppose I say that an action is good, though it promotes and is intended to promote no one's happiness, though it is intuitively approved by no one, though it makes no contribution to man's evolutionary progress however conceived, and though it is against the revealed will of God – if I make all these qualifications, do I not in effect virtually reduce to nonsense my original statement that the action is good? Any *one* such qualification does not, to be sure, invalidate the statement that the action is good; but, I would claim, *the more* such qualifications are made, *the more* it tends to be invalidated. 'Even if that action tends to promote the greatest happiness of the greatest number, it is one of a kind that I know intuitively to be wrong'; such an appeal to intuition against the general happiness principle makes perfectly good moral sense.

'To obey the Creator is good, even if to do so is to compass the
misery of every creature'; such an appeal to the will of God
against the general happiness principle, even if wrong-headed,
is at least intelligible. But to say that an action is good or right
though it fails not only on these counts, but on all the others I
have mentioned as well, surely is virtually to talk nonsense.
One might perhaps in some sense commend or prescribe such
an action; but to say that it was good, or that anyone ought to
do it, while admitting that it failed on all these counts, is surely
an abuse of words.

If my argument here is correct, it appears that, while value-
judgements do not logically entail propositions about any one
particular kind of matter of fact, they are not so logically
independent of matters of fact that you cannot render a value-
judgement so eccentric as to approximate to nonsense by
enough factual qualifications. I shall say that value-
judgements *loosely entail* certain kinds of statement of fact,
defining loose entailment, and contrasting it with strict entailment, as follows:

Statement A strictly entails statements p, q, r, and s, when to
affirm A and at the same time to negate p is a contradiction; and
similarly with q, r, and s;

Statement A loosely entails statements p, q, r, and s when to
assert A and at the same time to negate p (or any single one of
the others) is not to contradict oneself, though to assert A and to
negate p, q, r and s all together is either to contradict oneself or
to talk so eccentrically as to be unintelligible.

Suppose there is a six-legged table, constructed in such a way
that it can stand up on *any five* of its legs. Then if any single one
of the legs is unscrewed from the table, or folded up in such a
way that it no longer touches the floor, the table will go on
standing, provided that the other five are still in position. By an
argument parallel to that of Moore, a sophist could prove that,
since the table's standing depended on no one of the six legs, it
did not depend on any of them – or perhaps that the leg on
which it really stood was invisible and intangible. (The former
solution to the problem seems to correspond to the emotivist
and prescriptivist view that goodness is not a property at all;
the latter to Moore's own view that goodness is a simple
non-natural property.) The various properties of something

loosely entailed by the statement that it is good are related to its
goodness rather as the support given by each leg is related to
the standing of the table. Just because it is not true of any one of
the six legs that it must lend its support in order for the table to
stand, it does not follow that the table does not stand on its six
legs collectively; similarly, that the denial of any one of a list of
properties to anything does not invalidate the attribution of
goodness to it, does not entail that its goodness is something
logically quite independent of its possession of the properties
making up the list.

As John Wisdom has said, 'One thing may be a matter of
other things without being definable in terms of them'.[3] As a
matter of fact, as may be inferred from the account that I have
just given, many cases of loose entailment can be reduced to
strict entailment of a disjunction. But it does not appear that all
of them can be so, since – except in the case of terms which are
susceptible of exact definition and whose implications can
therefore be precisely specified – there is no particular degree of
qualification at which one can lay it down that a relatively
normal use has become eccentric, or a highly eccentric use
nonsensical. It is certainly the case that many statements are
subject to death by a thousand qualifications;[4] but this does not
imply that it is the last of the thousand that administers the *coup
de grâce* to a statement that previously retained a definite
significance. Most descriptive terms in ordinary language do
not have precisely specifiable conditions for their correct application; and hence the meaning of statements made in terms of
them cannot be exhausted in terms of strict entailment, even in
terms of strict entailment of a disjunction. Collingwood's comment is very much to the point: 'The proper meaning of a word
(I speak not of technical terms which kindly godparents furnish
soon after birth with neat and tidy definitions, but of words in a
living language) is never something upon which the word sits
perched like a gull on a stone; it is something over which the
word hovers like a gull over a ship's stern.'[5] It may be concluded that not all loose entailments are strict entailments of
disjunctions; but that all strict entailments of disjunctions are
loose entailments.

The naturalistic fallacy, when it *is* really a fallacy, is the
assumption that there is a relationship of strict entailment

between the statement that something is good and some one particular kind of factual statement about it. Prescriptivists and emotivists, so far as their position is based on acceptance of the validity of such arguments as Moore's, assume wrongly that when the possession by a thing of property B does not strictly entail its possession of properties or effects t, or u, or v, or w, its possession of property B cannot be *a matter of* its possession of properties or effects t, u, v, and w. One important assumption underlying their position seems to be that to give the meaning of a predicate 'B' is always to state what is strictly entailed by the possession of property B. I suggest on the contrary that to give the meaning of a predicate may be not only to say what is strictly entailed by possession of the coresponding property, but also, and sometimes only, to say what is loosely entailed by it. Referring to 'good', Hare writes 'that *the meaning which is common to all instances of the word's use* cannot be descriptive, and that *this common meaning* is to be sought in the evaluative function of the word'.[6] Two erroneous assumptions seem to be involved here: that there must be a single meaning corresponding to all instances of a word's correct use; and that all uses of the word 'good' have an evaluative function. As Philippa Foot remarks, it makes perfectly good sense to say 'You ought to do that; but I hope to God you won't', or 'I ought to do it; so what?'[7] and the same applies *mutatis mutandis* to 'good' as to 'ought'.

The loose entailments of 'X is B' constitute part at least of the meaning of 'B' in so far as, if one denies that 'X is B' has any one loose entailment which in fact it does have, one shows that one does not fully understand the meaning of 'B'. For instance, although of course it may be intelligibly claimed that a particular action is good though it causes and is intended to cause suffering, a man who claimed that it was in general morally good deliberately to cause suffering would thereby show, given that he was sincere, that he did not understand the terms he was using.

There are some qualities and effects of actions, like their tendency to diminish suffering and to promote justice, which *per se* constitute morally good reasons for performing such actions. The 'action guiding' aspect of moral judgements, which is often alluded to by prescriptivists, is due to their calling attention to these features, which are 'objective' in that they are qualities and effects of the actions concerned quite independently of the practical attitude which the agent or anyone else may actually take up to them. A man who does not know that to promote justice and to remove suffering are *per se* good, even if occasionally they may not be so *per accidens* (because of other qualities and effects of the actions concerned), does not altogether know what is meant by 'good'. Of course, it may be conceded to the prescriptivists that a man who does not know that to call something good *usually* has a commendatory function also does not know the full meaning of 'good'. I would not wish to claim that prescriptivism was any *more* erroneous than the crude forms of naturalism which actually were refuted by Moore's arguments.

There is a relationship of loose entailment between many of the statements of ordinary language; the connection is not peculiar to value-judgements and some restricted types of factual statement. In the famous and over-cited discussion of games in the *Philosophical Investigations*, Wittgenstein shows in effect that the statement that some human activity is a game does not strictly entail anything about it, but loosely entails a number of things about it, the absence of no one of which would disqualify it from being a game, but the absence of all of which would presumably do so.[8] There is a relation of loose entailment between statements about a man's character and statements about the way he behaves on particular occasions. That a man is irascible does not strictly entail that he will be angry in any particular set of circumstances; but it does entail that he will be so in a proportion of a sufficiently wide range of cases. Often a 'but' or a 'though' halfway through a sentence is a sign that affirmation of the proposition negated in the clause after it is loosely entailed by the proposition asserted in the clause before it. For instance, one is inclined to say 'He was a good general, *though* his conduct of one campaign was positively disastrous'; 'Toscanini's sense of tempo was phenomenal, *but* the minuet of the "Surprise" symphony is played at a ridiculous speed in one of his recordings of the work'; 'My daughter is a very intelligent girl, *though* she cannot achieve even the average proficiency in mathematics for her age'; 'He is very careless of his appearance, *but* at least he looked well turned out on the day of his wedding'. In such cases, the one qualification does not invalidate the original assertion, though evidently, the more such qualifications were made, the more they would tend to do so.

In the case of moral judgements, there are certain very general types of factual statement about an action or person which are loosely entailed by a moral judgement about it or him. These general types correspond to the various theories of ethics – intuitionist, utilitarian, theological and so on – which have been most widely held and which seem most plausible. Because these factual statements are loosely and not strictly entailed, all of these theories have proved liable to exception, and thus are inadequate claimants to provide an exhaustive and sufficient account of moral judgement. A good action characteristically corresponds to people's intuitions about what is good; but sometimes our 'intuitions' about the goodness of certain classes of actions is revised in the light of ascertained facts about their qualities and effects. Again, a good action is not characteristically an unkind one, or an infringement of the law; *but* in special circumstances, as in getting rid of somebody's illusions or resisting an unjust piece of legislation, it may be good to act unkindly or to break the law.

According to Hare, to call something 'good' is primarily to commend rather than describe it. The plausibility of this doctrine seems to me to be due to the fact that to describe anything as 'good' is as a rule to state that it has qualities and effects which render it objectively worthy of commendation. A distinction is to be made between non-arbitrary commendation, which entails the possession by what is commended of such qualities and effects, and arbitrary commendation, which does not do so. To commend things non-arbitrarily is to be able to support our commendations with assurances that they are useful or pleasant, that they contribute to the delight or fulfilment of men or (conceivably) other rational or sentient beings. But to state that things are, in the appropriate circumstances, useful or pleasant, is to describe them. In a sense, we can 'commend' anything whatever. But the desires and needs which are part of our human nature are such that there are only some things which prove non-arbitrarily commendable, or objectively worth commending; and it is these things which are properly speaking good. To call anything 'good' is usually to commend it non-arbitrarily; though, as is shown by the examples which I borrowed from Philippa Foot, in some cases it is not to commend it at all. The grounds for non-arbitrary commendation are various; but not any circumstance whatever can be grounds for such commendation. That some things, actions, persons and states of affairs are of such a kind as immediately or ultimately to satisfy or delight us, or alternatively to frustrate or disgust us, as individuals or societies, is the basis of all evaluation. And it is a given part of our human nature, as I have argued *ad nauseam* in the earlier chapters, to have certain basic needs and desires; we do not, in any useful sense, *opt* to have these. Whatever may be the case with merely arbitrary commending, if such an activity ever actually takes place, we may prove objectively to be speaking the truth or otherwise in calling something 'good'; and the truth-conditions characteristically have something to do with the fulfilment or frustration of human needs and desires. The use of the word 'good', or *mutatis mutandis* of the word 'ought', to commend something arbitrarily, would be definitely odd. If I say that a kind of chocolate is good, and everyone who eats it is nauseated; if I say that a medicine is good, and it turns out to hasten death in all who use it; if I say that a man is good, when he deliberately causes as much misery as he can to all those who have anything to do with him; I am shown by the circumstances to be objectively wrong in my statement, just as much as if I have described something as red all over which subsequent observation has determined to be blue all over. I do not say 'I was merely commending without committing myself to the truth of any proposition of fact about what I was commending'; I say rather, 'I was wrong. They were not good after all.'

Hare is surely right in drawing attention to the close connection between calling something good on the one hand, and commending and guiding choices on the other; but his analysis neglects, so far as I can see, that contribution by things, actions and states of affairs to human satisfaction that makes them worth commending. To say that anything frustrates or satisfies sentient beings is at once to evaluate and to describe it; the dichotomy between description and evaluation postulated by Hare and his predecessors seems to me to be due to neglect of this aspect of the matter. Hare does admit that the use of words like 'good' usually contains a descriptive as well as an evaluative element;[9] what I am concerned to show is that the evaluative element itself is in an important sense descriptive. What is at issue can be brought out very well in relation to an example discussed by Hare, that of the 'good sunset'. 'There is', he writes, 'general agreement among those who are interested in looking at sunsets, what a sunset has to be like to be called a good one (it has to be bright but not dazzling, and cover a wide area of sky with varied and intense colours, etc.)'[10] But it seems to me not merely that connoisseurs have determined criteria for the goodness of sunsets; but that it is a contingent fact that sunsets with the corresponding qualities give delight to many people, at least within our culture. It is this giving of delight to the beholder which makes them objectively worth commending, and hence 'good'. That the sunset gives satisfaction of this kind is what it is for it to be good; we do not merely *elect* to commend sunsets which have this particular set of characteristics, in such a way that we might just as well have elected to commend sunsets with quite a different set.[11]

We do not grade objects, or actions, or people, just anyhow; we grade them in general according to the way in which we deem them to foster or frustrate human needs and desires. Of course, ambiguity often arises in the application of this fundamental criterion. There is perhaps no one single set of properties, apart from this one of contributing somehow to the fulfilment rather than the frustration of rational and sensitive beings, that a good apple must have, simply because there are different ways in which an apple can give satisfaction – as an eater, or as a cooker, or as a missile at a political meeting. But what it is for an apple to be good, on the view that I am presenting here, is for it to be capable of giving satisfaction, in some way or other. Certainly, we *could* conceivably grade apples according to their average weight per cc, or according to the height above ground at which they grew on the tree. But such properties, unlike their ripeness or juiciness, bear no relation to the manner in which they characteristically give satisfaction; and it would therefore be eccentric to call apples good or bad, *tout court*, according to their grading on such scales. On Hare's analysis, it would appear that we might just as well have chosen to grade them on these scales, as on those on which in fact we do so.

It appears to me that the same general principles of evaluation apply to human beings and their actions. We do not merely opt to commend one kind of action, or to censure another, even at the level of greatest generality; or to have a pro-attitude to one, a contra-attitude to another; but we are so constituted, individually and socially, that some sorts of action tend to promote our satisfaction, others not to do so. The objective goodness of an action is a function of its tendency to promote such satisfaction, and not to frustrate it; a good man is one who deliberately cultivates in himself a disposition to perform such actions. His achieving and maintaining of the kind of effective freedom discussed at the end of the first chapter will be a necessary, though not a sufficient, condition for this. Hare rightly points out that it is only in the case of some things, which he calls 'functional', that it is true to say that to know what an X is is to know what a good X is. For instance, a knife is by its very nature for cutting, and a good knife is therefore one which cuts effectively; a servant is a servant by virtue of obedience to a master, and a good servant is one who is genuinely and consistently obedient. To be a servant or to be a knife is, logically, to have certain functions; to be a good servant or knife is to perform these functions effectively. But with other kinds of things, he adds, this is not the case; we can perfectly well know the meaning of 'sunset', or 'horse', or 'man', without knowing what it is to be a good sunset, or horse, or man.[12] I think that Hare's delineation of this contrast is both correct and interesting; but the contrast does not appear to me to affect the issue of the objectivity of value-judgements. To know what a good sunset, or man, or horse is, we have not only to know the meanings of 'sunset', 'horse' and 'man', but also in what manner things of each of these kinds characteristically contribute to the satisfaction of rational and sentient beings. A good sunset is pleasant rather than useful, a good horse useful rather than pleasant; a good man will set himself to foster the ultimate satisfaction and well-being of other men. Now this contribution to satisfaction, it seems to me, is of the very essence of goodness; it is not good merely because people very often commend such contribution. In fact, I should say, a man who did not admit

that at least *in general, other things being equal,* a man is morally
good so far as he sets himself to contribute to the well-being and
satisfaction of other men, would not know the meaning of the
phrase 'morally good', or at least would be using the phrase
'morally good' in a highly eccentric sense.

I argued early in this chapter that for an action to be good
loosely entails its contribution to the general happiness, its
being according to law, its being approved intuitively by
people, and so on. My later arguments have tended to assume
what I think can also be shown to be the case, that not all these
loose entailments are equally central or fundamental to the
meaning of 'good'. This may be shown by the following consideration. It makes perfectly good sense to say that a law is bad,
on the ground that its observance does not tend to promote the
general happiness; or that spontaneous 'intuitions' of value are
misguided, if actions to the approval of which they lead do not
tend to promote the general happiness. The general happiness
is a criterion for the goodness of laws and the correctness of
'intuitions' of value; but the goodness of the general happiness
(the very phrase is paradoxical) does not depend on such laws
or intuitions. And it is characteristic of believers in God that
they hold that to obey God's will is to contribute best to their
own ultimate happiness and that of others. *E'n la sua volontade è
nostra pace* (in his will is our peace), as Dante put it.

What is good in general is such by virtue of contribution to
the happiness or fulfilment of sensitive and rational beings; how
this contribution is made depends on the kind of good that is in
question.[13] In the special case of moral goodness, which is a
quality of agents and actions, I shall call deliberate contribution to happiness among rational and sensitive beings on the
one hand, and deliberate contribution to justice between them
on the other, *first-class conditions* of such goodness. Among
second-class conditions of such goodness I would include what is
demanded by law, what is according to the will of God, and
what people tend spontaneously to approve. Second-class conditions are such as *in general* may be justified in relation to the
first-class conditions of goodness, though in particular cases,
where they cannot be thus justified, they may provide independent grounds for saying that an action or the agent of such an
action is good. For instance, it is *per se* good to obey a law, even if

this particular law does not promote happiness or justice (always provided, of course, that it does not promote unhappiness or injustice); or to obey a law of which it is in general true that obedience to it promotes happiness and justice, even if in this instance it does not do so. The other second-class conditions of moral goodness which I have mentioned may be related to the first-class conditions in a not dissimilar manner. To go against anyone's spontaneous approval is so far to mar their satisfaction, and in any case what people spontaneously approve is seldom quite unrelated to what promotes happiness or justice or at least has done so in the past. Again, to obey God is deemed by those who believe in him to work for the ultimate happiness both of oneself and of mankind at large. Thus the second-class conditions of goodness are in general justifiable in terms of the first-class conditions. Any other condition of goodness will be so by virtue of such a relation either to a first-class or to a second-class condition.

It might be asked whether the consistent egoist can be said to have a real morality at all, on the account which I have given. I would prefer to approach the question from another direction, and ask how normal would be such a man's use of terms like 'good', 'ought' and their cognates, in describing and evaluating men and their actions. In effect, his actual use of these terms would be quite normal so far as he believed, as adherents of the great religions characteristically do believe, that any action of his that was designed to promote the ultimate happiness of his fellows in fact contributed to his own ultimate happiness. Even if he did not so believe, his 'morality' ought to be said to be rather eccentric than no morality at all, since, after all, his own happiness is one factor in the happiness and fulfilment of sensitive and rational beings in general. Of more practical interest is another question, of how far a man can be said to be moral whose criterion of goodness is happiness and justice only within the limits of his own class or race, and not those of human beings at large. I would say that the meaning of 'good' and cognate terms to such a man was not quite identical with their ordinary meaning. The claim that the lower classes of a society should have the same standard of living and cultural opportunities as the upper classes would seldom, I think, be dismissed as merely *pointless* by those upper classes. They would allege rather either that the lower classes would really derive no enjoyment from such privileges, or that these privileges were somehow not available to all members of the society, and that it was better that a few should enjoy them than that none should. I think that there are few human beings who do not at least pay lip-service to the principle that when any human being is debarred from happiness and fulfilment in any respect, justification is only possible in terms of the adverse effects of his enjoyment of them on the happiness and fulfilment of others. And in so far as anyone did not at least pay lip-service to this principle, I would say that his use of the terms 'good' and 'ought' in moral contexts was at least eccentric.

In his *System of Logic*, J. S. Mill describes how a term may become applied to a heterogeneous collection of things with nothing in common, and hence finally become bereft of any determinate meaning.[14] Once this has happened, he holds, the term ought to be redefined so that it connotes only a single quality, and denotes only those objects which have this quality in common, if it is any longer to be of any use in thought and communication. Now I would say that state of affairs which Mill describes actually is the case with moral and other value predicates; but I would deny that they have therefore become unserviceable for serious discourse. On the contrary, but for the imperfectly univocal significance that they have, they would not be able to perform the functions in human life and discourse that they do. Certainly, analysis of the meaning of predicates of value shows them to be not wholly homogeneous; but they are not totally heterogeneous either; they have the same kind of homogeneous heterogeneity that Wittgenstein brought to light in the case of the concept 'game', and Aristotle in the case of the concept 'healthy'.[15] Our notion of goodness is as it is on the assumption of the truth of certain very general propositions about human affairs – that in general what we intuitively approve, or what is in accordance with the Golden Rule, or what God demands (if we believe in him), will contribute to general happiness and well-being. But there are no ready-made rules, somehow latent in the meaning of the word 'good' as it is actually used, for applying the term when the usual criteria for its correct application come into conflict with one another. Even our use of the term 'oxygen', criteria for which are far more precisely delimited than is the case with the term 'good', depends on the contingent fact that an element of such-and-such an atomic weight has such-and-such sensible properties and undergoes such-and-such chemical reactions; if a specimen turned up tomorrow which had some properties supposed to be peculiar to oxygen, but lacked some of those previously supposed to be essential to it, there would be no infallible rule somehow latent in the meaning of the word 'oxygen' as it is now for determining whether this particular specimen should rightly be called oxygen or not. As Wittgenstein says, 'what today counts as an observed concomitant of a phenomenon will tomorrow be used to define it';[16] and evidently the converse holds as well. It happens that the world is such that the criteria for application of the term 'oxygen' seldom conflict; but in the case of 'good' it is often so. However, if I am right in my contention that one criterion is of more central importance than the others, many of these objectively ambiguous cases will be capable of some kind of satisfactory solution.

How is what one ought to do related to what is morally good? J. R. Searle has argued that in some cases at least what one ought to do can be inferred from merely factual premises.[17] For instance, in our society and in many others there is an institution of promising, that is, a convention such that I can lay myself under an obligation by a form of words. Then from the *fact* that promising is an institution within my society, and the *fact* that I have promised, it follows that I ought to act as I have promised. Thus what I ought to do can at any rate in this case be inferred from matters of fact alone.

However, it seems clear that to derive 'ought'-statements from premises which are merely internal to a particular institution is to be committed to conclusions which hardly anyone would actually accept. For example, let us suppose the existence in a society of a thoroughly bad instituion, such that I as a member of that society am obliged to shoot a man who has insulted me in a manner sufficiently grave.[18] It will hardly be claimed that I actually ought to shoot the man concerned in such a case; rather, I ought to refuse to comply with the demands of the institution. And yet it seems to follow, as a result of the argument outlined above, that I am in the circumstances under a moral obligation to shoot at him. But the objection can be met if one adds the condition that, for an institution to put a man really and not merely apparently under obligation, it should be, and be believed to be, an objectively good one by the criteria which I have mentioned.[19] Then I *ought* to do X, if according to some institution within my society one undertakes to do X by doing Y; if I have done Y; if the institution concerned is objectively a good one; if there are no circumstances which make this particular submission to it other than good; and if I know all these things to be the case. Any qualification on the last two counts lessens the degree of my obligation.

I have claimed that the relation between value-judgements and statements of fact in general is one of loose entailment. Exactly what kind of loose entailment is involved depends on the kind of value-judgement concerned; the case of moral judgements, which is the one which particularly concerns us here, is perhaps more complex than most others. An action is necessarily morally good when at least one of the relevant criteria is *pro*, and none is *contra*; it is necessarily bad when at least one of the relevant criteria is *contra*, and none is *pro*. Thus one cannot adequately represent in this case the relationship between goodness and the relevant properties by saying that a good action must have some of the relevant properties and not fail to have others; since what is in question, when it is uncertain whether an action is good, but it is agreed that it has at least one of the properties relevant to establishing it as good, is not whether it merely *fails to have* other relevant qualities, but whether it *has the contrary* qualities. If an act conduces to happiness, that it does not positively conduce to justice does not mitigate its goodness; but its positively conducing to injustice would certainly do so. For an action to have one of the relevant properties and none of the contrary properties is a sufficient condition of its being good; a necessary condition is its having one of the relevant properties. However, an action might be good while having some property contrary to one of the relevant properties. For instance, it is morally good to encourage someone to take an unpleasant medicine which will greatly improve his health, even though the unpleasantness involved in taking the medicine is acknowledged. This is because while there is one reason, perfectly good in itself, for not encouraging him to take the medicine, the reasons for encouraging him evidently outweigh this.

It may be inferred, from what I have said, that actions may be divided into the following four categories with respect to their moral quality:

(i) *Objectively Morally Good.* Some criteria *pro*, none *contra*, none facing both ways;[20] or at least an obvious preponderance *pro*.[21]

(ii) *Objectively Morally Ambiguous.* Some criteria *pro*, some *contra*; or one or more criteria facing both ways; no obvious preponderance in either direction.

(iii) *Objectively Morally Bad.* Some criteria *contra*, none *pro*, none facing both ways; or at least an obvious preponderance *contra*.

(iv) *Objectively Morally Indifferent.* No criteria *pro*, none *contra*.

Which actions fall within which categories is in no sense a matter of decision by the individual or by society or any part of it; it is to be determined by the kind of attentive, intelligent and reaonable assessment of the relevant data which was sketched in the first chapter; the relevant data include the material which has been surveyed in the intervening chapters.

We are now in a position to meet the famous difficulty raised by David Hume, of how any statement of the form 'one ought to do x' can be inferred from premisses which do not contain an 'ought' or any cognate term:

> In every system of morality, which I have hitherto met with, I have always remarked, that the author proceeds for some time in the ordinary way of reasoning, and establishes the being of a God, or makes observations concerning human affairs; when all of a sudden I am surprised to find, that instead of the usual copulations of proposition, *is*, and *is not*, I meet no proposition that is not connected with an *ought*, or an *ought not*. This change is imperceptible; but is, however, of the last consequence. For as this *ought*, or *ought not*, expresses some new relation or affirmation, 'tis necessary that it should be observed and explained; and at the same time that a reason should be given, for what seems altogether inconceivable, how this new relation can be a deduction from others, which are entirely different from it.[22]

I would answer that the 'relation or affirmation' expressed by 'ought' is not 'entirely different' in kind from what is the case 'concerning human affairs', or what God is deemed to have ordained. The first can be inferred from the second; we are always doing it in our reasoning from day to day; the general form of such inferences has to be set out, however, in a way which is not so crude as to be vulnerable to the usual counter-examples. When your doing X will evoke general approval, and your not doing it will evoke general disapproval, *ceteris paribus it follows that* it is morally good for you to do X. When your doing Y will bring about happiness as far as can be foreseen, and your failure to do Y will bring unhappiness (to yourself or others), *ceteris paribus it follows that* it is morally good for you to do Y. The same applies to the removal of injustice, the lessening of pain, and so on. *Ceteris imparibus*, where these principles conflict with one another (for example, where the happiness of the majority can be secured only by the perpetration of an injustice), there are cases of what one may call objective moral ambiguity. The effectiveness of our moral language in doing what it does depends on the fact that, in a very large number of instances, these criteria do not conflict with one another. The existence in a society of the relevant institution is what makes a morally good action one which a member of that society ought to perform.

I claim in this chapter to have shown that the usual arguments adduced by philosophers against the objectivity of value-judgements, which might be supposed to vitiate the line of reasoning followed by this book as a whole, are invalid.

7 Conclusion

I have tried to summarise and comment on a number of influential doctrines of human nature, with particular attention to their bearings on morality; it remains briefly to sketch how they might be used to form the basis of a science of morals.

In the first chapter, I argued that effective freedom was both satisfying in itself, and a virtually necessary condition for achieving other satisfactions of a lasting nature for oneself and for others. If the arguments sketched in that chapter, and elaborated in the sixth, are on the right lines, it may be inferred that to do good is very largely a matter of exercising and promoting effective freedom in oneself and others. The authorities whose work I considered in the intermediate chapters have all in effect, though not on the whole explicitly, been concerned with effective freedom, and its scope and limits in the light of man's inherited nature, his immediate social and economic circumstances, and his individual history. They all more or less presuppose that effective freedom is a paramount good, and suggest means by which it may be realised.

A man is effectively free, on the account suggested here,[1] so far as he is able to attend to a wide range of evidence available to experience on any topic; so far as he is able to envisage a wide range of explanations by which that experience might be accounted for; so far as he is able to make a judgement of fact or value by selecting the possibility most in accordance with the evidence; and so far as he is able to decide accordingly. He lacks effective freedom so far as his range of experience, understanding, judgement and decision are limited by habit, desire, fear, sloth, deference to public opinion, eccentricity for the sake of notoriety, and so on. Is effective freedom possible? Suppose someone were to deny that it is possible. Has he (or at least the authority on whom he relies) attended to the evidence on the issue? Has he considered a range of ways on which the evidence might be accounted for? Has he selected the account which best fits the evidence? Has he responsibly decided to make his views known accordingly? If any of these steps is missing, his denial is not reasonable or responsible, and there is no reason to take it seriously. If every one of these steps has been taken by him, he has exercised effective freedom in the act of denying its possibility. It may be concluded that effective freedom is possible, on the ground that the assertion that it is not so is self-destructive.[2]

The manner in which effective freedom may be compromised by one's position in society has been vividly described by Marx. A man is liable to avoid attentiveness, intelligence and reasonableness to a degree and in a direction which are such as to tend to yield judgements to the effect that he himself and his social group live as they do at the cost of the suffering and frustration of the vast majority of the other members of society; and even so far as he is honest enough to judge truly on the matter, he is liable to shirk responsible action in accordance with his judgement. So the more privileged persons in society either do not advert to the facts of exploitation, or rationalise them as desirable or inevitable. They will exert pressure on the exploited, in such a way that they are encouraged to accept the judgements of the exploiters on the prevailing scheme of things, and prevented by propaganda, or at worst by threats and punishments, from inquiring too closely into the relevant matters – for example, into whether a more equable distribution of ownership of the means of production is possible, or whether sophisticated technology can coexist with some other form of social organisation than the system of wage labour.[3]

So much for what is positively to be learned from Marx; there also appear to be oversights in his position which ought to be taken into account. To judge from inquiries into animal behaviour and individual human development, as represented by the work of Lorenz and Freud, Marx underestimates those tendencies to individual and group selfishness, and those predispositions to create adversary relationships, which appear an aspect of human nature as it has evolved up to the present.[4] To hold that dispositions to behaviour in human beings and other animals may to an indefinite extent be altered by training and education is to go against a central postulate of evolutionary theory, that the evolution of physical structure and of behavioural disposition take place *pari passu*. A cynic might suggest, not wholly implausibly, that the phenomenal success of Marxism is due largely to the way in which it encourages and justifies the adversary relationships which people are constitutionally predisposed to enjoy, due to the way in which man has evolved.[5]

It is of course of the utmost importance that rejection of an extreme interpretation of Marx's view should not lead to a denial that anything positive is to be learned from him. Even if tendencies to individual and group bias are not merely due to economic and social circumstances, but are to some extent inherited, it remains that some such circumstances, and perhaps especially those typical of capitalism and early industrialism in general, immensely increase these tendencies. Even if there is good reason to suppose that a society in which each spontaneously and effortlessly worked for the good of all, and all for the good of each, will never be brought about as a result either of revolution or gradual social change, at least it may be agreed that a society where this ideal is realised so far as possible ought to be the goal of social policy. Even if all labour which is in the least irksome to the labourer can never be done away with, at least effective freedom in work can be promoted as far as possible, and the 'alienating' labour that remains fairly shared. And there is evidently a need for something closely analogous to the 'Party' as envisaged by Marx and his followers – a body of intellectuals who make it their business to envisage clearly and direct effort towards the best possible state of society. However, as I have argued, it would be a mistake to follow Marx either in regarding such a body as uniquely representing one group or class within present society, even the largest or most worthy; or in thinking that a state of society is ever likely to be reached in which group bias will have disappeared, and so the activity of such a body of men become unnecessary.[6]

Much the same applies to the state: given the permanence in man of some predisposition to individual and group bias, and of some capacity for transcendence of it, one may infer that the state, or something closely analogous to it, need not be devoted exclusively to the interests of any one class here and now, and is likely for the indefinite future to have a function in acting against individual and group bias in the general interest. The possibility of a 'free-floating intelligentsia' as envisaged by Karl Mannheim,[7] which can criticise the immediate activities and long-range policies of 'Party' and 'State' as so conceived, would seem to follow from the existence of cognitive and moral self-transcendence; though, since everyone has an interest as an individual or a member of a group which is to some extent in conflict with the general interest, to be a member of such a body would presumably always involve a good deal of moral and intellectual effort.

In discussing the state of young intellectuals in Vienna at the end of the First World War, Bruno Bettelheim remarks that some, following Marx, thought that once social justice was achieved, individual enlightenment would take care of itself; while others, convinced rather by Freudian psychoanalysis, thought just the opposite.[8] If the argument of this book is on the right lines, both ends should be pursued at once, and neither will in the long run be possible without the other. Laing's work shows vividly how limited attentiveness, intelligence, reasonableness and responsibility in a parent, in regard to his own motives and to the treatment of his children, can drive the children to desperation if not insanity.[9] Freud has laid emphasis, some would say excessive emphasis,[10] on the importance of early infancy for the promotion or frustration in the individual of patterns of feeling, thinking and behaviour which will enable him then and later to act for his own overall satisfaction and that of his fellows. However controversial the detail of his findings, and however misleading the terminology in which he expresses them,[11] his basic account of successive stages in infancy, failure to traverse each of which satisfactorily will be liable permanently to impair the individual's effective freedom, seems supported by a great deal of independent evidence;[12] though the degree to which infantile experiences on the one hand, and present strategies for coping with the environment on the other, are significant in the causation of neurosis, is still very controversial.

Consideration of these later authorities, separately and together, increases one's astonishment at the genius of Aristotle as an ethical theorist. The satisfaction which seems the effective criterion of good in all the modern authorities, with which such evils as alienation and neurosis are contrasted, is the equivalent of Aristotle's 'eudaemonia' – that which is pursued for its own sake, and not for the sake of something else.[13] Aristotle falls neither into the Freudian trap of reducing man's intellectual and moral faculties to his sensual appetites;[14] nor into the Marxist error of underestimating what is common to men through changing economic and social circumstances.[15] The moral virtues as he described them seem just as applicable to the human situation now as in his time. There is necessary 'prudence', or right reasoning about what is to be done, by which a man has the capacity to judge what long-term ends of activity will prove truly satisfactory.[16] Thus a man who has a lifelong ambition, to which he devotes himself totally, but which proves worthless once he achieves it, is typical of those who lack 'prudence' in Aristotle's sense. But even those who have prudence need other moral virtues as well; even the best long-term plans will be useless, if one is swept away from one's planned course by immediate impulses of desire and fear. The capacities to curb immediate impulses of these kinds in the light of one's long-term ends are respectively the virtues of 'temperance and 'courage'.[17] To achieve these ends, one needs in addition relations of tolerable equality with other people, exacting no more, and Aristotle would add no less, than one's due; these are the province of the virtue of 'justice'.[18] It may easily be seen that the possession of effective freedom, and the use of it in the service of the general good, is equivalent to the practice of the moral virtues in Aristotle's sense.

In fact, Aristotle anticipated an important aspect of Freud's discovery of the unconscious and the effects of repression, as may easily be seen when one compares his account of the arts with that of Plato.[19] Plato had taught that much of the most admired art is bad for people, as it makes them cultivate feelings of grief, fear and desire, which they had rather to root out if they were to live rightly and according to the dictates of reason. Aristotle, however, regarded the effect of such arts on our feelings on the analogy of a purge; if, so to say, we excrete our pity and terror in the theatre, they will be less rather than more inclined to emerge suddenly and vitiate sound practical judgement in the running of our lives. That we had much better get clear about the nature of our emotions – that the effect of repression may in the long run be as bad or worse than indulgence – is perhaps the most important single practical conclusion to be inferred from the work of Freud and Jung, and is effectively agreed by virtually all schools of psychotherapy. Of course, the repression of an emotion and its indulgence are by no means straight alternatives; but without the work of Freud and his successors, the overwhelming importance of the difference between conscious control of an emotion or impulse on the one hand, and pretence that it does not exist on the other, would not be as clear or demonstrable as it is. The profound, if indirect, importance of the arts for morality may easily be inferred from this. One of the main functions of art is to show us human consciousness for what it is, both as tending towards effective freedom, and avoiding it in an infinitely various range of ways. As Collingwood pointed out, art and psychoanalysis have in common that they both counteract corrupt consciousness or self-deception.[20]

It is also highly characteristic of Aristotle, as opposed apparently to Plato,[21] that while insisting on the sovereignty of intellectual and rational consciousness in human living, he acknowledges at the same time that sensation and feeling should be allowed their place.[22] He would have agreed with Freud, that the dictatorship of the intellect would give scope to feeling and sensation.[23] It is not intelligent or reasonable, after all, to treat men as though they were beings wholly determined by intelligence and reason, and not at all affected by emotion or physical desire. However, Aristotle did not make Freud's mistake, which I have argued ultimately to be self-destructive, of regarding man's intellectual operations as simply an indirect route to the gaining of sensual pleasure.[24]

The development and exercise of the intellect, in practical as well as theoretical matters, is a good in itself, on Aristotle's view, as well as a virtually necessary means to other goods.[25] The autonomy of the subject, and the demand that he lays down principles for himself, rather than simply submitting to those imposed upon him from outside, is particularly stressed by Kant.[26] On the analysis suggested here, Kant is quite right to stress the autonomy and self-disposability of the agent as a criterion of good action; but does not take sufficient account of the general satisfaction which ought to be the aim of his action.

The reason for his oversight, I think, is to be detected in the very first sentence of the *Grundlegung*: 'Nothing can possibly be conceived in the world, or even out of it, which can be called good without qualification, except a good will'.[27] Even if it is true, as may perhaps be conceded, that the good will is the only thing which is good *in all circumstances*, it does not follow that the goodness of the good will is not a matter largely of its disposition to bring about general satisfaction and to diminish general frustration and suffering. Satisfaction, as I argued earlier,[28] is good *as such*, even if not *invariably* good. Its tendency to produce satisfaction, in the agent or in others, will always constitute good reason for performing an action; even though there may be other and stronger reasons against it. Much of what applies to Kant seems to apply also to those existentialist thinkers who rightly stress autonomy and self-determination as a good, but seem to neglect somewhat the fact that the attaining of these by the individual agent are not the only good. To be a good man is not only to be effectively free, so far as external circumstances allow, but to use one's effective freedom to promote the effective freedom and satisfaction of others.

In contrast to Kantians and existentialists, utilitarians have insisted that contribution to happiness or satisfaction is constitutive of good action and character on the personal level, good legislation and policy on the social. If the view argued for here is on the right lines, each party has grasped an aspect of the truth, and provides a useful corrective of the other. No doubt the account of human well-being proposed by some utilitarians, as a matter for example of a mere sum of pleasures together with absence of pains, is crude and inadequate.[29] But, as I have tried to argue, contribution to pleasure and avoidance of pain, however crudely conceived, *is* an essential criterion for judgement of what is good and bad, even if it is not the only one.[30] And in its insistence on the point, utilitarianism provides an immensely worthwhile corrective to those ways of thinking which entail that the difference between good and bad, right and wrong, is a matter on which the individual or the community in the last analysis simply has to decide.

Consideration of the nature of effective freedom sheds light on a famous view apparently defended by Plato, that a tyrant does not really do what he wishes;[31] and brings out why it is at once so profound and so implausible. It may be suggested that there are two sorts of circumstances in which a person may act tyrannically towards other persons in his power; when he lacks effective freedom on the one hand; and when he abuses it on the other. In the latter case, his range of experience, understanding, judgement and so on, is wide enough for him to have acted more for the benefit of those over whom he has power, if he had chosen to do so; but in fact he has decided to act wrongly towards them for his own selfish ends. In such a case as this, it seems an abuse of words to deny that the tyrant is doing what he wants, unless one is misleadingly to treat the phrase 'doing what one wants' as identical in meaning with 'doing what is good'. In the former case, it is much more plausible; it seems perfectly appropriate to say that to do what one wants is a matter of determining attentively, intelligently and reasonably what is the best thing to do, and acting accordingly. A tyrant may well be driven to act by immediate impulses of fear, lust or envy, since abuse of power may have enabled him to avoid the troublesome discipline of achieving or maintaining control over such impulses; and he may thus quite reasonably be said not to 'do what he wants' in this sense. The acquisition and maintenance of self-knowledge and self-control are always painful; and the greater one's power over other people, the more one's opportunities for shirking the unpleasantness involved. A tyrant of this kind is indeed closely analogous to the kind of neurotic whose 'gain from illness' is in fact the principal factor working against his cure.[32]

The acts of attention to experience, of envisaging possible explanations, and making judgements and decisions, which are constitutive of effective freedom, are to be known more clearly for what they are by what may be called 'introspection', for want of a better term. I may catch myself out, for example, in a malicious remark made to a member of my family or a colleague, which I have uttered on some pretext, offered to myself or if necessary to others, to the effect that it was really for the best. By investigating his own mental acts and states of the present or the immediate past, a man may become aware, often painfully so, of his refusal to attend to evidence relevant to a matter which concerns him, of his reluctance to think out or to consider inconvenient or frightening possibilities, or his failure to decide according to the value-judgement apparently best justified by the evidence, when this has gone against his immediate inclination, or his selfish long-term interest, or the prejudices of his social group or class, and so on. Now introspection has been out of favour in recent analytic philosophy, largely through the influence of Wittgenstein and Ryle.[33] These philosophers and their disciples are surely quite correct in stating that the *meaning* of terms referring to internal acts and states could not possibly be established *exclusively* by introspection, and without any reference to publicly observable states of affairs which characteristically accompany these internal acts and states. Short of such publicly observable states of affairs, one could not refer to such inner states as 'anger' or 'lust' in a public language, since, for all I knew, my private feelings which I named 'lust' might be totally different from your private feelings so named by you. Just the same would apply to the mental acts which are our direct concern here, of adverting to one's sensations and feelings, marshalling evidence on a topic, judging that one's previous beliefs or assumptions about something were erroneous, and so on. But that this argument is valid by no means entails that one cannot get clearer about the nature of one's conscious acts, and one's success or failure in the practice of them, by the kind of 'introspection' described earlier in this paragraph. And that such introspection is an important means to effective freedom seems in effect to be presupposed by almost all schools of psychotherapy.

Evidently such a scheme of ethics, in which promotion of the satisfaction of which effective freedom is a prime component provides the fundamental criterion of what is good, would be, as the philosphical jargon has it, 'teleological' as opposed to 'deontological', justified in relation to ends to be achieved rather than commending duty for duty's sake. A community or organisation and its rules may on such an account be evaluated in two ways; according to the degree to which they promote this kind of satisfaction within the group itself, and according to the degree to which they promote it in sensitive and rational beings who are not members of the group. A successful gang of robbers might well rate high on the first criterion, but only at the expense of a rating so low on the second as to outweigh its high rating on the first.

How on this account might one spell out the basis of the individual's obligation, if any, to obey the state of which he is a member? The state is to be submitted to on this view so far as it tends to promote the satisfaction of those subject to it, and does not do this at the cost of militating against the satisfaction of the rest of mankind. A typical example of a state which fulfilled the former condition, but not the latter, would be one that waged an aggressive war. Naturally a principle of such generality is not such that one can deduce from it in every case whether one ought to submit or not; but this does not imply that it provides no useful guidance whatever. An enactment by the state which promotes the interest of one individual or class against the general interest – where all these forms of interest are to be defined in terms of satisfaction and effective freedom – is an enactment which *ceteris paribus* does not lay anyone under obligation.[34] (It might conceivably do so *ceteris imparibus* – in a case where defiance of one unjust law, though the defiance were in other respects in the general interest, would lead to defiance of just laws to an extent which was ultimately against the general interest.)[35] The more such enactments the state is responsible for, the better is the case for saying that it ought to be destroyed or replaced, always supposing that there is a case for saying that as a result of such destruction or replacement general satisfaction and effective freedom would be better promoted. To revert to a distinction suggested in the fourth chapter, one has an obligation to submit to the state B; so far as it is a state A, one ought, so far as it is in one's power, to take steps to turn it into a state B or to replace it with one.

What has been said so far seems to shed some light on the question of the nature of crime, and of the extent to which it is merely relative to a social and legal milieu. It is sometimes argued that to say that someone is a criminal is not to say that something is objectively the case about him, but rather to 'label' him as a pretext for treating him as a less than fully privileged member of society – for example, by depriving him of his liberty or otherwise punishing him.[36] In dealing with this question, the following distinction may be made between true crime and pseudo-crime. True crime transgresses law, where that law tends to promote satisfaction and effective freedom, both in the community to which the law applies and in mankind at large. Pseudo-crime trangresses law where such law is against this general interest, but is in the service of short-term or individual or minority group interests. Such an account could be perhaps commended as a synthesis of the older view, which simply took for granted the objective justification of society's stigmatisation of the criminal; and the more recent view, which reacts to this with a total scepticism which would seem to make the essence of crime merely a matter of social *fiat*. The account just proposed, which distinguishes between infringements of law as such, and infringements of such law as really promotes satisfaction and effective freedom, would seem to enable one to avoid this bleak pair of alternatives.

The same question arises about mental disease as about crime, and a distinction of the same kind could be made to cope with it. True mental illness might be defined as a complex of thoughts, feelings and behaviour in a man which were such that he was incapable of effective freedom even where immediate external physical and social circumstances were such as to allow him to achieve it, at least without acting against the satisfaction and effective freedom of others in his environment. Pseudo-mental-illness would be such a complex of thoughts, feelings and behaviour which rendered one unable or unwilling to co-operate with those habits, conventions or laws of one's society or immediate group which might reasonably be held to militate against the general satisfaction and effective freedom.[37] These distinctions would not always be easy to apply in practice; but at least in theory they do seem to suggest a way out of the dilemma between dogmatism and relativism which appears, to one sympathetic outsider at least, to afflict much contemporary criminology and psychiatry.

There are some very general conclusions of a political nature which may be drawn. The political Left is rightly alive to the fact that the most fortunate members of society generally abuse their effective freedom in such a way as to allow very little effective freedom in the vast majority. The Right rather emphasises the danger that excessive state control may throttle effective freedom altogether. Now each party derives a great deal of pleasure, of a kind which has been pretty well accounted for by Lorenz and by Freud,[38] from stigmatising the other as a bunch of knaves or fools. It does not seem unreasonable to suggest that *both* may be aware of a real difficulty; and that *both* may be inclined to close their eyes to the real difficulty harped on by their opponents, who can always be plausibly accused of folly or bad faith in having the temerity to point it out at all. If the argument of this book is at all on the right lines, the crucial question of politics is, to what extent effective freedom can in general be fostered among the members of a society, without the strong abusing their effective freedom to deprive the weak of what little effective freedom they have. Marx thought, in effect, that after the revolution and the ensuing dictatorship of the proletariat, given the conditions of advanced technology and the social co-operation required to maintain it, there would be little or no temptation for the clever and the powerful to impose their will by force on other people.[39] But we have found reasons for doubting this.

It is no part of the object of this book to make any definite judgement as to the truth or beneficence of religion in general, or of any particular religion. But it would be wrong to leave the matter aside altogether, since religion and morality have generally been regarded as closely bound up with one another, and several of the authorities whom I have cited have had a good deal to say on the subject. I have suggested in effect that moral goodness is a matter of effective freedom exercised in such a way as to promote general satisfaction and effective freedom. If this is correct, it is clear that there is a readily available criterion for distinguishing between relatively good and relatively bad religion; whether the general effect of the beliefs and practices of the religion are such as to enhance such effective freedom in the religious believer and those whom he affects by his action, or such as to curtail it. I say 'relatively', because it is at least arguable that a religious system is bad, even if on the whole it does promote such satisfaction and effective freedom, if there are better reasons for thinking that it is false than that it is true; and conversely that a religious system is good, is such that one ought to be committed to it, even if on the whole it tends to lessen satisfaction and curtail effective freedom, if there are better reasons for thinking that it is true than that it is false. Of course, such states of affairs would be unusual and temporary on the view advanced here, according to which it is of the essence of effective freedom that it is a virtually necessary condition of finding out what is true as well as of doing what is good.[40]

I do not wish to attend to either extreme thesis, that religious belief always and everywhere fosters effective freedom, or that it always and everywhere militates against it; it appears to me that neither position can be maintained except as a result of blind partiality for or against religion. But it does seem worth giving some attention to the more moderate opposed positions, which may be set out as follows:

(a) Though religious belief may occasionally or in special circumstances be such as to foster beneficent effective freedom, it is necessarily opposed to it in the long run, when its full implications are realised.

(b) Though religious belief may be misinterpreted in such a way as to *seem*, or actually as thus misinterpreted, to *be* destructive of beneficent effective freedom, it tends to promote it in the long run, when its full implications are realised.

The former view, which was in effect maintained by both Freud and Marx, might be argued for somewhat as follows: 'To believe in God is to believe that what is good is dependent entirely on God's command, and not at all on what may be found out by human inquiry into the nature of man and society, and the way in which men may achieve happiness and fulfilment and avoid suffering and frustration. Humane religious moralists may try to base a morality on both sorts of principle; but their attempt to do so is doomed to failure. If God exists at all, his command is the sole basis for morality. If, on the contrary, the fundamental criterion of morality is the achievement of human happiness and fulfilment, the command of God is at best superfluous, so far as it conforms with a humane morality, at worst harmful, to the extent that it conflicts with it. The course of history shows that it is generally the latter.'

The exponent of the opposite view might commend it rather as follows: 'Given that God is our maker, and has given us commands not for his own benefit but for ours, it is only to be expected that there will be found to be a harmony between what God has commanded and what is found to be good as a result of an objective study of man. And this does not necessarily imply that special revelation is superfluous, given, firstly, that man has a destiny beyond this world which involves his acting for his own good in ways which cannot be directly inferred from his nature as a creature living within this one; and given, secondly, that even where our good within this world is concerned, we are prone to forego the use of our intelligence and reason or to pervert them for our selfish ends.'[41]

The argument between these two positions must be left to the theologians and their opponents. But it does seem as well to leave the reader with the hint that he might keep an open mind on the subject; and not assume too readily that the provision of a rational and objective basis for morality would either be completely destructive of religion, once its full implications were realised, or that it would be unquestionably and unequivocally harmonious with it.

References

1 Morality, Happiness and Epistemology

1. Cf. D. J. O'Connor, *Aquinas and Natural Law* (London, 1967) p. 30.
2. Ibid., p. 72.
3. In his *Utilitarianism*, J. S. Mill weakens his own position quite unnecessarily by trying to justify the principle of justice in terms of that of utility. Cf. A. D. Woozley, 'What is Wrong with Retrospective Law?', *Philosophical Quarterly* (January 1968) p. 51.
4. For the presentation of this argument in greater detail, cf. ch. 6 below.
5. Cf. Isaiah Berlin, 'Does Political Theory Still Exist?' in P. Laslett and W. G. Runciman (eds), *Philosophy, Politics and Society*, II (Oxford, 1962) p. 27.
6. M. Warnock, *Ethics since 1900* (London, 1960) p. 203.
7. Cf. G. E. M. Anscombe, 'Modern Moral Philosophy', *Philosophy* (1958).
8. Cf. Jeremy Bentham, *Principles of Legislation* (London, 1970).
9. See ch. 6 below.
10. E. Heimler, *Mental Illness and Social Work* (Harmondsworth, 1967) pp. 122–3. Since the writing of this work, Heimler has extended and refined his test; cf. *Survival in Society* (London, 1975). For the purposes of this discussion, I have confined attention to the test in its most primitive form; subsequent developments, though of some interest and importance, do not affect the immediate issue.
11. Heimler, *Mental Illness and Social Work*, pp. 125–6.
12. Ibid., p. 124.
13. R. D. Laing, *The Divided Self* (Harmondsworth, 1965), p. 27.
14. R. D. Laing, *The Politics of Experience and the Bird of Paradise* (Harmondsworth, 1967) p. 57.
15. Ibid., p. 24.
16. Ibid., pp. 28–9.
17. For a searching examination of this assumption, see Charles Taylor, *The Explanation of Behaviour* (London, 1964).
18. Cf., e.g., Book II of Aristotle's *Physics*, and Book XII of his *Metaphysics*.
19. For a witty presentation of this argument, cf. Bernard Lonergan, *Method in Theology* (London, 1972) pp. 16–17.
20. For example, D. M. Armstrong, Donald Davidson and U. T. Place.
21. Lonergan, *Method in Theology*, ch. 1. Cf. also Lonergan, *Insight. A Study of Human Understanding* (London, 1957),
22. Lonergan, *Method in Theology*, pp. 45, 114, 122 etc.
23. Ibid., p. 104.
24. Ibid., pp. 20, 53, 55, etc.

25. On 'ideology', cf. pp. 74–5 below.

26. It is 'virtually', rather than absolutely, necessary, in that one might, by chance, perform an action that was in some sense good, without knowing the relevant circumstances.

27. Plato, *Protagoras*, 357 B–E.

28. Lonergan, *Method in Theology*, pp. 20, 53.

29. Lonergan, *Insight*, pp. 619–24.

30. Cf. p. 20 above.

2   On Driving People Mad: Laing

1. See pp. 9–13 above.

2. I shall summarise Laing's views as presented in two works, *The Divided Self* (London, 1965) and (in collaboration with A. Esterson) *The Families of Schizophrenics* (1964); they will be referred to respectively as *DS* and *FS* in the following notes.

3. Cf. chapter 5 below.

4. For a clear and fair-minded account of problems of the nature and treatment of mental illness, cf. Anthony Clare, *Psychiatry in Dissent* (London, 1976).

5. Laing, *DS*, pp. 184, 189f; *FS*, p. 18.

6. Laing, *DS*, pp. 181, 183; *FS*, pp. 47, 52.

7. Laing, *FS*, pp. 21, 23, 26, 64, 67, 72–4.

8. On the use of the word 'really' in this kind of context, I have learned a great deal from Mr Peter Nokes. Cf. the assertion that the Ruritanian people *really* want to be forcibly liberated by the Puritanian army, and that the prima-facie evidence that they do not is due to the activities of agents in the pay of some third state.

9. Laing, *FS*, pp. 136f., 147, 152ff., 173, 182, 213f.

10. Laing, *FS*, pp. 20, 24, 40, 59, 64f., 98.

11. Laing, *FS*, p. 168.

12. Laing, *DS*, pp. 99, 75f., 11f; *FS*, pp. 28f.; *DS*, pp. 80, 84, 92.

13. This seems to me more naturally explicable in terms of Jung's theory of the development of mental life than Freud's. Of course such things *can* be explained in terms of Freudian theory, just as observed planetary motions *can* be explained if the earth is taken to be at the centre of the solar system. According to Jung, moral tendencies in the individual, and not merely biological urges, may be repressed. Cf. pp. 140–1 below.

14. Laing, *DS*, pp. 98ff., 104.

15. Laing, *DS*, pp. 113f., 140, 151, 153f.

16. Laing, *DS*, pp. 138, 147f.

17. Cf. the distinction in Heidegger's *Being and Time* (London, 1962) pp. 203–14, between *Sprache* and *Gerede*. Surely the alleged obscurity of this book largely disappears when one takes it as an exploration of the relation of the human agent to the world from the point of view of the agent himself.

18. Laing, *FS*, pp. 28ff., 52f., 187.

19. Laing, *DS*, pp. 36f.

20. Laing, *FS*, pp. 32, 43, 50, 63, 111.

21. Laing, *DS*, pp. 149f., 153.

22. Laing, *DS*, pp. 177f.

23. The similarity between dreams and delusions has often been pointed out; this kind of interpretation of delusions is evidently closely analogous to that suggested by Freud and Jung for delusions and dreams, and by Melanie Klein of children's play.

24. Laing, *DS*, pp. 180–4, 187, 192f.

25. Laing, *FS*, p. 174; *DS*, p. 159.

26. Laing, *FS*, pp. 163f.

27. Laing, *DS*, pp. 164–7. Many of these suggestions are confirmed in Morag Coate's *Beyond All Reason* (London, 1969), a first-hand account of schizophrenia. In the early stages of delusion, it is claimed, the schizophrenic may be helped a great deal by someone whom he knows and trusts; with the support of such a person he may become quite rational (p. 151). Psychiatrists, in Miss Coate's experience, seem much better at diagnosing mental illness than at establishing the kind of mental rapport which will really feel helpful to the patient; accordingly, they are apt to use physical treatments like drugs and electrotherapy as substitutes for rather than accompaniments to psychotherapy (p. 181). Anger with a doctor by a patient may be a promising sign that a personal relationship is building up between the two. Part of the doctor's role is, or should be as many patients see it, to accept a patient's anger without reacting with hostility or feeling hurt. 'If he cannot provide this service the patient may at some stage either go berserk or alternatively retreat into apathy and despair' (p. 191). (It ought, of course, to be remembered that what reassures or comforts the patient when he is ill is not necessarily what is most conducive to his recovery; though one would expect some correlation here, short of clear evidence to the contrary.)

28. One can hardly wonder at the findings of G. W. Brown in a study of ex-schizophrenic patients. He reported that those 'who returned to parents or wives did worse and were more likely to be re-admitted in the year after discharge than those returning to more distantly related kin or to lodgings.' Cf. *British Journal of Psychiatric Social Work* (1963) cited by E. Heimler, *Mental Illness and Social Work*, p. 76.

29. For my own part, I may mention that Laing's aspersions on T. Lidz's *The Family and Human Adaptation* (*The Politics of Experience*, p. 54) seem very unfair.

30. I owe these objections largely to Dr R. J. McGuire and Dr U. T. Place. The latter especially I have to thank for constant stimulus and useful criticism during the writing of this chapter.

31. Cf. pp. 27–8.

32. For a useful and not very sympathetic summary, cf. D. R. Davis, *An Introduction to Psychopathology* (London, 1966) pp. 55f.

33. Cf. pp. 27–8 above.

34. Cf. pp. 9–13 above.

35. Cf. H. Fingarette, *Self-Deception* (London, 1969) pp. 152–63.

36. Jung argued along these lines at the end of his life; cf. *The Psychogenesis of Mental Disease*, pp. 270ff.

37. That self-deception in a parent may lead to schizophrenia in a child is suggested by E. Berne, *Games People Play* (Harmondsworth, 1978) p. 90.

3 *Man as Animal: Lorenz*

1. Cf. pp. 1–4 above.
2. Lorenz, *On Aggression* (London, 1966) pp. 23, 186.
3. Ibid., pp. 143, 44–5.
4. L. Wittgenstein, *Philosophical Investigations* (Oxford, 1958) I para 7.
5. Lorenz, *On Aggression* pp. 53, 55–6, 129.
6. Ibid., pp. 145, 149, 15, 151–2.
7. Ibid., pp. 159, 165, 174–5, 179, 187.
8. Ibid., pp. 183–4, 186.
9. Ibid., pp. 177–8.
10. Ibid., pp. 207, 38–9.
11. Ibid., pp. 105, 107.
12. Ibid., pp. 33–4, 155, 209, 211, 242–3.
13. Ibid., pp. 41–3.
14. Ibid., pp. 212–13, 216, 221.
15. Ibid., pp. 68–9, 134, 138.
16. Ibid., pp. 233–4.
17. Ibid., pp. 207–8.
18. Ibid., p. 235.
19. Ibid., pp. 240–3.
20. Cf. the abundant literature on conversion, and on the time in the individual's life when it is liable to occur. E.g., G. W. Allport, *The Individual and His Religion* (London, 1951).
21. Cf. the discussion of this matter in W. W. Sargant, *Battle for the Mind* (London, 1957).
22. Lorenz, *On Aggression*, pp. 224–5, 227, 230.
23. Ibid., p. 106.
24. Wittgenstein, *Philosophical Investigations*, I, paras 7ff.
25. An undergraduate studying politics told me that his teachers condemned Lorenz's work on the ground that it was 'reactionary'. This is just the sort of criticism that is *not* relevant.
26. H. J. Eysenck, in his *The Scientific Study of Personality* (London, 1952), has some caustic and justified comments on the effect of these ideological preconceptions on research.
27. Cf. pp. 12–13 above.
28. I owe this point to the late Professor H. B. Acton.
29. Omer C. Stewart, 'Lorenz/Margolin on the Ute' in M. F. Ashley Montague (ed.) *Man and Aggression* (London and New York, 1968) pp. 103–15.
30. In this paragraph I am replying summarily to some of the more serious objections to Lorenz's thesis in the volume *Man and Aggression*. It is *not* a serious objection that all human behaviour is *affected by* environmental factors *as well as* innate predispositions, and that *therefore* no human behaviour is strictly speaking instinctive (*Man and Aggression*, Introduction), since Lorenz's argument in no way implies that *any* human behaviour is instinctive in this sense.
31. This fallacy was pointed out to me by Dr J. M. Cullen.

32. Geoffrey Gorer, 'Man Has No Killer Instinct' in Montague (ed.), *Man and Aggression*, pp. 27–36.

33. Cf. R. K. Jones, 'The Ethological Fallacy: A Note in Reply to Mr Meynell', *Philosophy* (1972) pp. 71–3.

34. An excellent discussion of the issues raised in this chapter is to be had in Mary Midgley's *Beast and Man* (Hassocks, Sussex, 1978). Cf. also E. O. Wilson, *Sociobiology: The New Synthesis* (Cambridge, Massachusetts, 1975) and W. H. Thorpe, *Animal Nature and Human Nature* (London, 1974).

4 Corrupt Society: Marx

1. K. Marx, 'Theses on Feuerbach' (1845). I shall give the *date* of each of Marx's works referred to on the first reference to it. This will enable the reader to see where an opinion which I attribute to Marx comes from a comparatively early writing, and where from a late and comparatively mature one. As a matter of fact, it does not seem to me, in spite of the claims of Louis Althusser and his disciples – cf. *For Marx* (Harmondsworth, 1969) – that Marx's views changed radically after 1844 on the matters with which I am concerned in this book.

2. K. Marx and F. Engels, *The German Ideology* (1846); quoted in D. McLellan, *The Thought of Karl Marx. An Introduction* (London, 1971) p. 125. I shall refer to this work, to which I am heavily indebted, as *TKM* in the notes which follow.

3. Ibid., pp. 127–8.

4. K. Marx, *Paris Manuscripts* (1844); *TKM*, p. 142.

5. K. Marx, *Capital, I* (1867); *TKM*, pp. 148–9.

6. Marx and Engels, *German Ideology*; *TKM*, p. 128.

7. Ibid., p. 129.

8. Ibid., pp. 129, 191.

9. K. Marx, *The Poverty of Philosophy* (1847); *TKM*, p. 130.

10. K. Marx, *Grundrisse* (1857–8); *TKM*, p. 134.

11. K. Marx, *Wage Labour and Capital* (1849); *TKM*, p. 130.

12. Marx, *Poverty of Philosophy*; *TKM*, pp. 129–30.

13. McLellan, *TKM*, pp. 124–5.

14. Mark, *Wage Labour and Capital*; *TKM*, p. 131.

15. Marx, *Grundrisse*; *TKM*, p. 134.

16. Cf. p. 16 above.

17. Cf. H. B. Acton, 'On Some Criticisms of Historical Materialism', *Proceedings of the Aristotelian Society*, supp. vol. XLIV (1970). Professor Acton made this point in discussion of his paper.

18. K. Marx, 'Contribution to a Critique of Hegel's "Philosophy of Right"' (1844); *On Religion. Writings by K. Marx and F. Engels* (Moscow, 1957) p. 41.

19. Cf. John Mepham, 'The Theory of Ideology in "Capital"', *Radical Philosophy* 2 (1972).

20. Ibid. pp. 12, 14.

21. This would be the case, for example, with Thomas Aquinas and all those who follow him on the matter. Cf. *Summa Theologica*, I, 2.

22. For example, the second and eighth of the 'Theses on Feuerbach'.
23. Cf. Marx, *On Religion, passim.*
24. Cf. pp. 188–90 below. I have considered the matter at greater length in 'The *Euthyphro* Dilemma', *Proceedings of the Aristotelian Society,* supp. vol. XLVI (1972).
25. McLellan, *TKM,* p. 154.
26. K. Marx, Inaugural Address and Rules of the Working Men's International Association' (1864); *TKM,* p. 147.
27. Cf. p. 16 above.
28. Marx and Engels, *German Ideology; TKM,* p. 160.
29. McLellan, *TKM,* p. 83.
30. Cf. p. 66 above.
31. Cf. note 19 above.
32. Cf. the title of an essay by Marx, 'Moralising Criticism and Critical Morality'; *TKM,* p. 162.
33. Several authors claim that the concept of alienation is central to the thinking only of the earlier, not of the later Marx. Cf. L. Althusser, *For Marx* (Harmondsworth, 1969). This claim is rebutted, in my opinion quite rightly, by D. McLellan (*TKM,* pp. 108–10).
34. Marx, *Paris Manuscripts; TKM,* p. 141.
35. Marx, *Wage Labour and Capital; TKM,* pp. 143–4.
36. K. Marx and F. Engels, *The Holy Family* (1845); *TKM,* p. 108.
37. K. Marx, 'Results of the Immediate Process of Production' (1865); *TKM,* p. 119.
38. Marx, *Capital,* I, *TKM,* p. 109.
39. Marx, *Grundrisse; TKM,* p. 114.
40. Marx, *Paris Manuscripts; TKM,* p. 112.
41. Marx, *Capital,* I; *TKM,* pp. 112, 116.
42. McLellan, *TKM,* p. 212.
43. K. Marx and F. Engels, *The Communist Manifesto* (1848) (CM).
44. K. Marx, 'Comments on Bakunin's "Statism and Anarchy"' (1875).
45. Marx and Engels, *Communist Manifesto.*
46. Marx and Engels, *Holy Family; TKM,* p. 213.
47. K. Marx, *Critique of the Gotha Programme* (1875).
48. K. Marx, *The Civil War in France* (1871).
49. Marx, *Critique of the Gotha Programme.*
50. McLellan, *TKM,* p. 214.
51. Ibid., pp. 215–16.
52. Ibid., p. 139.
53. Ibid., p. 140.
54. Marx, *Grundrisse; TKM,* pp. 139–40.
55. Marx, 'Inaugural Address and Rules'.
56. Marx, *Grundrisse; TKM,* p. 145.
57. Marx, *Civil War in France.*
58. Marx, *Capital,* III (1865).
59. Marx and Engels, *German Ideology.*
60. McLellan, *TKM,* p. 140.
61. Cf. chs 3 and 5 above.

62. Cf. Lonergan, *Insight*, pp. 218–25.
63. McLellan, *TKM*, p. 216.
64. Marx and Engels, *The German Ideology*, ed. C. J. Arthur (London, 1970) p. 104.
65. McLellan, *TKM*, pp. 123–4.
66. Marx and Engels, *Holy Family*; *TKM*, p. 127.
67. Cf. chs 3 above and 5 below.
68. Marx, *Grundrisse*; *TKM*, p. 133.
69. Cf. A. N. Manser, 'Rousseau as Philosopher' in G. N. A. Vesey (ed.), *Reason and Reality* (London, 1972) p. 119, quoting Rousseau's *Considerations on the Government of Poland*.
70. Cf. Marx, 'Comments on Bakunin', *TKM*, p. 222.
71. McLellan, *TKM*, p. 140.
72. As J. K. Galbraith says somewhere, the fundamental class distinction is between those who are expected to derive satisfaction from their work as such, and who, so far as they do not do so, are regarded as suitable objects of sympathy and even psychiatric treatment; and those who, like workers on some assembly lines, have jobs which are so obviously boring and soul-destroying in themselves that it is taken for granted that the only inducement for doing them is extrinsic and financial.
73. Marx and Engels, *Communist Manifesto*.
74. McLellan, *TKM*, p. 151.
75. This is not necessarily a criticism. An original genius may well show a looseness in the use of some terms which does not betray underlying inconsistency of thought; while 'terminological primness' is liable to be 'the solitary achievement of lesser minds' (B. J. F. Lonergan, *Grace and Freedom* (London, 1971) p. 142.)
76. Cf. the account of the matter at the end of *Capital*, III; *TKM*, p. 151.
77. McLellan, *TKM*, p. 155.
78. Marx and Engels, *Communist Manifesto*; *TKM*, p. 152.
79. Marx and Engels, *German Ideology*.
80. McLellan, *TKM*, pp. 155–6.
81. K. Marx, 'Letter to Kugelmann' (1866); *TKM*, p. 156.
82. Marx, 'Comments on Bakunin'.
83. Marx and Engels, *German Ideology*.
84. McLellan, *TKM*, p. 154.
85. K. Marx, 'Moralising Criticism and Critical Morality'; *TKM*, p. 161.
86. K. Marx, 'Letter to Weydermeyer' (1852); *TKM*, p. 156.
87. McLellan, *TKM*, p. 151.
88. McLellan, *TKM*, pp. 180–1.
89. Marx and Engels, *German Ideology*; *TKM*, p. 191.
90. Marx and Engels, *Communist Manifesto*; *TKM*, p. 182.
91. K. Marx, a review of 1850; *TKM*, p. 192.
91. K. Marx, 'The Alleged Splits in the International' (1872); *TKM*, p. 184.
93. My italics. Marx, 'Comments on Bakunin'; *TKM*, p. 195.
94. McLellan, *TKM*, p. 185.
95. Marx, *Civil War in France*; *TKM*, p. 193.

96. Ibid., p. 194.

97. V. I. Lenin, *The State and Revolution* (Moscow, n.d.) pp. 12, 18, 27–8, 30–31.

98. Cf. V. I. Lenin, *Selected Works,* vol. III (Moscow, 1971) pp. 150–63.

99. Marx and Engels, *German Ideology; TKM,* pp. 159–60.

100. Cf. the examples cited in A. Solzhenitsyn, *The Gulag Archipelago* (London, 1974).

101. Ibid.

102. As one would gather from what Solzhenitsyn says. Cf. also Karl Mannheim's view of the intellectual as, in effect, a specialist in self-transcendence.

103. Cf. 84 above.

104. Cf. Lenin, *The State and Revolution,* p. 17.

105. Cf. the first three of the *Theses on Feuerbach.*

106. The second of the *Theses on Feuerbach.*

107. Cf. p. 95 above.

108. Lenin, *The State and Revolution,* p. 17.

109. *Critique of Hegel's 'Philosophy of Right'* (1843); *TKM,* p. 187.

110. For a vivid and horrifying account of primitive group behaviour among members of the scientific community, cf. A. de Grazia (ed.), *The Velikovsky Affair* (London, 1966).

111. Lenin, *The State and Revolution,* pp. 20–1.

112. This is perhaps especially true of Durkheim. Cf. D. La Capra, *Emile Durkheim. Sociologist and Philosopher* (Ithaca and London, 1972) p. 7.

113. For some remarkable examples of the manner in which opposition between groups can immensely enhance the sense of well-being within them, cf. J. R. Searle, *The Campus War* (Harmondsworth, 1972).

114. 1850 and 1852; McLellan, *TKM,* p. 183.

115. Marx, *Grundrisse; TKM,* p. 183.

116. Marx, *Preface to a Critique of Political Economy* (1859); *TKM,* p. 196.

117. Marx and Engels, *Communist Manifesto.*

118. McLellan, *TKM,* p. 198.

119. Marx and Engels, *German Ideology; TKM,* pp. 159–60.

120. Marx, *Poverty of Philosophy; TKM,* p. 198.

121. Marx and Engels, *German Ideology; TKM,* pp. 198–9.

122. Marx, a review of 1850; *TKM,* p. 206.

123. Marx, 'Comments on Bakunin'; *TKM,* p. 210.

124. K. Marx, 'Speech at Amsterdam' (1879); *TKM,* p. 209.

125. McLellan, *TKM,* pp. 201, 209.

126. Ibid., p. 202.

127. Ibid., p. 168.

128. K. Marx, 'Letter to Paul and Laura Lafargue' (1870); *TKM,* p. 176.

129. Marx, 'The Alleged Splits in the International' (1872); *TKM,* p. 177.

130. Cf. the argument on pp. 80–6 above.

131. Cf. p. 98 above; and note 121.

5   *The Corrupt Individual Consciousness: Freud and Jung*

1. Cf. p. 12 above.

2. Freud, *Two short Accounts of Psychoanalysis* (Harmondsworth, 1962) pp. 31–8, 41–2.

3. Freud, *Two Short Accounts*, pp. 42–4, 46–7.

4. Ibid., pp. 39, 43–4, 52–3, 56; 'A Case of Hysteria', *Collected Works*, vol. VII (London, 1953) p. 18. Cf. *Introductory Lectures on Psychoanalysis* (London, 1933) pp. 51–2.

5. From about 1915 onwards.

6. See p. 115 below.

7. Freud, *Two Short Accounts*, pp. 104–5, 108, 111; *Introductory Lectures*, p. 189; S. Freud, 'New Introductory Lectures on Psychoanalysis', *Collected Works*, vol. XXII (London, 1964) pp. 69–77. I have deliberately referred a good deal to this work, which gives Freud's most mature and considered views on many aspects of psychoanalysis. Cf. *Introductory Lectures*, pp. 298–9.

8. Freud, *Two Short Accounts*, p. 137; 'New Introductory Lectures', pp. 59–61, 79. Cf. *Introductory Lectures*, p. 357.

9. 'Anxiety' is the accepted translation of Freud's 'Angst', which suggests a rather more intense emotion than that conveyed by the English term.

10. Freud, 'New Introductory Lectures', pp. 78, 93.

11. Cf. especially, S. Freud, *The Psychopathology of Everyday Life* (London, 1960).

12. Freud, 'New Introductory Lectures', pp. 95–7; *Introductory Lectures*, p. 17. Cf. S. Freud, 'Instincts and Their Vicissitudes', *Collected Works*, vol, XIV, pp. 118–25.

13. Freud, 'New Introductory Lectures', pp. 97, 103–10.

14. S. Freud, 'Three Essays on Sexuality', *Collected Works*, vol. VII, pp. 182–3; 'New Introductory Lectures', pp. 98–9.

15. Freud, 'New Introductory Lectures', pp. 99–100; *Two Short Accounts*, p. 75. *Introductory Lectures*, p. 352. 'Three Essays', pp. 153–4, 157, 160, 182, 210–11.

16. Stuart Hampshire, in a review of *The Freud-Jung Letters* in the *Observer*, 14 April 1974.

17. Cf. ch. 3 above. I have avoided the term 'instinct', as this term is sometimes used with the meaning 'predisposition to behaviour not at all subject to environmental influence'. At that rate, of course, man has few if any instincts, and certainly not a sexual one. However, I do not know of anyone who would seriously claim that much human behaviour is instinctive in that sense. Confusion on this point vitiates a lot of discussion of the important issue of the nature and strength of inherited predispositions to behaviour in man. For examples of such confusion, cf. Montague, *Man and Aggression*. Introduction and ch. 1.

18. Cf. K. Lorenz, *Studies in Human and Animal Behaviour*, vol. 2 (London, 1971) pp. 226–9.

19. Cf. p. 125. A certain unease on Freud's part as to the nature of curiosity, and how it can be accounted for on the basis of allegedly more primitive 'instincts', is to be found in the passage quoted.

20. Cf. p. 16 above.

21. J. A. C. Brown, *Freud and the Post-Freudians* (Harmondsworth, 1961) p. 2.

22. See p. 106 above.

23. Cf. p. 110 above.

24. Ibid.

25. Cf. W. H. Thorpe, *Animal Nature and Human Nature* (London, 1974) pp. 218–29.

26. Cf. p. 109 above.

27. An example of the methods and results of such studies are provided by Thorpe's discussion of bird song (Thorpe, *Animal Nature*, pp. 111–17).

28. Cf. pp. 47–51 above.

29. Freud, 'New Introductory Lectures', p. 7.

30. Ibid., pp. 18–19.

31. S. Freud, 'A Case of Hysteria', *Collected Works*, vol. VII, pp. 15, 65, 71; *Two Short Accounts*, pp. 60–63; 'New Introductory Lectures', pp. 11–12. Cf. S. Freud, *The Interpretation of Dreams* (London, 1954) pp. 121, 126, 127, 143–4, 160, 165, 277, 279, 284, 308.

32. Freud, 'New Introductory Lectures', pp. 18–21, 23. Cf. *Interpretation of Dreams*, pp. 49, 279, 308, 344.

33. Freud, *Introductory Lectures*, pp. 181–2; 'New Introductory Lectures', pp. 27–8; S. Freud, *Beyond the Pleasure Principle* (London, 1948) pp. 25, 39, 42. Cf. *Interpretation of Dreams*, p. 460.

34. Freud, 'New Introductory Lectures', p. 12; *Two Short Accounts*, p. 62; *Introductory Lectures*, pp. 128–30. Cf. *Interpretation of Dreams*, pp. 345, 353, 360.

35. Freud, *Introductory Lectures*, pp. 129–33. Cf. *Interpretation of Dreams*, pp. 354–6.

36. The words in brackets form part of the quotation.

37. S. Freud, 'The Acquisition and Control of Fire', *Collected Works*, vol. XXII, p. 191.

38. 'New Introductory Lectures', pp. 15–16; *Introductory Lectures*, p. 232.

39. Ibid., p. 133.

40. Freud, 'New Introductory Lectures', pp. 22–3.

41. Cf. L. Dupré, *The Other Dimension* (New York, 1972) p. 161.

42. Cf. p. 121 above.

43. S. Freud, *Totem and Taboo* (London, 1950) pp. 141–61.

44. Cf. ch. 3 above.

45. Freud, *Two Short Accounts*, pp. 71, 76–8.

46. Freud, 'A Case of Hysteria', *Collected Works*, vol. VII, p. 50; *Two Short Accounts*, pp. 74, 81; 'Three Essays', pp. 194, 239; 'New Introductory Lectures', p. 100.

47. Freud, 'New Introductory Lectures', pp. 61–4, 67–8. Cf. S. Freud, 'Group Psychology and the Analysis of the Ego', *Collected Works*, vol. XVIII (London, 1955) p. 116.

48. Freud, *Two Short Accounts*, pp. 80–1; 'Three Essays', p. 165.

49. Freud, 'Three Essays', p. 236; *Introductory Lectures*, pp. 302, 360.

50. Freud, *Introductory Lectures*, pp. 307–9.

51. Ibid., pp. 291–2, 301–2; Freud, 'New Introductory Lectures', pp. 120, 122, 126; Freud, 'A Case of Hysteria'. *Collected Works*, vol. VII, pp. 40, 42.

52. Freud, 'New Introductory Lectures', pp. 86–8. Cf. *Totem and Taboo*, pp. 141, 153.

53. Freud, 'New Introductory Lectures', pp. 116–20.

54. On this 'symbolic equivalence', cf. pp. 156–7 below.

55. Freud, 'New Introductory Lectures', pp. 120–22, 124–6, 128.

56. Melanie Klein claims, on the contrary, and surely with at least equal plausibility, that the superego in women is especially strongly developed. Cf. Klein, *The Psychoanalysis of Children* (London, 1949) p. 316.

57. Freud, 'New Introductory Lectures', pp. 129, 134–5; 'Three Essays', pp. 219, 221.

58. Freud, *Introductory Lectures*, pp. 368–74, 380–1. Psychotics cannot redirect libido, according to Freud, and so have no capacity to undergo the transference.

59. Freud, *Two Short Accounts*, pp. 135ff; *Introductory Lectures*, pp. 384–5.

60. S. Freud, *Civilisation and its Discontents* (London, 1930) pp. 20–3, 25, 35, 91. Cf. S. Freud, *The Future of an Illusion* (London, 1927) pp. 12, 30, 50, 54, 56–7.

61. Freud, *Civilisation and its Discontents*, pp. 90–1; 'New Introductory Lectures', pp. 110–11.

62. Freud, *Civilisation and its Discontents*, p. 143.

63. Freud, 'New Introductory Lectures', pp. 159–61, 163, 167.

64. Ibid., pp. 170–2.

65. Ibid., pp. 178–81.

66. Cf. pp. 122–4 above.

67. An admirably clear summary of the results of such an investigation is provided by E. H. Erikson, 'Growth and Crises of the Healthy Personality' in R. S. Lazarus and E. M. Opton (eds), *Personality* (Harmondsworth, 1970).

68. Cf. Freud's 'Leonardo da Vinci and a Memory of his Childhood', *Collected Works*, vol. XI (London, 1957).

69. Cf. p. 126 above.

70. See p. 114 above.

71. Cf. p. 127 above.

72. Cf. p. 132 above.

73. Cf. ch. 7, pp. 178, 189–90 below.

74. C. G. Jung, 'Freud and Psychoanalysis', *Collected Works*, vol. 4 (London, 1961) p. 125; 'Symbols of Transformation', *Collected Works*, vol. 5 (London, 1956) pp. 128–31, 136. Cf. Jung, 'Two Essays on Analytical Psychology', *Collected Works*, vol. 7 (London, 1956) p. 263; 'Freud and Psychoanalysis', pp. 112, 118–19, 125.

75. Jung, 'Freud and Psychoanalysis', pp. 113, 153–4, 197; Jung, 'The Psychogenesis of Mental Disease', *Collected Works*, vol. 3 (London, 1960) pp. 204–5, 207–8; Jung, 'Mysterium Coniunctionis', *Collected Works*, vol. 14 (London, 1963) p. xv.

76. C. G. Jung, 'Psychology and Religion', *Collected Works*, vol. 11 (London, 1958) pp. 76, 82, 179; 'Mysterium Coniunctionis', p. 520.

77. Jung, 'Symbols of Transformation', p. 297; 'Freud and Psychoanalysis', pp. 95–6, 134, 136–7, 179.

78. Jung, 'Freud and Psychoanalysis', pp. 168–70, 183, 209.

79. Jung, 'Psychology and Religion', p. 179; 'Mysterium Coniunctionis', pp. 474, 499, 520.

80. Jung, 'Symbols of Transformation', pp. 235, 304, 335, 356, 417; 'Freud and Psychoanalysis', pp. 155–6.

81. Jung, 'Symbols of Transformation', pp. 292–3; 'Two Essays', pp. 160, 182; 'Freud and Psychoanalysis', pp. 180, 184–5.

82. Jung, 'Two Essays', p. 192.

83. Jung, 'Symbols of Transformation', p. 141; Jung, 'The Archetypes of the Collective Unconscious', *Collected Works*, vol. 9, part 1 (London, 1959) pp. 277–8; 'Psychogenesis of Mental Disease', p. 219; 'Two Essays', pp. 235–6. Cf. 'Freud and Psychoanalysis', p. 202.

84. C. G. Jung, *Psychological Types* (London, 1923) p. 412.

85. Cf. H. J. Eysenck, *Dimensions of Personality* (London, 1950) *passim*; A. Storr, *Jung* (London, 1973) p. 77.

86. Jung, 'Archetypes of Collective Unconscious', p. 354; 'Mysterium Coniunctionis', p. 473.

87. Jung, 'Symbols of Transformation', pp. 97, 141.

88. Jung, 'Freud and Psychoanalysis', p. 201; 'Two Essays', p. 177; Frieda Fordham, *An Introduction to Jung's Psychology* (Harmondsworth, 1959) p. 103.

89. Jung, 'Two Essays', p. 110; 'Freud and Psychoanalysis', p. 146.

90. Cf. p. 146 above.

91. Jung, 'Archetypes of Collective Unconscious', p. 18; 'Symbols of Transformation', pp. 328, 396, 438–9; 'Psychology and Religion', pp. 166–7, 189–90.

92. Jung, 'Psychogenesis of Mental Disease', pp. 241–2; 'Psychology and Religion', p. 289.

93. The Supplement (1976) to the *Oxford English Dictionary* describes the 'mandala' as follows: 'a symbolic representation of a magic circle usually with symmetrical divisions and figures of deities, etc., in the centre, used by Buddhists in meditation and found in many cultures as a religious symbol.'

94. Jung, 'Archetypes of Collective Unconscious', pp. 10, 352, 357, 360–1; Jung and Kerenyi, *Essays on a Science of Mythology* (London, 1951) p. 18.

95. Jung, 'Archetypes of Collective Unconscious', pp. 125–7, 130; 'Symbols of Transformation', p. 345; 'Psychology and Religion', pp. 273, 294–5. Cf. Jung, 'Psychology and Alchemy', *Collected Works*, vol. 12 (London, 1953) p. 18.

96. Jung, 'Psychology and Religion', pp. 104–5, 294.

97. Cf. Calvin S. Hall and Vernon J. Nordby, *A Primer of Jungian Psychology* (New York and London, 1973) pp. 23, 36–8.

98. Jung, 'Symbols of Transformation', pp. 102, 294. Cf. 'Freud and Psychoanalysis', p. 151; 'Mysterium Coniunctionis', p. xix; 'Archetypes of Collective Unconscious', pp. 66, 79; 'Two Essays', p. 93. Cf. also the following from Jung's 'Civilisation in Transition', *Collected Works*, vol. 10, cited by J. Jacobi, *Complex/Archetype/Symbol* (New York, 1959), p. 37; 'Archetypes . . . are systems of readiness for action, and at the same time images and emotions. They are inherited with the brain structure – indeed they are its psychic aspect.'

99. Jung, 'Two Essays', pp. 76, 93; 'Mysterium Coniunctionis', p. 523; 'Psychogenesis of Mental Disease', p. 262.

100. Jung, 'Archetypes of Collective Unconscious', pp. 39, 285; 'Two

Essays', p. 205; 'Psychology and Religion', p. 30; 'Mysterium Coniunctionis', p. 186. Cf. Hall and Nordby, *Primer*, pp. 46–8.

101. The success of Alf Garnett seems to illustrate the point.

102. Jung, 'Archetypes of Collective Unconscious', pp. 260, 264–5; Hall and Nordby, *Primer*, pp. 49–51, citing Jung's 'Civilisation in Transition'.

103. Jung, 'Symbols of Transformation', pp. 277, 347, 382, 383; Jung and Kerenyi, *Essays*, pp. 38, 48–9; Jung, 'Archetypes of Collective Unconscious', pp. 117, 218, 221, 225, 227, 270.

104. Jung, 'Freud and Psychoanalysis', p. 26. The difference between the thesis that all psychic phenomena are *meaningful* on the one hand, and psychic *determinism* on the other, is crucial. J. A. C. Brown, *Freud and the Post-Freudians*, p. 191, writes: 'By the single assumption of psychic determinism, Freud brought every manifestation of the irrational into the sphere of psychic investigation.' But it seems that the correct assumption, which underlies Freud's real discoveries as opposed to his mistakes, is that such phenomena are *meaningful* rather than that they are *determined*. For a useful discussion of this question, cf. Paul Ricoeur, *Freud and Philosophy* (New Haven and London, 1970).

105. Cf. p. 121 above.

106. Cf. p. 152 above.

107. Cf. p. 140 above.

108. Cf. p. 127 above.

109. Cf. pp. 140–1 above; and many examples from Freud's *The Psychopathology of Everyday Life*.

110. Cf. p. 134 above.

111. Cf. pp. 150–1 above.

112. J. A. C. Brown, *Freud and the Post-Freudians*, p. 43. It is only fair to add that Brown does not content himself with this suggestion, but goes on to argue, erroneously as I have suggested, that Freud is far more scientific than Jung.

113. Cf. p. 113 above.

114. K. Lorenz, *Studies in Animal and Human Behaviour*, vol. 2 (London, 1971) pp. 164–88.

6 *The Objectivity of Value-Judgements*

1. Cf. pp. 1–3 above.

2. David Hume, *A Treatise of Human Nature*, III, i, 1; G. E. Moore, *Principia Ethica* (Cambridge, 1956) chs 1 and 2.

3. John Wisdom, *Philosophy and Psychoanalysis* (Oxford, 1953) p. 103.

4. Cf. A. G. N. Flew, 'Theology and Falsification', in Flew and R. C. MacIntyre (eds), *New Essays in Philosophical Theology* (London, 1955) p. 97.

5. R. G. Collingwood, *The Principles of Art* (Oxford, 1938) p. 7.

6. R. M. Hare, 'Geach: Good and Evil' in Philippa Foot (ed.), *Theories of Ethics* (London, 1967) p. 78.

7. Foot, *Theories of Ethics*, Introduction, p. 9.

8. Wittgenstein, *Philosophical Investigations* (Oxford, 1958) 1, sec. 66f.

9. Hare, 'Geach: Good and Evil', p. 79.

10. Ibid.

11. I have argued this at length in 'Remarks on the Foundations of Aesthetics', *British Journal of Aesthetics* (January, 1968).

12. Hare, 'Geach: Good and Evil', pp. 78–80.

13. On the notions of 'happiness' and 'fulfilment', cf. pp. 1–5 above.

14. J. S. Mill, *System of Logic*, I, viii, 7. Cf. A. N. Prior, *Logic and the Basis of Ethics* (Oxford, 1949) pp. 10–11.

15. Wittgenstein, *Philosophical Investigations*, I, 66f.; Aristotle, *Metaphysics*, III, 2.

16. Wittgenstein, *Philosophical Investigations*, I, 79.

17. J. R. Searle, 'How to Derive "Ought" from "Is"', reprinted in Foot, *Theories of Ethics*, pp. 101–14.

18. Foot, *Theories of Ethics*, Introduction, p. 11.

19. The ruling of Thomas Aquinas, that the unjust prescriptions of a tyrant put no one under obligation, is closely comparable (*Summa Theologica*, Ia, IIae, xc, 1).

20. Cf. cases where the happiness of some is promoted at the cost of the unhappiness of others; or where an act is intuitively bad to one set of persons and not to another.

21. Exactly at what point the 'obvious preponderance' ceases to be such is impossible to determine. But that the boundary between the categories is not sharp does not imply that the categories themselves are useless or the distinction they mark illusory. To take an analogy, it is impossible to determine exactly where in England the Midlands end and the South begins, but this does not prevent, say, Nottingham from being quite definitely in the Midlands and Winchester being quite definitely in the South.

22. Hume, *A Treatise of Human Nature*, III, i, 1.

7   *Conclusion*

1. Cf. p. 22 above.

2. Cf. pp. 12–13 above.

3. Cf. ch. 4 above.

4. Cf. chs 3 and 5 above.

5. Cf. p. 55 above.

6. Cf. pp. 80, 84–5, 90–5 above.

7. K. Mannheim, *Ideology and Utopia* (London and New York, 1940) pp. 138ff.

8. B. Bettelheim, *The Informed Heart* (London 1970) pp. 16–17.

9. Cf. ch. 2 above.

10. Cf. p. 140 above.

11. Cf. pp. 136, 156–9 above.

12. For a recent account of evidence bearing on this matter, cf. A. and A. Clarke, *Mental Deficiency: The Changing Outlook* (London, 1974).

13. Aristotle, *Nicomachean Ethics*, I, 4.

14. Cf. pp. 106, 115, 117 above.

15. Cf. pp. 83–4 above.

16. Aristotle, *Nicomachean Ethics*, VI, 5.

17. Ibid., III, 10–12, 6–9.

18. Ibid., V, 1–9.

19. Plato, *Republic*, Books III and X; Aristotle, *Poetics*, 1449b.

20. R. G. Collingwood, *The Principles of Art* (Oxford, 1938) pp. 217–21.

21. Cf. Plato, *Phaedo*, 82C – 83B; Plato, *Gorgias*, 496C – 497A.

22. Aristotle, *Nicomachean Ethics*, X, 1–5.

23. Cf. p. 134 above.

24. Cf. p. 115 above.

25. Aristotle, *Nicomachean Ethics*, X, 7.

26. Cf. especially Kant's *Groundwork of the Metaphysics of Morals*, available in English under the title *The Moral Law*, tr. H. J. Paton (London, 1961).

27. Cf. Kant, *The Moral Law*, p. 61.

28. Cf. pp. 161–2, 170–1 above.

29. Cf., for example, Jeremy Bentham, *Principles of Legislation* (London, 1970) chs IV and V.

30. Cf. pp. 169–70 above.

31. Plato, *Gorgias*, 468 B – E.

32. Cf. p. 132 above.

33. Cf. especially Wittgenstein, *Philosophical Investigations*; G. Ryle, *The Concept of Mind* (London, 1949).

34. Cf. Thomas Aquinas, *Summa Theologica*, Ia, IIae, xcvi, 4.

35. On the contrast between 'act utilitarianism' and 'rule utilitarianism', cf. Foot, *Theories of Ethics*, pp. 14–15.

36. On 'Labelling', cf. Howard S. Becker, 'Labelling Theory Reconsidered', in P. Rock and M. McIntosh (eds), *Deviance and Social Control* (London, 1974).

37. On difficulties on thought and practice in relation to mental illness, cf. Anthony Clare, *Psychiatry in Dissent* (London, 1976).

38. Cf. pp. 54–5, 133 above.

39. Cf. pp. 77–8 above.

40. Cf. pp. 12–17, 20–2 above.

41. I discuss this point at some length in 'The *Euthyphro* Dilemma' (symposium with D. M. McKinnon) *Proceedings of the Aristotelian Society*, supp. vol. XLVI (1972) pp. 223–34.

Index